THE POLITICAL ETHICS
OF ALEXANDER CAMPBELL

The Political Ethics
of
Alexander Campbell

———◆———

HAROLD L. LUNGER

———◆———

1954

The Bethany Press

ST. LOUIS, MISSOURI

Printed in the United States of America

To my
MOTHER and FATHER
whose
Example and Faith
have been a constant
Inspiration and Encouragement

ACKNOWLEDGMENTS

These chapters were presented as the Spring Lectures at The College of the Bible, Lexington, Kentucky, April 13-18, 1953. They are based upon a dissertation on the same subject presented to the faculty of Yale University in 1949 in partial fulfillment of the requirements for the degree of Doctor of Philosophy.

I shall be forever in debt to the leaders and members of the Austin Boulevard Christian Church, Oak Park, Illinois, for the sabbatical leave and monetary grant in 1946-47 which permitted me to complete residence requirements at Yale University, and for the patience and understanding shown during the months back in Oak Park while I carried on the research out of which this volume has grown.

Gratitude is also hereby gladly expressed:

To the committee at Yale University under whose direction my dissertation was prepared *in absentia*—Dr. H. Richard Niebuhr, Dean-Emeritus Luther A. Weigle, and Dean Liston Pope;

To R. Frederick West, who had gone over much the same field a few years earlier studying another phase of Campbell's thought, for wise counsel and encouragement;

To the staffs of the Newberry Library and the libraries of the University of Chicago and the Disciples Divinity House, Chicago, Illinois, and the Disciples of Christ Historical Society, Nashville, Tennessee, for their fine cooperation;

To the typists in Oak Park and Tucson who helped with the various drafts of the thesis and of this volume—Mrs. Dorothy Bell and Mrs. Mary Schmidt in Oak Park, and Mrs. Guida Thomas in Tucson;

To my associates, Russell M. Fuller and James B. McKendry, for relieving me of many responsibilities and thus aiding in the preparation of this volume;

To President and Mrs. Riley B. Montgomery and members of the faculty and student body of The College of the Bible for many courtesies and constructive criticisms during my days there;

To Walter B. Sikes, and especially to my brother, Irvin E. Lunger, for valued suggestions based upon their critical reading of the manuscript;

To Norman and Connie Lunger, who for many months put up with a father preoccupied with matters of little interest to growing children; and

To my wife, Alberta Huff Lunger, who reviewed most of the chapters in this book many times at various stages of their development and has been very helpful with her suggestions and encouragement.

H. L. L.

Tucson, Arizona
December, 1953

CONTENTS

10 CONTENTS

INTRODUCTION

For over forty years, Alexander Campbell was the recognized leader of what Henry Clay, in 1847, characterized as "one of the most important and respectable religious communities in the United States"[1]—a group which came to birth on the frontier, has been generally thought of as a peculiarly *American* religious movement, and is today one of the larger religious bodies in the nation—the Disciples of Christ. He and a majority of his followers were located along the two axes around which the chief political issues of his period revolved— the frontier and the Mason-Dixon Line. From 1811 to the time of his death in 1866, Campbell lived in the panhandle of what is now West Virginia, almost at the intersection of these two axes.

He was not primarily a political philosopher. James Madison once expressed a high regard for his abilities in debate upon the fundamental principles of government, but continued: "It is as a theologian that Mr. Campbell must be known."[2] When he came to deal, in the *Millennial Harbinger,* with so urgent a problem as slavery, Campbell once felt it necessary to apologize for giving so much attention to a subject "not being so directly in the train of our labors."[3]

Yet as a Christian moralist and American citizen he took a lively interest in the social and political issues of his time. When occasion presented itself, he was not unwilling to give a "push to the car of liberty."[4] In the course of his full life as editor, lecturer, preacher, and teacher, he expressed himself on many political matters. In addition he sought and won a seat in the Virginia Constitutional Convention of 1829-30 and entered into its debates with zest and conviction.

Did he have a consistent political ethic? What were the sources of his norms for political action? How did

he stand in relation to the issues raised by Jacksonian
democracy, and on questions like slavery, Roman Catholicism, public education, capital punishment, and war?
What were his attitudes toward the political theories and
tendencies of the Presbyterian church in which he was
nurtured and of the Baptists with whom he was affiliated
for a while? What light, if any, does he throw upon
the emergence of a distinctively American Christian political ethic? These are questions of interest to present-
day Disciples of Christ and to other students of American culture and religion.

Students of American democracy distinguish two main
streams of influence: one, primarily philosophical and
political, the natural rights philosophy of John Locke
mediated through Madison and Jefferson; the other, essentially religious, the left-wing Protestant tradition
mediated through the Baptists under the leadership of
Roger Williams. Locke was himself deeply influenced by
this left-wing Protestant movement.

In general Campbell represents an uneasy blending of
these two streams. His understanding of the nature of
the church, the relations between church and state, and
the principles of Christian conduct is essentially that of
left-wing Protestantism, while his views of the nature of
the state and the forms and elements of government are
those of Locke's natural rights philosophy. His political ethics represent a merging of these two principles.

In the Johnson Memorial Lecture, *Church, Denomination and Sect,* Joachim Wach makes a distinction between three sociological types of Christian fellowship:
the *ecclesiastical body* (the "church-type" of Ernst
Troeltsch's familiar classification), represented by
Luther, Zwingli, Calvin, and the Anglicans; the *sect*
(Troeltsch's "sect-type"), represented by the Anabaptists, Quakers, and Brethren; and the independent body
or *denomination,* represented among others by present-
day Baptists, Congregationalists, and Disciples of Christ.

The third, Wach maintains, is the characteristic American church form.[5]

The denomination is neither as exclusive as the sect, nor as broad and all-embracing as the ecclesiastical body. Unlike the sect, it does not claim to be the only true church. Nor does it, like the church, insist upon a preferential social and political status in relation to other religious bodies. It is content, either from principle or necessity, to be "one among many" and looks upon itself as more or less of an equal in relation to other religious groups.

With regard to political orientation the denomination neither seeks to dominate the state, as the ecclesiastical body frequently does, nor to withdraw completely from the state—the typical sect response. It shows "a reserve toward and criticism of the state which [it] shares with the sect,"[6] while at the same time, like the church, it accepts the state and seeks to establish a *modus vivendi* with it.

The violent struggle which exists between some ecclesiastical bodies and sects and the state has no counterpart in denominational history, not necessarily due to a greater amount of connivance on the side of these groups but because their principle of organization does not afford the basis for a clash between two totalitarianisms.[7]

A distinction may also be drawn between the three sociological types in terms of the source of their norms for social and political ethics. The ecclesiastical body usually derives its political norms from the natural law, while the sect attempts to derive all its norms from the Bible—usually from the New Testament and, within that, the Sermon on the Mount. The denomination, at least in the area of political action, usually finds it necessary to supplement biblical norms with principles derived from natural law.

In his political ethics Campbell represents the emergence of the denominational form of Christian fellowship.[8] Toward the state he showed a peculiar ambivalence which oscillated between an attitude of sectarian withdrawal and one of rather enthusiastic acceptance and accommodation. As for his norms of political action, Campbell made use of both the Bible and the natural law as reinterpreted, under the Englightenment influence, by John Locke. He took the New Testament as the rule book for the church as a fellowship and for the Christian as an individual citizen, and the natural law as the source of norms for the state itself. As a consequence, there was often an element of tension as between what he felt called upon to do as a Christian and what he considered best as a "politician" or "citizen."

Professor Wach characterizes Disciples of Christ today as "an independent body [or denomination] with sectarian features."[9] At the stage of development which Campbell represents, it is probably more accurate to say that his was *a sect position with emerging denominational features*.

Since he was primarily a religious leader, Campbell's views of the church and the principles of Christian conduct will be looked into first. Then attention will be directed to his views of the social compact and the principles of government, followed by some of the problems of practical political ethics with which he dealt.

In a sense Part One represents the sect elements in Campbell's thought, Part Two the ecclesiastical body elements, and Part Three the denominational attempt at synthesis. From another point of view, Part One represents his thought and concern as a churchman, Part Two his views as a member of the body politic, and Part Three his efforts to combine the two as a Christian citizen facing the concrete problems of political life. There is a certain chronological significance also to this division, inasmuch as Parts One and Two deal generally with the earlier stages of his thought, and Part Three with that to which he evolved in his more mature years.[10]

Religion is the development of a man's moral and spiritual obligations to God; morals, his duties and obligations to man; and politics, his duties and obligations to the state, or social compact, in which he lives and moves and has his being.

A temporizing politician is bad; an equivocating moralist worse; but a compromising Christian, worst of all.

Alexander Campbell

Part One

The Christian Church and the Principles of Christian Conduct

CHAPTER I

CAMPBELL'S HERITAGE FROM LEFT-WING PROTESTANTISM

HISTORIANS have come increasingly to recognize the decisive influence upon American Christianity and culture of those left-wing religious groups which insisted upon the separation of church and state and denied the latter any authority in matters of religion. In the early days of the Reformation this meant the radical sects only, since Luther, Calvin, and the Anglicans alike favored establishment on a territorial basis and were therefore "ecclesiastical bodies" in terms of Joachim Wach's threefold classification. Under the peculiar political conditions prevailing in the British Isles and, more especially, in the United States, most of these bodies came eventually to accept the free-church principle. Among the major religious groups in America in the early nineteenth century, the Baptists advocated in their purest form the sect principles of a voluntary church, religious liberty, and the complete separation of church and state.

Alexander Campbell can best be understood against the background of the "ideal type" of left-wing Protestantism classically exemplified by the Anabaptists and Spiritual Reformers of sixteenth-century Europe. Roland H. Bainton describes four characteristics of this radical sect wing of the Reformation: the ethical note, or the ideal of a pure church; Christian primitivism, or

17

the attempt to restore primitive Christianity on the basis
of a biblicism of either the Old or New Testament; a
heightened sense of eschatology, which in some instances
passed over into revolution but more often took the form
of a passive and patient enduring of present evils while
awaiting the early coming of the millennium; and the
radical separation of church and state.[1]   All four of
these notes were present in the thought of Campbell, and
each helps us better to understand his political ethics.
Some were modified during the 1830's and early 1840's
as he made the transition from a radical sect position to
a more denominational point of view.

Campbell was a primitivist who looked upon the New
Testament as the only valid source of doctrine, church
polity, and norms for Christian conduct.   He thought of
the church as a pure church, composed of regenerate persons, completely autonomous, and self-governing.   He
was almost fanatical in his insistence upon the radical
separation of church and state.   His eschatology helped
contribute to a relatively low estimate of the importance
of political life and decisions in his middle period; although in the long run it helped bring him around to a
somewhat more positive attitude toward government and
the state.

While his thought shows striking similarities to the
classical left-wing Protestantism of the sixteenth century, it would be wrong to assume that Campbell drew
his inspiration or got his views directly from that source.
As a student of church history he was familiar, at least
in a cursory way, with the sect-type of Christianity exemplified by the Novatians, Donatists, Paulicians, Wal-
denses, and Albigenses.   In his debate with John B.
Purcell he paid tribute to these sects by name for keeping alive "the spirit of true religion" during the period
of Roman apostasy.[2]   But he seems to have felt little
affinity with the Anabaptists, for in his debate with N. L.
Rice he was careful to dissociate himself from them, and

more particularly from the "Munster fanatics." "What have we to do with the Anabaptists?" he asked.[3]

Campbell would have claimed, and with some measure of truth, that any similarities between his own views and the classical left-wing position were purely coincidental. He went back for his teachers not to the sixteenth century but to the first. Given his New Testament primitivism, he would have said that his other left-wing characteristics were derived directly from the New Testament.

Nevertheless, certain formative influences in his life did stem from the left wing of the Reformation and help to explain his own left-wing tendencies. Reared in the Seceder branch of the Presbyterian church, Campbell came under Independent (or Congregational) and nascent Baptist influences in Ireland and Scotland and became associated with the Baptists soon after his arrival in the United States. Each of these associations represents a stage in the development of his thought.

HIS SECEDER BACKGROUND

Campbell was born in 1788 in County Antrim in the province of Ulster, North Ireland. His mother was descended from French Huguenots who fled from their native land in search of religious liberty in 1681. On his father's side his ancestors came originally from West Scotland, but had been natives of Ireland for three generations. His grandfather was a Roman Catholic, who later became a member of the Church of England. His father, in turn, forsook the cold formalism of the Episcopal church for the warmer and more devotional fellowship of the Seceder Presbyterians. Alexander himself was brought up in Anti-Burgher Seceder Presbyterianism.

Presbyterianism had been established as the national religion of Scotland in 1690. In 1733 Ebenezer Erskine and a considerable number of followers withdrew from the national church in protest over some of the evils of

establishment—particularly the practice of lay patronage, whereby ministers were forced upon local congregations without their consent. The seceders formed the
Associate or Secession church. In 1747 they divided over
the question of the burgess oath, required in some of the
towns of Scotland, which bound those who took it to
defend "the true religion presently professed within
this realm, and authorized by the laws thereof." The
Burghers saw no wrong in the oath, claiming that it
merely bound them to support Protestantism in general.
The Anti-Burghers interpreted it to refer to the national
church; to take the oath would be to sanction the very
abuses of establishment against which the Seceders had
always protested.

In Ireland, where the Anglican rather than the Presbyterian church was established, these divisions were
largely carry-overs from the mother country and had less
relevance and urgency.

For this reason too far-reaching conclusions must not
be drawn from Campbell's early background. The fact
remains that he was brought up in a religious fellowship
which had come into being in opposition to the principle
of establishment, and in the wing of that church which
went farthest in rejecting any church-state alliance.

THE INFLUENCE OF INDEPENDENCY

In the opening years of the nineteenth century Campbell came under the influence of a movement still further
to the left. This was Independency, which represented a
merging of Calvinist and Anabaptist elements.

In Scotland, Independency stemmed from the work of
John Glas and Robert Sandeman who left the Church of
Scotland in 1727 to establish churches along congregational lines, reviving and exemplifying "the order and
discipline of the primitive church." Congregational
principles were more widely popularized by the great
evangelistic mission launched by James and Robert Hal-

dane in 1798. These brothers finally broke with the national religion and advocated a voluntary church, locally autonomous and free from subservience either to hierarchy, synod, or state, and such other left-wing elements as lay preaching, New Testament primitivism, and the right of private interpretation of the Scriptures. Robert Haldane became one of the founders of the Scottish Congregational Union; James later adopted Baptist principles.

Irish Independency had its rise in 1799 under the leadership of John Gibson of Rich Hill and George Hamilton of Armagh, who became ministers of Independent congregations, and Alexander Carson of Tobermore, who started out as an Independent but later became a Baptist. Campbell's father lived on a farm near Rich Hill while conducting an academy in that village and ministering to the congregation at Ahorey. Sunday evenings he occasionally attended services of the Independent church in Rich Hill where he heard the sermons of John Gibson and of such visiting preachers as Rowland Hill, James Haldane, Alexander Carson, and John Walker. Once when the latter preached, Thomas Campbell and his son Alexander had an interview with him and doubtless took advantage of the opportunity to learn more about the Independent position, although neither gave up his Seceder connections at this time.

In 1807 Thomas Campbell emigrated to the United States where the Associate Synod of North America assigned him to the Presbytery of Chartiers in western Pennsylvania. The following year he sent for his family, but the ship on which they set sail was wrecked on the Scottish coast. Thwarted in their plans and with winter almost upon them, the family settled in Glasgow where Alexander enrolled in the university. There he became acquainted with Greville Ewing, a disciple of Glas, Sandeman, and the Haldanes. Ewing introduced him to Robert Haldane, and the young student frequently visited in the Haldane home during his stay in the city. As a result of these associations Campbell became more and more committed to the principles of Independency and finally came to an inward break with Presbyterianism.

Even before going to Glasgow he had come in contact with English Independency through the writings of John Locke. The *Letters on Toleration* he had read as a boy. In his debate with Robert Owen in 1829, Campbell paid high tribute to this "essay" as the thing that "first burst the chains that held England and Europe fast bound under a religious and civil despotism."[4] In 1844 he said of Locke's First Letter on Toleration: "Few compositions of so humble dimensions . . . have exerted a mightier influence in the cause of human liberty and civilization, than this briefest but most puissant production of the great Christian philosopher."[5] While studying at Glasgow, if not before, Campbell became acquainted with the views of another advanced English Independent, John Milton. In the Owen debate he referred to Locke and Milton as two of the foremost architects of the free institutions of Europe and America.[6]

Two other influences which contributed to his left-wing views may be noted here, although the men themselves were not connected with Independency. They were William Chillingworth and Soame Jenyns, both of whom were often quoted by Campbell. Their influence, added to that of English, Scotch, and Irish Independency, helped prepare him for the extreme left-wing views which he came to espouse as a Baptist.

EXTREME BAPTIST POSITION

After almost a year in Glasgow, Campbell, with the rest of the family, set sail once more for the United States. He landed in New York on September 29, 1809, and a month later reached Washington, Pennsylvania, where his father had settled. Although he brought with

him credentials certifying that he was a member of the
Secession church in good standing, he later declared:
"My faith in creeds and confessions of human device was
considerably shaken while in Scotland.'"[7]

When Alexander and his father met and exchanged
experiences and views, each was pleased to find that
the other had arrived, by a different route, at convictions
similar to his own.   Alexander told of his alienation from
Seceder principles.   His father recounted the steps
leading to his separation from the Associate Synod of
North America and the organization of the Christian
Association of Washington.   Thomas Campbell had with
him some of the proof sheets of the *Declaration and
Address,* which had been adopted by the Association and
ordered printed less than two months before.   The
younger Campbell read them eagerly and with delighted
approval.

The *Declaration and Address* was a stirring plea for
Christian unity upon the basis of a return to New Testament Christianity.   There was a strong note of Christian primitivism running through it, as for example in
the declaration: "Nothing ought to be received into
the faith or worship of the Church, or be made a term of
communion amongst Christians, that is not as old as the
New Testament."   The note of the pure church appeared
in a couple of places, as when it was affirmed that

none should be received as members but such as . . . do profess
their faith in Christ and obedience to him in all things according to the Scriptures; nor . . . be retained in her communion
longer than they continue to manifest the reality of their profession by their temper and conduct.

The left-wing note of separation of church and state
was implied throughout and made more specific at
certain points, as when gratitude was expressed for "a
country happily exempted from the baneful influence of
a civil establishment of any particular form of Christianity."

Most of the forces that led the elder Campbell to the views stated in this document, of which he was the chief author, had been operative upon his son as well, and had led him toward much the same conclusions. The *Declaration and Address* seems to have confirmed young Campbell even more strongly in his new convictions and may have helped crystallize opinions which were as yet tentative and unformed.

In this new country he continued his study of "the Scriptures, ecclesiastical history, and systems of Divinity, ancient and modern," until July 15, 1810, when he delivered his first sermon, on the last section of the Sermon on the Mount. During the following year he preached frequently throughout western Pennsylvania and in neighboring communities in Virginia and Ohio, while carrying on his work as a farmer.

By his study of the New Testament Campbell was led to question and finally reject the institution of infant baptism. On June 12, 1812, he was immersed by a Baptist elder. He was immersed, he points out, "when as yet I scarce knew a Baptist from Washington to the Ohio, in the immediate region of my labours."[8] This may be a significant point, not only for his views on immersion but for his views on the church generally and its relation to society and the state. He was convinced in his own mind that he owed his Baptist conclusions not to any strictly Baptist source but to his own study and reasoning. He wrote to an uncle in Newry in 1815: "I am now an Independent in church government . . . and a Baptist insofar as respects baptism. . . . What I am in religion I am from examination, reflection, conviction, not from '*ipse dixit*,' tradition or human authority."[9] It is probably true that Campbell was influenced far more by the Scotch and Irish Independents, many of whom were themselves moving on to the Baptist position, than he was by American Baptists, at least at this early stage.

Even after he had accepted the Baptist practice in regard to immersion, Campbell had no thought of joining the Baptists. The reason he gave was: "The perfect independency of the church and the pernicious tendency of human creeds and terms of communion were subjects to me of great concern." But after attending the meeting of the Redstone Baptist Association in 1812, he entered that association in 1815 with the understanding that he would not compromise his own convictions.[10]

Campbell was never really at home among the Baptists. His theology was more Arminian than theirs. He differed from them on the matter of creeds and on the operation of the Holy Spirit. He held more radical views of the independence of the local church. Nevertheless, by his association with the Baptists from 1812 to 1830, and through his continued study of the Bible and church history, he was further confirmed in many of his left-wing views. His Baptist period, during the last seven years of which he was publishing his *Christian Baptist,* represents his most extreme sect phase.

CHAPTER II

NEW TESTAMENT PRIMITIVISM

B Y HIS own word Alexander Campbell began his career in this country "under the conviction that nothing that was not as old as the New Testament should be made an article of faith, a rule of practice, or a term of communion amongst Christians."[1] That is to say, he was a primitivist who went back to the New Testament for the normative patterns of Christian faith and practice.

HIS APPROACH TO THE BIBLE

From his home and Seceder background Campbell had acquired a profound respect for the Holy Scriptures. In his diary for 1809 he wrote: "The word of God, which is contained in the Old and New Testaments, is the only rule to direct us how we may glorify and enjoy him." Again he asked: "Do not the Scriptures of truth furnish the only established law or way for Christians, whether in an individual or church capacity, to walk to heaven in?"[2]

Campbell was convinced that the Bible must be interpreted in an intelligent manner by applying to it the same rules of interpretation that are used in understanding any other piece of literature. He insisted upon the right of individual interpretation and made an important distinction between matters of "faith" and those of "opinion." In all this he showed his indebtedness to the Scotch and Irish Independents, Chillingworth and Locke,

26

and acted in harmony with the *Declaration and Address,* which declared that "nothing ought to be inculcated upon Christians as articles of faith; nor required of them as terms of communion, but what is expressly taught and enjoined upon them in the word of God."

For Campbell and the movement generally only those things that were set forth "in express terms or by approved precedent" were considered matters of "faith" and therefore binding upon all members of the church. Other inferences and deductions from scriptural premises fell into the category of "opinion" and could not be made terms of communion. This distinction, taken together with the principle of individual interpretation, and carried over into the field of ethics, meant that for Campbell a church could take a stand *as a church* on a moral issue only where the Bible's commands were clear and unmistakable. Social ethics, therefore, remained largely a matter of individual interpretation and judgment.

In spite of the liberalizing elements in Campbell's approach to the Bible, his biblicism was extremely verbalistic, due largely to his views of the operations of the Holy Spirit. In the *Christian Baptist* for March, 1824, he took a stand against current views of the Holy Spirit as "some invisible, indescribable energy exerted upon the minds of men . . . independent of, or prior to, the word believed." This popular emphasis upon the Holy Spirit seemed to open the way to "raging enthusiasm." He urged his readers to open their Bibles and "hearken to the voice of God, which is the voice of reason." He continued with a statement which gives the heart of his teaching regarding the operations of the Holy Spirit: "God now speaks to us only by his word. By his Son, in the New Testament, he has fully revealed himself and his will. This is the only revelation of his spirit which we are to regard."[3]

THE NEW TESTAMENT, THE LAW FOR CHRISTIANS

Campbell was not just a Bible primitivist; he was a New Testament primitivist. The second of his rules of interpretation calls attention to his distinction between the three dispensations—patriarchal, Mosaic, and Christian:

> In examining the contents of any book, as respects precepts, promises, exhortations, &c., *observe who it is that speaks, and under what dispensation he officiates.* Is he a Patriarch, a Jew, or a Christian? . . . This rule is essential to the proper application of every command . . . in Old Testament or New.[4]

In his Ireland and Scotland days Campbell had been influenced by the Covenant Theology of Cocceius and Witsius, which was then having quite a vogue in the Seceder branch of the Presbyterian church. Following the principles of this theology, he came to emphasize the idea of development in God's relations with man and the sharp distinction between the three dispensations—especially that between the Old Testament and the New. In his references to the Bible as the rule of faith for Christians, he usually qualified or limited his reference to the New Testament. Here again he found the *Declaration and Address* quite in line with his own thinking, for its fourth proposition declared: "The New Testament is as perfect a constitution for the worship, discipline, and government of the New Testament church, and as perfect a rule for the particular duties of its members as the Old Testament was for the worship, discipline, and government of the Old Testament church."

In a letter to his father in 1812, Campbell decried the way Christian ministers "run to Moses" for their "forms of worship, ordinances, discipline, and government in the Christian church." He was convinced that all these things "must be learned exclusively from the *New Testament.*"[5]

His classic statement of the relation between the Old
and New Testaments is to be found in his famous "Sermon on the Law," delivered September 1, 1816, at a
Baptist association meeting, at Cross Creek near Wells-
burg, in what is now West Virginia. He examined the
Law of Moses, its nature and limitations, and pointed
out that it was given to the Jewish nation and to none
others. Then he distinguished between the Law and the
Gospel, declaring that Christians are under the latter
and not the former.[6] This radical contrast between the
Old and New Testaments set Campbell off from all those
who, on the basis of a "level Bible," incorporate Jewish
theocratic ideas into their Christian political theories.

This distinction between the Testaments was elaborated more fully, and its implications for social ethics
brought out more clearly, in the course of his debate
with Robert Owen in Cincinnati, Ohio, April 13-21, 1829.
At one point Campbell devoted what amounts to twenty-
seven pages in the published debate to outlining his
theory of the three dispensations.[7]

The Three Dispensations

The relations between God and man, he declared, have
fallen into three ages or dispensations: "the Patriarchal
[which] continued from Adam to Moses; the Jewish,
from Moses to the Messias; and the Christian, from the
Messias till now, and is never to be superseded by another."[8]

More particularly, the patriarchal age began with the
creation of Adam and Eve and continued to the time of
the Mosaic covenant. It corresponds to the family stage
of society. God stood in relation to the whole family of
mankind in the role of a Father, and the positive religious
and ethical commands were related to the familial or
tribal situation.

The second, or Jewish, dispensation commenced with
the Mosaic covenant. Having despaired of the human

family as a whole, God became King of one nation to see
what he could make of that. The framework of Jewish
religion and ethics thus was national, instead of tribal
or familial.

The Christian dispensation, or the kingdom of God,
commenced after the ascension and coronation of Jesus
as Messiah and his enthronement at the right hand of
God. It will never end, although it will enter a new
phase with the coming of the millennium "sometime
soon, perhaps in the present century."[9] It embraces the
welfare of all mankind.

While Campbell thus made a sharp distinction between
the three dispensations, he also called attention to the
continuity which underlay them. There were three dispensations, but only one religion and one ethic. The
elements of piety and morality, he declared, are immutable and are summed up in the two principles of love
to God and love to one's neighbor.[10] But the positive
laws "prescribing the *forms* of religious and moral action
. . . have been changed, and may again be changed."[11]

He seems to have believed that the changes which have
taken place from dispensation to dispensation are chiefly
in ritual. Yet even in the area of morality, the commands of the New Testament sometimes countermand
those of the Old, one of the clearest examples being in
regard to war. The Bible "certainly commanded and
authorized war amongst the Jews," he said; whereas
"the precepts of Christianity positively inhibit war."[12]

These modifications, however, were only such as were
required by changed religious or social situations. As
the social reference changed, the objects of religion and
ethics changed correspondingly. Speaking of the three
dispensations, Campbell declared: "The first formed
good individuals; the second, while held sacred, made a
happy nation, and comparatively a moral people; but
the third . . . will terminate in, a pure and happy
world."[13]

THE SOURCES OF ETHICAL NORMS

The ultimate source of ethical norms in all dispensations is the will of God, but there are differences as to the mediate or proximate source.

In the early part of the patriarchal age ethical norms were derived immediately and directly from God. Campbell made much of the fact that Adam was created as an adult, and that God conversed with him and taught him *viva voce* to speak. In the same manner God taught man to eat and gave instructions covering all his moral obligations. When Campbell later discussed the basis for capital punishment, he examined Cain's penalty (Genesis 4:14) and the command to Noah (Genesis 9:5f). In both instances it was the *spoken* word of God that was decisive.[14] After the fall God "no longer conversed with man, face to face." Thereafter men were dependent upon the *traditions* in which the earlier revelations were embodied and passed on from generation to generation.[15]

In the Jewish age the basis of religion and morality was the Covenant which, Campbell pointed out, was "precisely what we call a *constitution*."[16] He insisted that the Covenant was "a *political* constitution, though [both] religion and morality are delineated in it."[17] It was "written by the *Finger of God,* upon two tables of stone." The religious and moral precepts of this age were revealed by God intermediately through this basic political instrument, and through the other moral and religious laws which were afterward prescribed and recorded in the Old Testament. These latter "were not of the same high character with those thus written on the two tables." Those on the tables of stone comprised the "constitutional" laws to which other and later regulations were subordinate.[18]

In the Christian dispensation ethical and religious norms are derived from the commands of "the present King of the universe,"[19] Jesus Christ, as set forth in the

New Testament—either in his own words or in the words of the Apostles. Again the norms are to be found in a written document, as was the case in the Jewish dispensation.

Still there are differences between the ethics of the Jewish and Christian dispensations. ''The Jews were under a government of *precepts*—we are under a government of *principles*.'' For the Jews moral and religious duties were ''accurately defined to the utmost conceivable minutia . . . nothing was left to discretion—nothing to principle.''[20] But Christians ''have very general rules, left to be filled up by our own reflection and reason.''[21]

Within the New Testament a significant distinction was made between the relative authority of the Gospels and that of Acts and the Epistles. Since Christ's kingdom began at his coronation in heaven following the resurrection, the laws of his kingdom ''must be learned from what the Apostles published to the world, after the ascension and coronation of the King, as they are recorded in the Acts of the Apostles and Epistles.'' The laws of the Christian kingdom will not be found ''antecedent to the day of Pentecost; except so far as our Lord himself, during his life time, propounded the doctrine of his reign.''[22]

This ''except'' might have opened the door to a rather liberal use of the Gospels and the Sermon on the Mount. For actually, as Campbell pointed out, ''the principles of any reign or revolution are always promulged, debated, and canvassed before a new order of things is set up. A party is formed upon these principles before strength is acquired.'' Just as ''republican doctrines were promulged and debated'' before the setting up of the American republic, so Jesus during his ministry set forth the principles of his kingdom in advance of its actual inauguration.[23]

But Campbell seldom made use of the Gospels in his social and political ethics. He seems to have reasoned that where there are divergences between the teachings of Jesus and of the Apostles, Jesus himself has authorized a modification of his earlier commands to meet the exigencies of the new situation. There may well have been a temperamental factor also in his preference for Acts and the Epistles. The rather conservative social and political views of the Apostles were for the most part more congenial to him than the radical teachings of Jesus.

In any event, Campbell was not so much a New Testament primitivist as an Acts-Epistles primitivist. This preference for Acts and the Epistles *within* the New Testament played a very important role in his social and political ethics. Except in the case of war he relied almost exclusively upon the Epistles for his "precepts" and "approved precedents" in social matters. He made almost no use whatever of the Sermon on the Mount. This helps account for his wide divergence from what are thought of as typical left-wing social and political views, and also for the ease with which he arrived at a denominational synthesis on many specific issues.

SUBJECTS OF THE THREE LAWS DISTINGUISHED

Campbell distinguished sharply the subjects of the three dispensations, seeking to make it clear that the Christian is not bound to obey the Mosaic law. He roundly criticized those who called the decalogue "THE *Moral Law,* and made it the law of the whole spiritual kingdom; affirming . . . that it is now, and ever will be, the law of the whole spiritual world."[24] The decalogue and the Mosaic law were "delivered . . . *as a rule of life to the Jews only.*"[25] They were the laws for a particular nation, and only the Jews were obliged to keep them.

As for the relation of the Christian to the Mosaic law, the comparison which he used in 1816 in the "Sermon on the Law" he still considered *apropos* and reiterated in 1830.

Under the English constitution and law these states once existed. After the Revolution new constitutions and laws were adopted and promulged. In the new governments many of the principles and laws of the old government were retained, and repromulged, but emanating from a new authority and adopted and enforced from new considerations.

As the people of Pennsylvania or Virginia are not now "under the English law as a rule of life, or under the English constitution as a form of government. . . . Neither is the law of Moses, in whole or in part, a rule of life to christians." Only such parts of it are binding as have been "promulged" anew by the present monarch of the universe, Jesus Christ.[26]

The Christian must follow the New Testament where pertinent commands are given. In other cases he is at liberty to follow the principle of expediency, which may mean accepting the Mosaic norm,[27] or—more often— going back to the patriarchal dispensation, since these commands were given not to one particular nation but to the whole human race. Upon rare occasions Campbell appealed to what he called "the tendency of christianity,"[28] although his extreme literalism made this approach very uncongenial. His views on a great many subjects might have been quite different if he had used it more.

Just as the Jewish ethic was binding only upon Jews, so the Christian ethic is binding only upon Christians. "The laws of this kingdom, like the laws of every other kingdom, are obligatory only on the citizens," he insisted.[29] In his discussions on moral societies and slavery, Campbell frequently pointed out that we cannot impose Christian standards and laws upon those who are **not** the subjects of Christ.[30]

CHRISTIAN PHILANTHROPY VERSUS "SOCIAL SELFISHNESS"

Campbell made a sharp distinction between the spirit of Christian philanthropy and the various forms of "social selfishness," of which patriotism is one.

The principle of every moral law, he declared, is love. But the object and scope of this love has broadened with each successive dispensation. In the patriarchal age it included only the family or tribe. For the Jews the object was the welfare of the nation and one's fellow-citizens. Christian love embraces the whole world and enjoins us to imitate the universal benevolence of our Creator.

Most systems of morality have been "attempts to promote good will amongst a few—whom nature, interest, solemn pledges, climate or country had united." Christian morality "grows from another root"—from the knowledge that we and our fellows are all "redeemed by the same blood, bought by the same Lord, purified by the same Spirit, embraced in the same love of the Father. . . . This is that fountain, the streams of which are pure morality."[31]

In the *Millennial Harbinger* for 1832 he set out to distinguish Christian philanthropy from the "love of country" of soldier, statesman, and patriot. His thesis was that the philanthropy of these latter is "of a different genus. Disguise it as their admirers may, it is but an enlarged and somewhat refined selfishness." The patriot, Campbell viewed as a lover of his native soil rather than a real lover of men. Nor is the "statesman" a true philanthropist, for "the very soul of politics is cold, calculating selfishness. . . . It is ourselves, our country, perdition whom it may. The products of our soil, our industry, our genius must be protected, impoverish whom it may." Even "the patriot soldier," who is willing to give his life in defending the rights of his fellow citizens and posterity "to life, liberty, and independence"—even he "knows not the name, feels not the impulse of that philanthropy" which belongs to the follower of the Prince of Peace. Christian philanthropy, Campbell declared, is the love of *man*, irrespective of country, friends, interests, partialities, sects, divisions, casts.   Its meets and boundaries are not leagues and commercial treaties, political alliances, the artificial ties of affinity, nor the stronger natural cords of consanguinity.   It regards *man* as the workmanship of God. . . . It loves man purely for man's sake.[32]

Campbell frankly recognized that the spirit and injunctions of Christianity sometimes conflict with what would be considered "good patriotism," although at other times he believed the dictates of Christianity and patriotism are, as he put it, "in conjunction."[33]

No Christian Political Ethic

The whole trend of his thought thus far leads to the typical sect position that Christianity offers no basis for a Christian state.   This conclusion Campbell did not hesitate to draw.   "The Christian system contemplates love as supreme, and makes no arrangements nor provisions for keeping together a carnal, worldly, selfish, self-willed population."[34]   With reference to the slavery issue, he said: "Each individual State has made laws for itself.   The United States have made laws for themselves.   Jesus Christ has made laws for neither of them."[35]   In another connection he declared that "the nations, not owning Jesus Christ, are disowned by him; he leaves them to themselves, to make their own institutions, as God anciently did all nations but the Jews."[36]

In 1833 he quoted "one well versed in the policies of nations, and in the laws of Christian ethics," to the effect that

No nation can be governed by the New Testament alone, nor by the principles which it inculcates; for were we to take Jesus for our King, the Romans or some unchristian kingdom would come and destroy our country and government; for Jesus would not allow us to have a sword or cannon by which to avenge our wrongs.

Continuing in his own words, Campbell said:

Grant it in all its force; and what follows? That no one kingdom can become a kingdom of Jesus Christ until all kingdoms become his; and then it follows that the New Testament is only adapted to Christians while citizens of other kingdoms, being under the governments of those who know not God. . . . Hence the New Testament is only written and adapted to Christians in a suffering state—not as triumphant, not as having the reigns of government in their hands.

In the same vein he went on to say that Christianity "never can mount the throne, nor become a court religion" until Jesus returns on the clouds of heaven. "When Christianity gains the throne, Jesus will place it there himself; and wherever he sets up his throne, from that place shall go forth the law adapted to his subjects in their triumphant state."[37]

Chapter III

SEPARATION OF CHURCH
AND STATE

WITH HIS New Testament primitivism, Alexander Campbell quite naturally shared two other related positions characteristic of left-wing Protestantism—the ideal of a pure church and the principle of the separation of church and state. Fundamental to both was his concept of the local church as a voluntary and autonomous society.

"The Perfect Independency of the Church"

One of the reasons Campbell gave for his reluctance to join forces with the Baptists was his great concern for "the perfect independency of the church." In his early days he was an independent of the independents. "The church" for him never meant the presbytery, synod, or association, but always a local congregation "statedly meeting together in one place." This local body had exclusive authority to order its own life and select its own leaders. It was not subject to "any tribunal on earth called ecclesiastical."[1] His extreme emphasis upon this point set Campbell apart from Presbyterian theory, and also in some measure from Baptist practice, since both of these bodies placed considerable power in the synod or association. So extreme was he that at times he made no distinction whatever between the Episcopal form of church government and the more democratic procedures of the Presbyterians and Baptists.

38

THE IDEAL OF A PURE CHURCH

His emphasis upon a pure church probably grew out of the Seceder stress upon discipline and his own study of the New Testament. It was also a prominent feature of American church life at the time, especially among the Baptists, where discipline of members occupied much of the attention of frontier churches.

On June 19 and 20, 1820, Campbell held the first of his public debates with John Walker, a Seceder Presbyterian minister, on the subject of infant baptism. In the Appendix to this debate, published the same year, Campbell added a rather extended discussion of the evils of infant baptism, in which his radical sect views stand in sharp contrast to the church-type views of those who practiced infant sprinkling.

To begin with he contended that infant baptism "has *carnalized* and *secularized* the church more than any other innovation since the first defection in Christianity." The actual tendency of infant sprinkling, he said, "is to open the gates of the church as wide as the gates of the world, and to receive into its bosom all that is born of women." This is obvious when we consider that if all children were

"initiated into the church" as soon as born, by the rite of sprinkling, then . . . the discrimination between the world and the church would be lost; its gates would be as capacious as those of the world, and without the necessity of regeneration, every member of the human family in that region or country, would have a place in the church.

This was actually the case, he contended, in Scotland a hundred years before and throughout all of western Europe in the thirteenth century.

In those days and while those principles prevailed, the church was secularized, the church and state completely amalgamated; and all the follies and vices of childhood, manhood, and old age, were engrafted upon the stalk of Christianity.[2]

To this worldly church Campbell contrasted the Church of New Testament times. Then the members were char-

acterized as "saints" and "*a peculiar people.*" The
descriptions given of the churches in the Epistles "will
not apply to a church that admits all the infants born
of the members, to membership."[3]

His criticism of the system of infant baptism at this
point, and of the whole theory of the ecclesiastical body
or church-type of Christian fellowship with which it is
associated, Campbell stated more concisely a little later
when he said: "It necessarily confounds the radical distinction betwixt the church and the world, by making
baptism a birth-right privilege, and thereby bringing the
world into the church."[4]

The *Declaration and Address* in its twelfth proposition had declared:

That all that is necessary to the highest state of perfection and
purity of the Church upon earth is, first, that none be received
as members but such as having that due measure of Scriptural
self-knowledge . . . do profess their faith in Christ and
obedience to him in all things according to the Scriptures; nor,
secondly, that any be retained in her communion longer than
they continue to manifest the reality of their profession by their
temper and conduct.

Disciples of Christ as a whole have placed far more
emphasis upon the first of these points—voluntary adult
membership and its implementation by means of immersion—than they have upon the second—discipline to
maintain within the church certain minimum standards
of Christian conduct.

Campbell frequently stressed the necessity of church
discipline and urged the disfellowshipping of those who
failed to abide by the commands of Scripture. He maintained that speculation and failure to pay one's debts
should be cause for church discipline. Even business
dealings which do not constitute violations of the laws of
the land, but which are "opposite to the spirit and tendency of christianity" ought to be examined and dealt
with, as should cases of church members who are keepers

of "a tippling house" or "dram-drinkers, julip-sippers, [and] chronic tipplers." In his later years the instances in which he most frequently urged discipline were those involving a master's violation of his duties to his slaves.[5] As for the procedure in disciplinary matters, he advocated, like most Baptists of the time, following the scriptural rule of Matthew 18:15-17.

In his efforts to preserve the purity of the church, Campbell also followed the typical sect line of urging that Christians limit their marital, social, and business relations to other Christians and "transact, as far as possible, all the business of life" within "the household of faith."[6]

INFANT BAPTISM THE ENEMY OF RELIGIOUS AND CIVIL LIBERTY

Certain of his other objections to the sprinkling of infants deal more directly with political ethics as such. Infant baptism, he declared, violates the liberty of conscience of the child thus baptized, for it "imposes a religion upon the subjects of it, before they are aware of it, and thus deprives them of exercising the liberty of conscience in choosing that which they have examined, and in refusing that which they disapprove."[7]

It was for this reason that he was so disturbed in 1843 by the decision of Ellis Lewis in the case of *Commonwealth vs. William Armstrong* in Lycoming County, Pennsylvania. The defendant, William Armstrong, had prohibited William S. Hall, a Baptist minister, from immersing his minor daughter of seventeen, who had already been baptized in the Presbyterian church. This prohibition was accompanied by threats of personal injury to the minister if he baptized her. The complainant, however, proceeded to immerse the girl and then went to court to secure legal protection against the father's threats. The Judge compelled the father to post $500 bond, but ruled that the minister had interfered with the lawful authority of the father and directed him to pay the costs.[8]

After quoting the Judge's decision in full, Campbell launched into an extended analysis of the rights and duties of the parties involved in the case—minister, father, and daughter. One of his major objections to the decision was that the authority claimed for parents in the argument and decision "annihilates personal responsibility, the rights of conscience, and political freedom, at 'one fell swoop.' " The decision also violated the right of ministers of the gospel to preach and perform the "sacred functions" of their sects "without any molestation or annoyance."[9] To this case Campbell devoted thirty-three pages in the *Millennial Harbinger*. It was doubtless with some satisfaction that he noted more than a year later: "Judge Banks, of Pennsylvania, has confirmed, in the main, my Review of Judge Lewis' Decision, by deciding a similar case in direct contravention of the opinion of Judge Lewis."[10]

Another of his objections to infant sprinkling was that it has "uniformly inspired a persecuting spirit." Not that every "pedo-baptist" has a "persecuting spirit." Nor is every church which practices infant baptism "necessarily a persecuting church." There are "many honorable exceptions." Nevertheless Campbell took it as a fact that "infant sprinkling has, as a system, inspired all the parties that embraced it with a persecuting spirit at one time or other, and they have manifested it, as far as the civil authority supported them."[11]

This last phrase is significant, for he affirmed a bit further on that it was the "native tendency" of infant baptism to unite church and state, so that

persons who disobeyed the former became necessarily responsible to the latter. . . . Thus in all cases of obstinacy, where ecclesiastical persecution ended, civil persecution began, and the excommunicated became the subject of civil penalties.

This generalization Campbell made after citing numerous examples of persecution in his own state of Virginia, where civil disabilities, imprisonment, or ill treatment had been meted out upon Quakers, Baptists, and others. At the same time he recognized that there was less persecution in his day than there had been in the past, "in consequence of the pleadings of the celebrated Milton, Locke, and others."[12]

In these early days Campbell consistently spoke of the Baptists as advocates of civil liberty and "pedo-baptism" as tending toward a denial of both religious and civil liberties. "There is nothing more congenial to civil liberty," he declared, "than to enjoy an unrestrained, an unembargoed liberty of exercising the conscience freely upon all subjects respecting religion."[13] So significant was this point that in concluding his debate with Walker he offered to meet any "pedo-baptist" minister of any denomination who would deny "that infant sprinkling is a human tradition and injurious to the well-being of society, religious and political."[14]

This became one of the major issues in the debate with W. L. Maccalla in 1823.[15] Again in his debate with Rice, Campbell noted with pride that

those who concur with us in our views of Bible interpretation, creeds, and church organization, were the patrons and promulgers of the principles that originated our political institutions; and infused into the mother country, and into this, the true doctrines of civil liberty.[16]

Campbell viewed the political implications of the Baptist (or sect) and the "pedo-baptist" (or ecclesiastical body) systems as follows: the Baptist theory leads by way of religious liberty to civil liberty; the other theory leads through denial of freedom of conscience to an established church and the suppression of both religious and civil liberty.

In discussing the political ambitions of American churches Campbell sometimes characterized the Catholic,

Episcopal, and Presbyterian bodies as three "royal sects." These churches in America, he affirmed, "are the same as in Rome, England, and Scotland, only under the control of different circumstances." If the circumstances were changed and they had the chance, he was confident that they would follow the same course here. "If the mother sect was a tyrant, the daughter will ape her temper; and when of mature age and reason, she will imitate her practice."[17]

Until well into the decade of the 1830's, Campbell looked upon the Presbyterians as the most dangerous of the "royal sects." Then he turned his attention more in the direction of the Catholics. The Methodists, too, he regarded as *potentially* a "royal sect." With regard more particularly to Catholics, Anglicans, and Presbyterians, he declared: "The creed must be changed, and its spirit cast out, before I dare trust my civil liberties in the hands of the best members of any one of these three royal sects."[18]

The temper of this rather undiscriminating attack upon all non-Baptist groups is indicative of the great anxiety which Campbell, as an extreme left-wing Protestant, felt over even the least danger of religious establishment in this country. Some grounds for his fears are suggested by a modern church historian who agrees that Catholics, Anglicans, and Presbyterians, in colonial America at least, advocated the separation of church and state from policy only, and not, like the Baptists, from principle.[19]

THE MORAL SOCIETY AND SUNDAY MAILS ISSUES

The same fanatical fear of anything looking in the direction of a church-state alliance is to be seen in Campbell's opposition to the moral societies, which were a force to be reckoned with in the early decades of the nineteenth century.

In 1812 a society was organized in the state of Connecticut for the purpose of promoting the observance of the Sabbath and temperance reform. In the years that followed, similar organizations sprang up in many places, stimulated, in part, by discussions and actions of the General Assembly of the Presbyterian church.

On April 4, 1815, a number of citizens of Washington, Pennsylvania, met and formed the Washington Moral Society "for the suppression of immorality." Among the rules adopted was one making it the duty of every member

actively to promote the objects of the Association by giving information against anyone known to be guilty of profane swearing, Sabbath-breaking, intoxication, unlawful gaming, keeping a disorderly public house, or any other active immorality punished by the Commonwealth.[20]

Though the society was ostensibly merely an organized band of informers, emboldened by the submission of the populace, its members soon began to make arrests without legal authority and otherwise infringe upon the civil and religious liberties of the people.

For a time the moral societies had everything their way. In 1820 the situation reached a stage where Campbell felt obliged to take a stand. In the *Washington Reporter* of April 27 an article by him was published under the pseudonym of "Candidus," in which he criticized a statement previously issued by the Moral Society of Middletown. Others came to the defense of the societies in the columns of the *Reporter,* and Campbell's articles continued to appear intermittently until February 25, 1822. The issue was also brought up by both Walker and Maccalla in their debates. Many good citizens were incensed that a religious leader should oppose these societies. The Middletown group itself charged "Candidus" with being a "friend to immorality, etc."[21]

In his second article Campbell affirmed that the moral societies were "anti-evangelical, anti-constitutional, and anti-rational." "There is no precept or command in the New Testament to compel by civil law, any man who is not a Christian to pay any regard to the Lord's Day, any more than to any other day," he declared. "To compel men destitute of faith to observe any Christian institution . . . is commanding duty to be performed without faith in God" and is therefore "anti-evangelical or contrary to the Gospel."[22]

That the proceedings of the moral societies were "anti-constitutional" seemed self-evident. The Constitution gives the right to all to worship God according to their own consciences, and the observance of the Sabbath or any other day must be a matter of individual choice. Campbell took the position that "officers of the church" have no right either to interfere with the properly constituted authorities in the performance of their civil duties, or to use the agencies of government to enforce church standards of morality.[23] To exclude ecclesiastical power from the civil realm, he found it necessary, like Luther, to insist upon the competency and even sanctity of the civil authority in its own realm.

The moral society issue became nation-wide in its scope in 1828 when there arose a movement for the abolition of the Sunday mails. In 1810 the Postmaster General had instructed postmasters to keep their offices open for delivery of mail on Sunday in cases where mails were received on that day. The next session of Congress received numerous remonstrances and petitions against the carrying and delivery of mail on the Sabbath, but no nation-wide organized attack upon the Sunday mails occurred until the year 1828 when the "General Union for Promoting the Observance of the Christian Sabbath" was formed in New York. This organization arose, at least in part, in response to the plea of a prominent Presbyterian minister, Ezra Stiles Ely, for "a new sort of union, or, if you please, *a Christian party in politics."* Stimulated by this organization, petitions and memorials began to pour into Congress urging an end to the Sunday mails as a desecration of the Sabbath. In the Senate these petitions were referred to a committee, headed by Colonel Richard M. Johnson, of Kentucky, who rejected the demands with a resounding statement of religious liberty.

In the *Christian Baptist* for April, 1829, Campbell published this report in full, declaring: "The following Report is *rational, politic,* and in the spirit of our constitution. It is one of the ablest state papers on the question, we have ever read. It cannot be resisted by good logic or sound policy."[24] As a "preface" to this document, he reprinted a *"proclamation* of the Right Reverend Ezra Styles Ely, D.D." in which Ely attempted to assess the political power of the Presbyterian church. Campbell minimized somewhat the doctor's claims, but recognized the dangerous tendency of his aims and spirit.

Richard M. Johnson, Esq. and such men, who will not, by act of congress, sanctify the *First* day of the week, or make a *Jewish* Sabbath of it, will have to seek some new country, if they wish to wear their heads. For my part, I would as lief live a door neighbor to the Spanish *spiritual* court of Inquisition, as live next door to a council of such spirits [as Ely and the Sunday mail remonstrants].[25]

A reading of the Sunday mails report will make clear why Campbell endorsed it so enthusiastically. It is quite in harmony with his own views on Sunday observance, moral societies, and the separation of church and state. Still the evidence seems to refute the thesis, tentatively advanced by Robert Richardson, and accepted uncritically by most Disciple historians, that Campbell was Richard M. Johnson's ghost writer and the actual author of the document.

Campbell continued to be critical of moral societies and similar enterprises throughout his life. One of his fundamental objections was that they brought Christians into a "confederacy" with the world. As he wrote later:

It was not any hostility to benevolent enterprise . . . nor to temperance . . . which sharpened our pen against these gigantic combinations. It was the alliance sought and courted between the visible subjects of the kingdom of Satan and the professed followers of him whose kingdom is not of this world, by the patrons and managers of these . . . institutions. . . . The landmarks between the kingdom of Satan and the kingdom of God are wholly defaced.[26]

Another objection was that the very organization of moral societies seemed to imply the inadequacy of the church itself as an agency of moral and spiritual reform. In a "Letter to England" in 1837 he explained that "our brethren generally regard the church as the only moral or religious association which they can lawfully patronize." If missions, education, tract distribution, Bible distribution, temperance, antislavery, or antimasonry are good works, "they belong to the church in their own proper character; and every member of the church is, as a *Christian*, obliged to promote these objects as far as he has the means and the opportunity."[27]

A third ground for his opposition to such societies was his fear that they might ultimately lead to an alliance of church and state. In 1823 he reprinted portions of a tract published by the National Tract Society which stressed the utility, in time of war or other crisis, of a national creed or religious establishment. This, he said, makes clear the real designs of the promoters of these "great religious engines," and he called upon "the Christian and republican" members of the community to arouse themselves against all such "jesuitical schemes."[28]

THE RADICAL SEPARATION OF CHURCH AND STATE

Campbell gloried in the American tradition of separation of church and state and in the constitutional guarantees of religious liberty. In his debate with Maccalla he spoke of the Constitution as a "shield" to protect "the true professors of the Christian religion from the flood of persecution which tyrannical governors, infuriated by blinded, biggotted, blood thirsty priests, have [elsewhere] issued forth against the disciples of the primitive faith."[29]

He was convinced that religious liberty is something far more fundamental than a grant of any government, however enlightened. It is a natural right. Campbell rebuked those "who ask the civil authorities to *tolerate* all or any religious opinions," because

The mere asking for *toleration,* recognizes a right which no civil government possesses, and establishes a principle of calamitous consequences; viz., that opinions contrary to the majority, or the national creed, are a public injury, which it is in the power of government to punish or tolerate, according to their intelligence and forbearance. Civil rulers have no right to tolerate nor punish men on account of their opinions in matters of religion.[30]

So jealous was he of this tradition of religious liberty and separation of church and state that he sounded the alarm whenever he saw anything that seemed even remotely to threaten it. He protested exploitation of the religious affiliations of prominent political figures either by themselves in seeking election or by their religious parties in seeking prestige. It seemed to him an ominous sign that supporters of Andrew Jackson, during the campaign of 1824, should try to make political capital of the fact that his wife was a "pious Presbyterian" and that "the General himself either was or was about to be, a *ruling elder.*" A few months later he published a rebuke directed against the Presbyterian church in Brownsville, Pennsylvania, for seeking to capitalize on Jackson's political prestige upon the occasion of a visit to that city.[31]

More serious were the occasions upon which partisan religious zeal seemed to be encroaching upon the proper domain of government. He early condemned the practice of church synods in passing resolutions approving particular acts of the government, for in doing this they assume the right and reserve the power "to pass resolutions disapprobatory of the proceedings of government, when either their temper or the times require it."[32]

Campbell kept what he characterized as "a sharp lookout" for evidences of sectarian influence in political appointments. In one instance, after apologizing to the Postmaster General for having given currency to charges of partisanship which he later discovered to be unfounded, he excused himself by saying: "We deem it our duty, even on probable evidence, to notice and expose every encroachment upon our religious and civil liberties, without respect of persons."[33]

His greatest concern seems to have been to prevent religious bodies from securing public funds to advance their sectarian interests. Twice at least in his *Christian Baptist* days he objected to the incorporation and making of grants to schools of higher education for this reason. When the legislature of Kentucky had before it a bill "for the incorporation of a University at Danville . . . and for vesting the whole institution, its government, and control, in the Presbyterian synod of Kentucky," Campbell expressed strong opposition.[34] Again after the Ohio legislature had granted a charter to Western Reserve College, he decried the action on the grounds that

if the legislature of Ohio appropriate twenty thousand dollars in cash or public land for such an institution, they make every poor man pay his quota to furnish a splendid system for the rich man's son to be educated; and when this is given to be controlled by an aspiring sect, it is making the Baptist, the Methodist, and the Quaker pay for making Presbyterian or some other sectarian Divines![35]

He carried the doctrine of separation of church and state to such an extreme that he opposed the incorporation of churches. The chief reason for a church's seeking incorporation, he believed, is to enable it to ''compel, *by the arm of flesh,* those who do not willingly contribute to the 'Lord's treasury.' '' The truth is that

an unincorporated congregation . . . cannot raise or collect funds from those who promise, and afterwards repent, by any legal process. But when incorporated . . . they can compel every man to pay whatever he once promised; they can receive legacies; they can raise, and husband, and appropriate funds, as any other company, for building roads, canals, or bridges.

Incorporation, he concluded, ''is the best substitute for a religious establishment in this country, and in a certain degree has answered all the purposes.''[36]

Like most men Campbell was not without his inconsistencies. In his efforts to keep a ''sharp lookout'' for violations of the principle of separation of church and state in other quarters, he was sometimes blind to violations of that principle close at home. In July, 1827, he noted with some satisfaction the establishment of a post office in his home. This carried with it certain franking privileges which he enjoyed through the years and the loss of which he lamented when the law was changed in 1851.[37] He seems not to have considered that this subsidy of his extensive publishing enterprise represented an indirect subsidy of his own ''sectarian'' movement.

Campbell's left-wing theory required the radical and complete separation of church and state. Although he never attempted to define terms, it is clear that his views of the nature and function of government were essentially those of John Locke, who defined the commonwealth as ''a society of men constituted only for the procuring, the preserving, and the advancing their own civil interests,'' and asserted that the power of civil government is confined to the things of this world and has nothing whatever to do with religious matters.[38] This is essentially what Campbell meant when he spoke of the American government as *"purely political"* and designed to *"* secure only man's political rights and promote his political happiness.*"* *"*This government,*"* he declared, *"*regards this world only as the appropriate object of its supervision and protection. . . . Here the affairs of another world are left to themselves.*"*[39]

His views of the nature and function of the church were also similar to Locke's—*"*a voluntary society of men, joining themselves together of their own accord, in order to the publick worshipping of God,*"* with its powers limited to the spiritual relationships of its own members. Locke had also acknowledged the right of the church to discipline and even excommunicate those of its members who failed to measure up to its standards, but insisted that the church has no right to *"*damnify*"* the ejected persons *"*in body or estate,*"* or to exercise any jurisdiction whatever over those who are not joined to it.[40]

Campbell shared Locke's too-simple theory of the separation of church and state in terms largely of the mutual noninterference of magistrates and clergy in each other's realms.[41] He never dealt adequately with the problem of the layman who is at once a member of the church and a citizen of the state.

Ernst Troeltsch writes that *"*Locke feared nothing so much as priestly domination, whether it be Catholic, Anglican or Presbyterian in form.*"*[42] This fear was almost a *"*phobia*"* in Campbell's case, as is seen from his almost neurotic fear of the Presbyterian clergy. It will be noted that he became less nervous on the subject as the years passed, and as his own energies became more fully absorbed in the tasks of constructive churchmanship and responsible citizenship.

CHAPTER IV

THE CHRISTIAN'S RESPONSIBILITY TO GOVERNMENT

A LEXANDER CAMPBELL'S views of the Christian's responsibility toward government and the state can best be understood in relation to the fourth characteristic note of left-wing Protestantism—eschatology. A strong millennial note appears in his thought, though not the "wild eschatology" of Millerism and other contemporary movements. He had little concern for the setting of dates, but did reveal a strong sense of the imminence of the millennial age and an eager longing for the same.[1]

Two things combined to fill him with despair for the institutions of this world and to intensify his millennial expectancy in the opening years of the 1830's. One was the sad and apparently hopeless state of affairs within organized Christianity—highlighted for him by the failure of his efforts at reform within the Baptist fold, and the widespread expulsion of the "Campbellites" from Baptist congregations and of "Campbellite" churches from Baptist associations. This was quite largely completed by the end of 1830. The other, which came to a head a year or two later, was the ominous trend of political events in the world as a whole and even in this "best government on earth." Interpreting these developments in the light of Bible prophecy, he concluded that the millennial age was at hand.

Temperamentally Campbell was too much of an activist to sit passively by and wait for the Lord to usher in his new age singlehanded. He had something of the spirit which led the Munster Anabaptists into revolutionary political activity. At the same time, he was too much of a moralist and to deeply grounded in other left-wing traditions to find in political action an adequate or congenial channel for his millennial energies.

In the 1830's and early 1840's, Campbell presents the interesting picture of a religious leader whose millennialism found revolutionary and aggressive expression in the ecclesiastical sphere, at the same time that it helped contribute, at least theoretically, to quietism and relative indifference in the political sphere. His actions were not always consistent with his theories, for he participated much more fully and enthusiastically in political activity than his left-wing principles and preachments would warrant. This foreshadows the emergence of a denominational position in relation to the state.

THE CHARACTER OF HIS MILLENNIALISM

In 1829 Campbell decided to discontinue the *Christian Baptist* and launch, with the beginning of the new decade, a new and more ambitious periodical to be known as the *Millennial Harbinger*. According to the "Prospectus" for this journal, it was to be devoted "to the destruction of Sectarianism, Infidelity, and Anti christian doctrine and practice" and would have for its object "the developement, and introduction of that political and religious order of society called THE MILLENNIUM, which will be the consummation of that ultimate amelioration of society proposed in the Christian Scriptures."[2]

Fourteen years later, when Millerism was at the height of its influence, and some of his own followers were adopting Miller's premillennial views, Campbell expressed regret that his "title of *Millennial Harbinger*" had been taken so literally by "some of our brethren" as connoting "an immediate Millennium." Still, he declared, "I expected, as I yet expect, a Millennium—a thousand years of a triumphant Christianity, and at no very distant day."[3]

In a series of articles on ''The Coming of the Lord'' in 1841, he portrayed what he called the ''Protestant Theory'' of the millennium in these glowing words:

The Millennium . . . will be a state of greatly enlarged and continuous prosperity, in which the Lord will be exalted and his divine spirit enjoyed in an unprecedented measure. All the conditions of society will be vastly improved; wars shall cease, and peace and good will among men will generally abound. . . . Genuine Christianity will be diffused through all nations; crimes and punishments will cease; governments will recognize human rights, and will rest on just and benevolent principles. . . . [There will be] one extended and protracted series of revivals . . . [and even] the seasons will become more mild; climates more salubrious, health more vigorous, labor less, lands more fertile, and the animal creation more prolific.[4]

To this glorious consummation Campbell looked forward with eager longing—with perhaps more confidence in the 1830's than later. ''Nothing can be more exhilarating,'' he wrote in 1842,

than the thought that within the short period of two years from this date, all our misfortunes, cares, vexations, sins, sorrows, and afflictions will be for ever past. . . . Who would not desire that such a consummation was just at the door. . . . [Yet, he continued] we have . . . to regret that the evidence on which it is proposed to us is, in our esteem, insufficient.[5]

Unlike Miller, Campbell looked for the millennium ''to precede the coming of the Lord,'' rather than to follow it.[6] On the basis of his reading of Revelation 20, he affirmed that ''John's Millennium is not to be preceded by the coming of the Lord, but by the descent of an angel.''[7] In 1843 he wrote: ''I have never been, and am yearly less disposed to be, dogmatical in affirming how, or by what means and instruments this glorious period is to be ushered in.''[8] He did not anticipate any cataclysmic, overnight transition from the present to the millennial age, but rather a more gradual transformation of man's earthly existence by the permeation of life and society with the teachings and spirit of the gospel.

BUILDING A "MILLENNIAL CHURCH"

By 1830 the rather unstable union between the "Campbellites" and Baptists had broken down, and two years later the groundwork had been laid for the union of the "Disciples of Christ," as Campbell preferred to have his followers known, and the "Christians," whose leader was Barton W. Stone of Kentucky. The opening years of the decade thus saw the movement, of which Campbell was the most eminent leader, emerge from its position as a party within the Baptist fold to the status of an independent religious body of considerable strength. These developments compelled him to take a more constructive attitude toward matters of practical churchmanship than he had shown as a negative critic and "reformer" within the Baptist fellowship.

His eschatology was pushing him in the same direction. As a *post*millennialist, he stressed increasingly the role of the church in preparing the spiritual and moral climate for the coming millennium. As early as February, 1825, he had declared in the *Christian Baptist* that the "Millennium" had already "commenced" to the extent that New Testament Christianity had been restored.[9] In the Owen debate he asserted:

There wants nothing . . . but a restoration of ancient christianity, and a cordial reception of it, to fill the world with all the happiness, physical, intellectual, and moral, which beings like us in this state of trial could . . . enjoy.[10]

With the launching of the *Millennial Harbinger*, Campbell turned almost at once with great zeal to the establishment of a "millennial church" on the New Testament pattern. Prior to 1830 he had looked upon the Baptists as one religious body near enough to New Testament principles to hold some promise of reformation. Now he seems to have concluded that it would be more practicable to restore primitive Christianity by establishing a new religious body than by reforming any of the existing churches. He therefore shifted his efforts from reformation to restoration.

His views of the *nature* of the church remained, for a while, largely of the sect type, even as his *concern* for the development of ecclesiastical structures and institutions began to approach that of church-type Protestantism. In the course of time he gradually abandoned or modified many of his extreme sect emphases and came finally to espouse characteristic denominational features.

POLITICAL DESPAIR

Shortly after his disillusionment with existing religious institutions, Campbell underwent a similar disillusionment with political institutions as well—even in "this best government on earth." As will be noted in more detail later, the early years of the 1830's were for him a period of deepening pessimism over the trends in politics and social life in general.

He seems to have sensed a relationship between his millennial hopes and this political despair, for upon several occasions he treated them together. "The political affairs of the nations are approaching some momentous crisis," he declared in 1831. "The Lord will ere long avenge the infidelity, ingratitude, injustice, and blasphemy of the nations so long visited with his oracles."[11] In 1833, he wrote:

We begin to doubt the permanency of our own political institutions; and men are now proving that no parchments, constitutions, or forms of government can throw efficient barriers in the way of the cupidity, ambition, and pride of man. . . . Politicians stand aghast; but the students of the Bible know that the atheism, infidelity, and mammonism, which inwardly work in all the governments of the Old World and the New, must consign them all to perdition.[12]

The next issue of the *Millennial Harbinger* carried the first in a series of seven articles by S. M. McCorkle on Christ's second coming.

A month later Campbell again bemoaned the fate of this government "purchased with the blood of our ancestors." "How rapid is the progress of corruption, and how certain its consummation!" he exclaimed. Such pessimistic utterances were frequent over the next several months, until finally, in a mood of frustration if not of despair, he asked:

What then is to be done? Wait the coming of the Lord, despair of better times, submit to the rulers of the darkness of this world; or shall we fight on, and combat the good combat, in the firm persuasion that our labor in the Lord shall not be fruitless? Most assuredly this ought to be our unshaken determination.[13]

Campbell was not one to buy a white robe and sit down to wait for March 21, 1843—or any other day—to dawn and bring with it the millennial age. He felt himself compelled to fight the good fight—but with the weapons of the gospel and constructive churchmanship rather than of political action.

THE CHRISTIAN'S PARTICIPATION IN GOVERNMENT

During his *Christian Baptist* days, Campbell was as negative in his attitude toward government as he was toward religious institutions. To be sure, he rejoiced in "the rights of man," gloried in the freedoms granted under American democracy, and was very nervous about anything that seemed to jeopardize religious liberty or the separation of church and state. But further than that he did not go—at least as a religious editor. He gave little attention to the positive aspects of government and the responsibilities of citizens thereto. Nor did he in the next decade and a half, for in his disillusionment he saw no constructive course of action.

His quietism was further strengthened during the 1830's by his belief that the restoration of primitive Christianity would itself bring in the millennium with its transformation of all human institutions, including the political, and also by the fact that his energies were so completely absorbed in the building of a millennial church. Furthermore, as long as he held to his sect views of the church he had no valid theoretical basis for political action.

MAY THE CHRISTIAN HOLD PUBLIC OFFICE?

In 1839 a correspondent raised the question of the extent of the Christian's participation in government. From Jamestown, Ohio, M. Winans wrote:

Some honest-hearted well-meaning men . . . have found doctrines in the scriptures, or think they have found doctrines, which prohibit Christians from taking any part in politics. According to these doctrines a Christian must not hold any office in the political government, nor must he vote for any officer in said government. . . . This doctrine, when carried out, makes salvation to depend on being separated from all political governments.

Having presented this full-fledged sect point of view, which, he said, "is supposed to be fully taught in the Lord's Sermon on the Mount," Winans asked for Campbell's opinion.[14]

This inquiry was turned over to Thomas Campbell, whose answer was published in the *Millennial Harbinger*. Judging from scattered but oft-repeated remarks, Alexander Campbell agreed with his father that it was better for the Christian to abstain from political affairs. Even in his later denominational phase he had little appreciation of the good that a Christian might do in public office. In this he followed the usual sect pattern, although for him it was not so much a matter of scriptural prohibition as it was a pragmatic judgment, related to his eschatological views, and therefore in the realm of "opinion." It was not that a Christian dare not hold public office, but rather that if he has a true sense of values, he will not want to hold public office. He will devote himself, instead, to more important religious interests.

Campbell often referred to the incompatibility of the spirit of politics and that of Christianity. In 1838 he wrote: "Politics are a moral pestilence. . . . Christians, keep yourselves from IDOLS!"[15] A few months later, in reflecting upon his experiences on a visit to Washington, D. C., he explained why he had never preached in Washington.

Among other reasons, one is—that I know of nothing more antipodal to the gospel than politics. . . . It is about as hard for a Christian man to please unchristian constituents, as it is for any one to serve God and Mammon. The true politician rises by descending to cater for the lusts and passions of men.[16]

He frequently revealed his low esteem for the law and for politics as a vocation. In 1831 he rejoiced when Richard M. Johnson's brother, John T., forsook politics for the ministry, declaring: "Sir, in *descending* from the forum and legislative hall to proclaim a crucified Saviour, you have *ascended* far above all earthly crowns."[17] Later he expressed his sorrow that Colonel Caperton, of Kentucky, "a gentleman of large and liberal mind, distinguished both as a statesman and a lawyer," was "whirling round in the fearful vortex of political strife" and "wrangling in wordy combat on the oft-perplexed questions of *meum and tuum*," instead of yielding to the claims of "an inheritance uncorruptible, undefiled, and unfading in the bright heavens of eternal glory."[18]

Campbell's attitude toward the Christian seeking public office appears to have been the same as that of his co-editor Robert Richardson who, in 1856, in a rather lengthy and carefully developed discussion of "Christian Politics," declared that "it is the affairs of the Redeemer's kingdom alone that constitute his 'politics.' "[19] In warning his readers against turning "politicians" and deciding questions of state policy, Campbell said: "We have, as *Christians,* little to do with such matters. Political governments, in their best form, are but mere tents for pilgrims to lodge under while on their journey to the great King and Lord of all."[20] Elsewhere he referred to government as merely "the present scaffolding of humanity" which is of use only "while the Christian temple—that building of God's own Son—is in progress of erection."[21]

In yet another connection he spoke of family, state, and church as the three "sublimely Divine and powerful institutions" which "have the destinies of the world in their hands." He went on to point out, however, that these institutions stand in the order, respectively, of "positive, comparative, and superlative" in their "degrees of moral influence."[22]

MAY THE CHRISTIAN VOTE?

Winans' second question dealt with the use of the franchise. Should the Christian vote? Campbell affirmed that he should—but seldom urged him to do so. When queried in 1846 about his own political allegiance, he replied, "that there were certain principles and policies to which I sometimes gave my suffrage, but that neither parties nor men were worshipped by me with any blind devotion."[23] This seems to be a fair self-appraisal of his attitude as revealed in the pages of the *Millennial Harbinger*.

He had no use for political partisanship. Disgusted by the party strife in connection with the campaign of 1840, Campbell likened it to "the pestilential blast from the desert." He called attention to the way the "mania of President-making" had sown the "fierce demon of discord" even in the church and then went on to picture the relative unimportance of the results of such an election:

To see men who profess to be on their way to a celestial throne fighting in partizan fury about the waiter at table, in an Inn at which they have stopped for a single breakfast, is sage wis-

dom and sound discretion compared with the conduct of some
who contend with heated zeal for four years of X in preference
to four years of Y, in a period of a thousand million of ages.[24]

With this introduction he asked: "Ought Christians to
take an active part in politics—in the present politics of
this country?"

This is a question of as easy decision [he replied] as it is of
great moral importance. I am decidedly of opinion that they
ought not. . . . Would to God that they would set their affection
on the politics of heaven, and leave the politics of earth to those
who cannot soar above the Allegheny mountains.[25]

While he had little concern for "parties" or "men,"
he did put some emphasis upon the importance of voting for "certain principles and policies." This relatively late emphasis reflects an emerging denominational
attitude toward the state. Even then only on rare occasions did he call upon others to vote in favor of specific
policies. In his address on "Common Schools" in 1841
he urged his hearers to take definite political action to
advance the cause of common school education; here he
appealed to them as citizens rather than as Christians.
In his "Tract for the People of Kentucky" in 1849 he
urged the use of the franchise to secure the elimination
of slavery. In this case the appeal was to Christians
both in their capacity as citizens and as disciples of
Christ. For the most part his references to the Christian's use of the ballot were rather halfhearted. In
fact, the franchise seems sometimes to have been suggested merely as a preferable alternative to more radical
and direct forms of action. In rejecting the program of
the abolitionists in 1840, he reminded his readers that
if they felt that the laws governing the institution of
slavery were "cruel, unjust, unrepublican, and unchristian, they have at the polls, in their citizen character, a
right and a duty to seek for their amendment or abrogation"—but let them seek changes in this manner,
rather than by extralegal action.[26]

Campbell's mature thought on the subject is summed up in a statement from the year 1857 in which he declared:

In our country and government, every man is responsible for his vote. When, therefore, in his horizon, there is a question or a crisis involving, as he judges, any good, or the prevention of any evil, it is his duty to God, who gives him a vote, and it is his duty to man, to use, or to give that vote, to that person, or to that measure, which will, in his judgment, inure to the most good, or of two evils to prevent the greater, by voting for the less.[27]

The conclusion of the matter is that while Campbell did not adhere to the radical left-wing position that the Christian *dare not* hold public office or participate in political decisions by the use of the franchise, he did discourage Christians from becoming candidates for political office and minimized the importance of the ballot in the life of the Christian. Such little encouragement as he gave his followers to "vote like Christians" came in the later period and reflects an emerging denominational attitude toward political life.

No Christian Social Action

For Campbell there was no basis or motivation for what is known today as Christian social action. As he said in connection with the slavery issue, "The Church cannot constitutionally undertake to reform the State. It may seek to convert the citizens; but can never assume, by any political expedients, to reform the State."[28] It apparently has no responsibility for giving its members guidance on matters of practical Christian citizenship or even of leading them, through the discussion of concrete problems, to a better understanding of the issues involved. In fact Campbell tended to discourage the bringing of political issues into the church in any form.

His opposition even to the discussion of controversial political issues, at least in the case of slavery, was motivated in part by a desire to prevent any disturbance of the unity or harmony of the church—a denominational characteristic. But in general his attitude roots in his left-wing background. Since he was a New Testament primitivist, who found in the Scriptures no divinely revealed pattern for political life, political judgments were left in the area of "opinion" rather than of "faith," and were therefore a purely individual matter. Moreover, the issue of social action for him and his readers presented itself largely in terms of participation or non-participation in the various moral and reform societies—especially abolition and temperance. His objections to moral societies, on the left-wing grounds that they "defaced" the "landmarks between the kingdom of Satan and the Kingdom of God," have already been noted.

Now with his growing emphasis upon churchmanship, Campbell had another reason for opposing such participation. It was obvious to him that energies given to moral societies by Christians subtracted from the resources available to the church for the accomplishing of its millennial objectives.

Instead of putting it in the church's power to do that good, you weaken her power just so much as you give of your time, your means, or your favor to these institutions. Every shilling you give to a Temperance Society, as such, you, as a professed Christian, abstract from the church. . . . Also, every hour you spend . . . in said society . . . you . . . give . . . away forever from your Christian and church duties.[29]

In connection with the slavery controversy of 1836, he expressed regret that "in this partizan and political age it is expected that every man must join in some of the popular crusades against some one of the hundred evils that afflict society." Pointing out that the great Christian reformers "preached Christ crucified and inculcated the principles which struck at the root of every moral and every political evil," Campbell said he chose rather to direct his energies

to the root of the tree; while others who can handle the axe or the saw better than the mattock, delight in lopping off the branches. I wish them all success who oppose any religious, moral, or political evil [he declared]; but I do not think it my duty to devote myself to any one branch of evil or to any one branch of virtue.[30]

He had nothing but scorn for what he called the *"one idea* class of good men," who were flaming evangelists for some one particular social or political reform.[31]

In all this he was quite consistent with his view of the way in which the social benefits of Christianity are mediated to the community at large—that is, through the influence of the church and of individual Christian lives. In his debate with Owen he had affirmed:

The direct or the reflex light of this holy religion affects almost every man in the region where it shines. It shines into the hearts of some, and in their lives it is reflected as from a mirror upon all around. And thus some are *christianized,* more are *moralized,* and all are, in some degree *civilized,* by its light.[32]

This is why, on a particular social issue, Campbell could say that while "the Church cannot constitutionally undertake to reform the State," it may seek to "convert the citizens." For him that was the surest method of reform. It was the way Christians might prepare for the millennial age.[33]

Part Two

The Social Compact and the Principles
of Government

Chapter V

CAMPBELL'S DEBT TO LOCKE'S "NATURAL RIGHTS" PHILOSOPHY

$\mathbf{A}$ S A LEFT-WING Protestant, Alexander Campbell could find no authoritative Christian pattern for the state. If he were to face the practical problem of helping establish the principles and institutions of government, what would he do? Fortunately this is no hypothetical question. Campbell's statements and acts as a member of the Virginia Constitutional Convention of 1829-30, which are a matter of official record, make it clear that his views of the social compact and the principles of government were essentially those of John Locke and the natural rights school of social and political philosophy. That is to say, in his political theory Campbell stood in the natural law tradition of right-wing, "church-type" Christianity, as that tradition was modified by the Enlightenment.

There seems to be no conclusive evidence that he actually studied Locke's *Two Treatises of Government*, but he probably did so since he was familiar with both of Locke's other major works. In any event he was a close student of James Hay Beattie's *Elements of Moral Science*, which restates much of Locke's social and political theory, though with some modifications. As a result, when Campbell landed in the United States in 1809, he had a common "universe of discourse" with the American people whose political bible from colonial times had been the writings of Locke. When he spoke or wrote on political matters, Campbell worked within the framework of the same political philosophy which had found expression in the Declaration of Independence and the Bill of Rights.

The Theories of John Locke

Locke held that there is planted in the heart of man a God-given "law of Nature," discernible by reason, and adequate to guide him in all his social and political relationships.

By this law of nature men enjoy certain "natural rights," chief among them being the rights to "life, liberty, and estate." In the state of nature, men were "free, equal, and independent." Even then reason taught man that he should not harm another "in his life, health, liberty or possessions," but that each has the duty to preserve his own rights and come to the aid of others whose rights might be threatened.[1]

The state of nature was not one of war, as Hobbes had maintained, but there were certain obvious "inconveniences." "The execution of the law of Nature [was] put into every man's hands," and there was wanting "an established, settled, known law . . . to be the standard of right and wrong . . . a known and indifferent judge, with authority to determine all differences according to the established law," and "power to back and support the sentence . . . and to give it due execution." As a result, the individual's enjoyment of his rights was "very uncertain and constantly exposed to the invasion of others." In short, the state of nature was "full of fears and continual dangers."[2]

Civil government was "the proper remedy for the inconveniences of the state of Nature." It arose when men, by common consent and agreement, united "for the

mutual preservation of their lives, liberties and estates,''
each ''quitting'' his natural powers to preserve his own
rights and to punish offenses against the natural law,
and handing them over to the community itself. It was
a cardinal doctrine of Locke that government arises out
of a compact and rests upon the consent of the governed.[3]

Government, or ''commonwealth,'' is established to
secure for the individual advantages which he could not
hope to enjoy so fully in a state of nature. Political
power exists ''for the regulating and preserving of
property'' and ''the defence of the commonwealth from
foreign injury, and all this only for the public good.''[4]
But government is limited to the particular ends for
which it is established. It must be guided by principles
of natural law and must respect the natural rights of its
members—rights which men brought into civil society
and were not conferred upon them by society. It was
upon these grounds that Locke insisted upon the right of
the majority and the principle of no taxation without
the consent of the people or their representatives. When
rulers exceed their powers, the governmental compact
may be dissolved—but only by act of the majority of the
people. In this event political power reverts not to the
individual citizens but to the community as a whole,
which may then proceed to establish such new institutions
of government as the majority shall determine. Other
points of importance in Locke's political theory include
the retention of supreme political power in the hands of
the people, the supremacy of the legislature, the rule of
law, and the separation of powers.

It is obvious that Locke stood in the tradition of natural law, ''church-type'' thinkers like Aquinas, Luther,
Calvin, and Hooker. Yet there were important differences between Locke's understanding of the law of nature
and that of most earlier writers of this school. Fundamentally these differences rooted in the individualism of

Locke as over against the organic view of society held by most "church-type" thinkers.

Locke's thought was probably closer to that of Calvin than of any other in this tradition, but there were significant differences resulting from Locke's utilitarian and empirical point of view and his preoccupation psychologically with the ideas of individual freedom and equality. Nevertheless, the similarities between Locke and Calvin are great enough to help account for those which will appear between Campbell and Calvin in their views of the state and other political matters.

THE VIEWS OF JAMES BEATTIE

If Alexander Campbell worked within the general framework of the political philosophy of Locke's *Two Treatises,* many of the specific formulations and illustrations which shaped his thinking were drawn directly from Beattie's *Elements of Moral Science.* In his political theory Beattie was a rather close follower of Locke, although he also stood in the line of the Scottish "common-sense" philosophy of Thomas Reid.

While a student at Glasgow, Campbell is reported to have copied extracts from Beattie on law, civil government, right, obligation, and justice. His addresses at the Virginia Convention and his writings on strictly political subjects furnish many evidences of his indebtedness to this Scottish poet, who served as professor of moral philosophy at the University of Aberdeen.

Beattie introduced his discussion of politics by defining law as "the declared will of a person, or persons, in authority." There are two kinds of laws—divine and human. Laws of God are of two types: natural or moral, discernible by the right use of reason; and positive or revealed, discernible only by revelation.[5]

Even in the state of nature there was society, according to Beattie, "because man is a social being. But men, being liable to ignorance and error, and much inclined to wickedness, would find the state of nature exposed to great inconveniencies, which could be prevented in no other way, than by establishing government, subordination, and human laws.''

The state of nature is not wholly an imaginary concept, he believed.

Independent nations, who acknowledge no superior but God, are in a state of nature with respect to one another. And a number of persons, mutually independent, thrown by shipwreck into a desert island, would, at first, be in a state of nature; though, no doubt, they would soon find it necessary to make regulations; which would introduce a sort of government.[6]

Two forces tended to bring men into political society. The first was the natural admiration which the weak and inferior have for men of superior abilities. The weak looked to the strong for advice and assistance, and thus conferred upon the latter a certain authority or preeminence. All this presupposes a diversity of human character and an inequality in regard to abilities of mind and body.[7]

The second factor leading to the establishment of government was the ''inconveniencies'' of the state of nature. Men, being fallible, mistook their rights and disagreed among themselves. Thus arose the need for an impartial arbiter. Men were also wicked. They injure one another today in spite of the sanctions of both divine and human law. Remove these sanctions and they would be still more injurious. Such was the case in the state of nature. ''Hence the necessity of men divesting themselves of the freedom of the natural state, uniting in society, appointing a sovereignty, entrusting it with certain powers for the public good, and supporting it in the exercise of those powers.''[8] Like Locke, Beattie had a purely utilitarian theory of government and presupposed a social compact.

A significant passage, which may be the one Campbell copied on the subject of civil government, analyzes the processes of the social compact as follows:

The independence and equality of men in the natural state, being alienable rights, may be parted with, for valuable considerations. Men quitting that state, in order to establish policy [or civil government], would accordingly part with them; and either expressly or tacitly enter into a mutual agreement, to the following purpose. First: every individual would engage to unite himself with the rest, so as to form one community; whose conduct, in matters of public concern, is to be determined by the will of those who shall be entrusted with the sovereignty.— Secondly: it must be further agreed, that the government shall be of some one particular form; that is, that the sovereignty shall be lodged in the body of the people, which is Democracy; or in the more distinguished citizens, which is Aristocracy; or in one man, which is Monarchy; or that the government shall be made up, as ours is, of two or more of these forms mixed together. For different forms of government are supported by different systems of law; and therefore, till the form be ascertained, it cannot be distinctly known what laws would be expedient.— Thirdly: the form being agreed on, they who are entrusted with the sovereignty would become bound to provide for the common interest, and the subjects would be bound to allegiance and obedience. And from this contract would arise the sovereign's right to command, and an obligation on the rest of the community to obey.[9]

Beattie classified forms of government, according to the scheme of Montesquieu, as republics, monarchies, and despotisms. Like the French philosopher he considered democracy and aristocracy as variant forms of republics. Democracy is founded on an equal distribution of property, especially in land, is suitable only for small territories, and requires special provisions for voting and making and enforcing laws, since the citizens are both sovereigns and subjects. A democracy is not favorable to cultural advance, and is very unstable since inequalities are bound to appear and increase from generation to generation. "So the Democracy will gradually resolve itself into Aristocracy; and this, by a similar, and almost unavoidable, degeneracy, into Oligarchy; which will probably end in Despotism.'' Commerce, which helps generate inequalities between men, is dangerous to a democracy.[10]

In a democracy, terms of office must be short so that each citizen will have a chance at being a magistrate. Then too, ''if any one citizen remain in office too long, he will acquire too many clients, and consequently too much power.'' It is further expedient in a democracy, where

offices of public trust are to circulate through the whole body of the people, that every citizen receive such an education as may qualify him for serving his country as a magistrate, as well as a subject. For this reason, all the citizens should receive the same education . . . [and] education ought to be the care of the public.[11]

A democracy, Beattie declared, ''cannot act with expedition or secrecy; because many people must be consulted before it can act at all.'' It is, therefore, no match for a monarchy in war. These considerations, he continued, ''joined to what was formerly said of the natural inequality of mankind, in respect of abilities and character, seem to prove, that republic, especially as the world is now constituted, is neither a desirable, nor a natural, form of government.''[12]

Beattie next disposed of despotism, and then turned to monarchy—''government by one person who is subject to law.'' Such a government, Beattie believed, has many advantages over any other form.

With respect to foreign nations, it may, by vesting the executive power in the king, act with more secrecy and expedition, than any of the republican forms; and it is less liable to dangerous contentions at home; because it is the interest of all ranks of persons in it, mutually to maintain the privileges of one another; and because, the executive power, in the hands of one person, can operate with more energy, than when it is committed to a senate, or to a number of magistrates.[13]

Like some more recent Christian writers who claim to derive their principles of politics from natural law (e.g., Emil Brunner), Beattie came out at last with a eulogy of his own country's political system—in his case, British constitutional monarchy—as the finest example of government according to the divine law of nature!

In spite of the fact that this Scottish moral philosopher's political theories were at some points out of harmony with the concepts of his adopted land, Campbell never forgot the lessons he learned out of the *Elements of Moral Science*.

OTHER EXPONENTS AND CRITICS OF THE NATURAL RIGHTS PHILOSOPHY

He also owed a considerable debt to Montesquieu, with whose works he apparently had a firsthand acquaintance and from which he often quoted. One discovers in Campbell, for example, such characteristic Montesquieuan emphases as the importance of the separation of powers and a system of checks and balances in the structure of government, and the influence of climate, geography, social customs, and religion upon the forms of political institutions.

Campbell was also familiar with Voltaire and Rousseau, the latter of whom reacted rather strongly against certain aspects of the Lockean natural rights philosophy. His references to both of these French thinkers were usually in relation to their views of religion, but he was too much of a Lockean to have accepted Rousseau's view of the community as having a collective good apart from the private interests of its members, and many of his other characteristic emphases.

Of other English writers in the field of politics and ethics, Campbell quoted from the works of William Godwin, Jeremy Bentham, David Hume and Edmund Burke. Although many of the extreme views of Godwin were not acceptable to him, he was impressed by Godwin's emphasis upon individualism, his opposition to coercive and oppressive institutions, and his ardent advocacy of peace. Campbell specifically opposed many of the views of Hume and Burke, as, for example, their insistence that the rights of man are purely conventional.

Among American political writers, he always showed the highest esteem for James Madison, sharing the former President's constitutionalism and emphasis upon government by laws rather than by men. He recommended the reading of the *Federalist,* by Madison, Hamilton, and Jay.

In his earlier years he had great respect for the political theories of Thomas Paine and Thomas Jefferson, although he was critical of their religious views and became increasingly so with the years. Of Paine he said that he was *"sane in politics,* but *insane in religion."*[14] He often eulogized "the immortal Jefferson" and followed him at many points, although in his later years this enthusiasm for Jefferson also seems to have cooled.[15]

In general, though, Campbell followed rather closely the Locke-Beattie version of the natural rights philosophy, and based his views of the state and government upon its presuppositions.

CHAPTER VI

AT THE VIRGINIA
CONSTITUTIONAL CONVENTION

IN SPITE of his vigorous statements on the separation of church and state and his nervousness in the presence of anything looking in the direction of clerical interference in politics, Alexander Campbell was a delegate to the Virginia Constitutional Convention which met in Richmond from October 5, 1829, to January 15, 1830.[1] It was here that he gave fullest expression to his views of the social compact and the fundamental principles of government, although he also dealt with many of the same issues in the same general period in articles in the *Christian Baptist* and *Millennial Harbinger*.

BACKGROUND AND PROCEDURE OF THE CONVENTION

With the election of Andrew Jackson as President in 1828, new and liberalizing forces came into power in the national government. Jacksonian democracy represented the political self-consciousness and emergence of the common man—the frontiersman of the West and the urban industrial worker of the East.

The conflict between conservative and liberal forces within the nation as a whole had its counterpart in the internal politics of many individual states. In none were the issues more clearly drawn than in Virginia. Geographically the state was divided into four sections: Tidewater, Piedmont, Shenandoah Valley, and Trans-Allegheny. The sectional controversy in Virginia went through three phases. In colonial days it was a struggle for power between the Williamsburg area and the older counties north of the James River. Later it centered around the demands of the newer settlements in the Piedmont counties. This phase ended with certain adjustments made in the convention of 1829-30. The third phase—the struggle of the Shenandoah Valley and Trans-Allegheny sections for a just share of political power—came to the fore in the debates of 1829-30 but was not settled until the Civil War brought the dismemberment of the state.

Charles H. Ambler says of the sectional controversy of this middle period:

It was a contest between an older society with its peculiar institutions and a newer society fundamentally different from the older and inadequately represented in the law-making bodies. It was a contest between the owners of large estates and the owners of small farms; between a population largely English and one composed of various nationalities; and between a people whose economic interests and relations were with the South and a people whose interests and relations were mainly with the North.[2]

In the years leading up to the convention of 1829-30 this conflict of interest had become apparent between the western and eastern portions of the state on many particular issues—especially slavery, the tariff, and internal improvements. The East defended the slave system, which was the foundation of its economy, while the West was beginning to question it. The West had begun to support protective tariffs, which the East opposed, and to look to the federal government for internal improvements, which the state government had refused to grant. In short, the West was beginning to advocate nationalism and "the American system," both of which were anathema to the East.

The convention "was the result of a half-century of conflict between the east and the west over representation, suffrage, and abuses in the state and local governments."[3] The East, with a total population of 348,873, had 134 representatives in the House of Delegates in

1828, while the West, with a total white population of
254,195, had only 80. As for suffrage, the possession of
twenty-five acres of improved land was a requirement
for voting, with the result that in 1829 only about 45,000
were entitled to vote whereas at least 31,000 male tax-
payers of legal age were excluded. Other moot points
involved the conduct of the legislature, the existence and
character of the governor's council, the county court
system, and the operation of the sheriff's office.

When the convention was called and each of the twenty-
four senatorial districts was allowed to elect four delegates, Campbell became a candidate for election from
his district. According to his friend Robert Richardson
he did so, reluctantly and with some misgivings, in response to the urgent insistence of his friends and fellow-
citizens.

"You may ask, What business had I in such matters?"
Campbell wrote to William Tener of Londonderry upon
his return from the convention.

I will tell you. . . . I consented to be elected . . . because I was
desirous of laying a foundation for the abolition of slavery . . .
and of gaining an influence in public estimation to give currency to my writings, and to put down some calumnies afar
off that I was not in good standing in my own State.

In the same letter he disclaimed any "taste or longings
for political matters or honors." But since the making
of a constitution was "one of the most grave and solemn
of all political matters, and not like the ordinary affairs
of legislation," his participation, he thought, was "not
incompatible with the most perfect gravity and self-
respect."[4] This is quite consistent with his general
position. As a constitutionalist and believer in government by laws rather than by men, he felt at liberty to
help debate and determine the fundamental principles of
government, even though he kept aloof from partisan
politics.

Campbell was chosen, along with Philip Doddridge, Charles Morgan, and Eugenius Wilson, to represent the district consisting of Ohio, Tyler, Brooke, Monongalia, and Preston counties.

When the delegates assembled, some of the foremost statesmen of Virginia and of the nation were present. Among them were former Presidents James Madison and James Monroe, Chief Justice John Marshall, Governor W. B. Giles, two United States senators (John Tyler and L. W. Tazewell), eleven representatives in Congress (among them John Randolph, C. F. Mercer, P. P. Barbour, and Philip Doddridge), and a number of judges, including William A. G. Dade, John W. Green and Abel P. Upshur.

The convention was significant not alone for the stature of the participants but also for the range of topics under discussion. Charles E. Merriam declares that, "In the Virginia Convention of 1829-30, there was an animated and extended debate in which almost every phase of political opinion was represented."[5] A participant in the convention would reveal his opinions on most of the fundamental issues involved in the ferment of Jacksonian democracy.

When the convention met, it resolved itself into four committes, each composed of one delegate from each senatorial district. To each committee was given the task of considering a particular phase of the constitution of 1776 and recommending the changes which it felt should be made. One committee was charged with considering the Bill of Rights, another the executive branch of government, a third the legislative, and a fourth the judicial. Alexander Campbell was appointed to the last of these committees.

From October 24 to December 16, 1829, the convention sat as a "committee of the whole" considering the recommendations of the four subcommittees. After debating and amending the subcommittees' recommendations the delegates convened as the "house." First they acted upon the amendments to the resolutions of the sub-committees, and then on the resolutions as amended by the committee of the whole. They then committed these actions to a drafting committee which drew up the proposed constitution. This in turn was taken up, beginning January 5, first as a committee of the whole, then as the house. Thus the delegates covered all the major issues several times. Only when they sat as the house were the votes of individuals recorded.

CAMPBELL'S ADDRESS ON
THE BASIS OF REPRESENTATION

After all committees had presented their reports, the first major topic called up for discussion, on motions of Doddridge and Campbell, was that of the basis of representation. The resolution of the committee on the legislative branch proposed "that in the apportionment of representation in the House of Delegates, regard should be had to the white population exclusively."[6] No sooner had this resolution been brought to the floor, than an amendment was proposed by John W. Green to strike out the concluding word "exclusively" and add, in lieu thereof, *"and taxation combined,"* the effect of which was to give eastern slaveholders a larger share of political power. Debate on the amendment continued for almost three weeks. During this time most of the more prominent delegates delivered one or more major addresses, covering not only this particular topic but many other aspects of political philosophy and practical politics as well.

After Judge Green had defended his amendment at some length, Campbell arose to offer "a remark or two in relation to the order of the Committee's proceedings." In a statement which was to be characteristic of his whole approach to the issues before the convention, he rebuked his fellow delegates for their unwillingness "to settle those fundamental principles, the sub-basis, as they might be termed, of the fundamental law of the community.'' The occasion for his rebuke was the refusal of the committee the day before to act on the recommendations of the committee on the Bill of Rights before plunging into the consideration of other committee reports.

Either adopt the principles in the Bill of Rights as canonical, and base all your subsequent proceedings upon them [he advised]; or, if those principles are considered unsound, let them be modified or amended; or else let gentlemen propose other principles as a substitute for them.[7]

These remarks and later statements in a similar vein show Campbell's view of government as based upon certain immutable principles. His subsequent addresses were given over largely to defending the basic principles of the Virginia Bill of Rights and seeking to deduce therefrom correct procedures of practical politics.

As the debate continued, addresses were given by Messrs. Upshur, Doddridge, Barbour, Baldwin, Powell, and Morris. On October 31 Campbell arose to deliver his first major address on the topic still under consideration—the basis of representation.

As a debater and orator Campbell seems to have made quite an impression. His ideas were not particularly unique, but he had a colorful personality and a vivid and forceful way of speaking, which compelled his opponents to take note.[8] As a result, some of the most prominent figures in the convention crossed verbal swords with him—Marshall, Randolph, Upshur, and others—and students of the debates, like Ambler, and of general political theory, like Merriam, have picked up and quoted many of his phrases.

Campbell opened his address on the ''basis question'' with a touch of humor and another lament that ''we did not first establish the principles ... on which the frame of Government should be based, before we attempted to

form the Constitution."[9] He then set forth four important items which the remarks he was about to offer
would "tend to establish."

1. That the principles of the friends of this amendment
   are based upon views of society, unphilosophic and anti-
   republican.
2. That the basis of representation, which they advocate, is
   the common basis of aristocratical and monarchical Governments.
3. That it cannot be made palatable to a majority of the
   present freeholders of Virginia; And,
4. That the white population basis, will operate to the advantage of the whole State.[10]

Instead of developing these points in logical fashion
he assumed it was his duty, rather, to counter the arguments of those on the affirmative. After refuting the
arguments of Richard Morris and John W. Green, he
directed his attention to the position of Abel P. Upshur,
of Northampton. He rejected Upshur's "postulate, that
there are two sorts of majorities; of numbers and interests; in plain English, of men and money." There are
also "majorities of talent, physical strength, scientific
skill, and general literature," which are all "more valuable than money, and as useful to the State." Why
ought not these majorities in the community have "as
much weight as mere wealth?" Carrying the arguments of his opponents to a *reductio ad absurdum,* Campbell asserted that "the property basis of representation,
never can become tolerably rational, until each vote is
valued at a given sum, and every man have as many votes,
as he has the stipulated price." He also rejected Upshur's assumption that "there are *no principles* in Government" but that "men are governed by *interest* only.
. . . by mere cupidity."[11]

It was in meeting the arguments of Philip P. Barbour,
of Orange, that Campbell gave his clearest statement
regarding natural rights and the nature of the social

compact. In defending the right of the majority he admitted that

men roaming at large, over the forests, could have no idea of majorities. . . . But, so soon as men form a social compact, it is one of the first things, which, from nature itself, would present itself to them. The true origin of this idea, is found in the nature and circumstances of men. Man is a social animal, and in obedience to this law of his nature, he seeks society, and desires the countenance of man.

Differences of opinion are bound to arise on matters of common interest. When this happens, one part must yield.

But, which . . . ? All nature cries, the inferior to the superior; the weaker to the stronger; the less to the greater. It is, then, founded on the nature of things . . . that, in case of a struggle, the minority must yield to the majority.[12]

At the same time each man deserves as much voice in the affairs of government as every other. In underscoring this point Campbell pictured a foreign enemy invading this country and spreading devastation, ruin, and death through the land. A few citizens escape and flee to the "wilds" beyond the Rocky Mountains. After having lived some two or three years unknown to each other, five of them meet to form a social compact.

A, in making his escape, had snatched a bag of dollars; B had taken his wife; C, his rifle; D, his children; and E had nothing but himself. They are about to form a social compact. They have brought some of the old ideas with them, from their former society.

A, an old Virginian, begins the discussion: "Gentlemen, Government is chiefly for *the protection of property,* and every man ought to have influence according to his property. I, therefore, contend for an influence, proportioned to my wealth." B argues that since he has a wife he deserves twice as much political power as A. C disagrees with both: "My *Rifle,* Sir, is of as much use, and my skill to use it, as either of your possessions."

Since the safety of all their persons and possessions may depend upon him, C claims a preponderance of political power. D then asserts his claims:

I have no money, no rifle, it is true; but I have seven sons and daughters coming forward. They will be able yet, Sir, to create wealth, and to defend the community. I insist upon it, gentlemen, if any man in this community has a right to *any* more than his own voice . . . I have *seven* good reasons to offer, why I should have seven times more than he.

E claims power equal to any of the others on the grounds that in case of a misunderstanding with the Indian tribes his knowledge of their languages will make him the most valuable member of the community as interpreter and peacemaker. After all have spoken, the "old Virginian" rises to say:

Gentlemen, I see we all have claims for various portions of political power. I think we must abandon the idea of forming a social compact, upon these principles. I will claim only my single vote . . . and will yield my pretensions, if every other gentleman yields his. I will agree, that we all surrender ourselves, our property, our talents, and our skill, *pro bono publico;* that each man shall have his own personal influence, and in all contributions for the public service, each man shall contribute in his own way, according to his respective ability.[13]

The right of suffrage, Campbell went on to say, "is not a right derived from, or conferred by, society; for it is a right which belongs to him as a man." It is nothing more or less than the right of a man's "thinking, willing and expressing his will. A vote is neither more nor less than the expression of a person's will." These powers were given to man by God and the right is therefore a natural right, which man brings with him into society.

No men could form a social compact, without first exercising what we must call the Right of Suffrage. It is [therefore] a right *natural* and *underived,* to the exercise of which, every man by nature has as good a reason as another.[14]

Turning then to "the great question, now pending before us," Campbell declared that if the amendment should succeed he would consider the principles of the Bill of Rights as having been abandoned.

A new principle will be sanctioned; the very principle on which the aristocracies and monarchies of the old world have been founded. Give men political power according to their wealth, and soon we shall have a legalized *oligarchy;* then come the thirty Tyrants; then follow the Quin decemviri; then the decemviri; then the triumvirate; and last of all, comes Julius Caesar.

"Men love power, and in proportion as they possess it, does that love increase."[15]

If the issue had become one of power, Campbell contended that the "white basis" would vest it "in the very hands of those who ought to hold it as umpires between the rival interests of the east and the west." He quoted figures to show that both the East and the West would lose and the middle gain representation on the white basis. This was proof that the delegates from the West, in supporting this proposal, were contending not for power but for principle.[16]

Campbell next took up the argument, advanced by his opponents, that if the white basis obtained there would be "endless discontentment among many of the citizens of this Commonwealth." In rejoinder, the said that "if the *black basis,* or the *money basis,* as it should be called, should obtain," this would neither diminish nor terminate "discontentment or complaint," for then a large majority of the freeholders "would be irreconcileably discontented." If there must be "discontents, murmurs and complaints," whichever way the issue was settled, "the question is, whether in policy and in justice, they had not better be confined to the minority, than spread through the majority of the citizens of this Commonwealth."[17]

In conclusion he expressed the opinion that the policy of his opponents was not only "anti-republican" but shortsighted as well. "That policy which augments the power of wealth, which tends to make the rich man richer, and the poor man poorer, is the worst policy for such a community as this is.'' He urged the wealthy to think of their own children, reminding them that ''riches are ever making to themselves wings,'' and that if they thus restricted the rights of the poor, their own descendants in one or two generations might be among those to suffer. ''My views of men, and of revolutions in human affairs, make me a republican. My love for my own posterity would prevent me from voting for the amendment, if I had no other considerations to govern me.''[18]

When Campbell finished, there were further addresses on the basis of representation and several amendments were proposed to the Green amendment. All were defeated as was the Green amendment itself on November 14. The liberal view prevailed—but by a very close vote of 49 to 47. The delegates then turned their attention to the second major problem, that of suffrage.

After completing the debates and actions on the remainder of the committee's recommendations the body returned to the discussion of the basis of representation on November 30. By this time the eastern group had gained in strength. The reformer Robert B. Taylor, from Norfolk, had resigned when his constituents opposed his liberal views, and he was replaced by a conservative, Hugh B. Grigsby. Madison and Marshall, at first neutral and inclined toward liberalism, had become more conservative as the debates proceeded. Some of the Piedmont delegates had reconciled themselves to eastern proposals which gave them most of the increases in representation, and there followed what amounted to a ''sell-out''' by John R. Cooke and Richard Henderson who had been the leaders of the ''white basis'' group.

Various plans were presented or revived by eastern delegates designed to supplant the ''white basis'' resolution still before the committee. They were presented by their sponsors, allegedly, "in the spirit of compromise." Campbell resented this portrayal of the situation and arose to declare: "We have heard nothing proposed as yet, which deserves the name of *compromise.*" "In the true spirit of conciliation and compromise," he therefore proposed a scheme of his own. This would have put representation in *both* houses on a white basis.[19] It was a futile gesture, as he seems to have recognized.

The plan finally adopted, known as the Gordon amendment, ignored the basic question entirely. Instead it made an arbitrary division of seats between the four major sections of the state. The delegates then considered various procedures for reapportioning representation periodically to meet shifts of population. At this juncture, on December 5, Campbell moved to submit the question to the people. His substitute amendment was defeated, and the motion of Upshur approved, providing that the legislature should have power to rearrange representation in both houses at stated intervals upon a fair average of the ratios of white population and federal numbers.

Later when the delegates faced the same issue as "the house" and the Cooke amendment was proposed—to reapportion representation once in ten years *within* each of the great districts, but not to disturb the balance *between* them—Campbell burst forth with one of his angriest statements. In the words of the reporter, he declared that

if he had been put to the torture to devise a mode of perpetuating the injustice done by the present scheme of apportionment between the Eastern and Western portions of the State, he could not have invented a more effectual one than that which had been proposed by the gentleman from Frederick. . . . It forever precluded . . . all hope of any redress of existing grievances.[20]

Madison offered a more flexible rule giving the legislature authority, "two-thirds of each House concurring, to make re-apportionments of Delegates and Senators throughout the Commonwealth.'' Even this, Campbell declared, was not satisfactory since ''there was no hope of getting two-thirds of the Legislature to assent to any equitable principle of apportionment whatever.'' He went on to propose a substitute amendment giving the General Assembly power to reapportion representation in both houses ''so that the number of Delegates in each of the four grand districts, shall bear the same proportion to the whole population of each district, which the present apportionment bears to the whole population of each district.''[21] The motion to strike out to make way for Campbell's amendment was defeated 42 to 33.

Campbell's votes on the basis of representation were cast in harmony with the principles he espoused in his addresses and remarks.[22] Twenty-four record votes of the convention dealt directly or indirectly with the principle of representation. In every instance Campbell voted the same as the other three delegates from his district—Doddridge, Morgan, and Wilson. The quartet voted with the majority only six times. Another ten votes dealt with readjustments of representation within the major districts of the state under the Gordon formula. In the logrolling involved in these decisions Campbell and the others from his district divided only once. On this subject, then, his views coincided with those of the secular politicans from his own district and with his own sectional interests.

Address on Suffrage

The second major issue to be taken up by the committee of the whole was that of suffrage. Paragraph three of the legislative committee's report recommended extension of this right to certain leaseholders and householders but still left 30,000 men of legal age without the franchise. After general debate and some minor changes, Eugenius Wilson, from Campbell's district, offered a substitute amendment which would have given the vote to practically "every free white male citizen of this Commonwealth, of the age of twenty-one years, and upwards, who shall have resided in this State two years, and in the county where he proposes to vote, one year."[23] After almost two days of debate, this was defeated by a vote of 53 to 37. Whereupon Campbell arose and offered a substitute amendment, similar to Wilson's, but with certain additional safeguards. According to his plan, natives would have to attain the age of *twenty-two* to qualify, and newcomers to the state would be required to make a declaration of their intention to become permanent residents.

Immediately after introducing this amendment, on November 19, Campbell launched into his second major address. This time he organized his thoughts more systematically and was less inclined merely to refute arguments of his opponents. The question, *"who shall be a citizen of this Commonwealth?"* he declared, was the basic issue confronting the convention.[24] Denying that his resolutions introduced any new theory, he affirmed: "I only wish to see the principles already defined, understood, and canonized [in the Bill of Rights], carried out to their proper extent." In these words Campbell showed again his deep desire to get back to "first principles." In a sense he revealed in political matters a Bill of Rights primitivism which paralleled his New Testament primitivism as a churchman. His reference to the Bill of Rights led him to declare: "I am more attached to the Bill of Rights, than I was before the late discussion commenced. I have seen that this instrument has been our palladium, and the only bulwark against the demolition of our republican citadel." He concluded this disgression with another fervent reference to "this now more than ever dear to me instrument."[25]

His resolutions "only developed the meaning of the 6th section of the Bill of Rights; the plain English interpretation of the words," he said. If a single idea "not founded on the fairest and most just interpretation of these words" were discovered in any of those resolutions, he hoped it would not be retained.[26] These statements suggest that he was about to apply to the Bill of Rights the same methods of exegesis which he customarily applied to the Bible. This is exactly what he proceeded to do with the phrase in the sixth article, "that all men, having sufficient evidence of permanent common interest with, and attachment to the community, have the right of suffrage."

Taking first the phrase *"common interest,"* he observed that these words do not mean *equal* interest. *"Common* interest admits of the greatest variety in the extent and value of that interest." This he illustrated by imagining a number of individuals with a great diversity of wealth and other interests, embarked on the same boat. All are equally interested in the safety of the ship. So in government. "No two interests are precisely equal, yet all have a *common interest.*"[27]

Next he examined the implications of the word *"permanent,"* which is at best, he held, a relative factor. "Our interests in the State are as transient and as uncertain as our lives." The possession of a "freehold of any given extent" is no guarantee of permanent interest, for the owner may "either sell or spend it in a very short time, and if we make his tenure of that estate the test of his permanent interest in the State, we have fixed upon as great an uncertainty as can be well conceived."[28]

The third word to be considered was *"attachment."* This is the *end* to which "permanent" and "common" are the *means*. "Property in the earth" is one proof of attachment but it is not the only or the strongest one. "Nativity is a stronger . . . and a more invariable evidence of attachment to a community, than wealth or

any other consideration." That was the basis of his
second resolution, which would extend the right of suffrage to every free white male of the age of twenty-two
years born within the state. He had fixed upon the age
twenty-two rather than twenty-one, he explained, to meet
the "fastidious objection" that at twenty-one a young
man has given no

evidence of permanent, common interest with, or attachment to,
the community . . . inasmuch as he has, till that moment, been
under the guardian and compulsory authority of his parent
or guardian. His living one year after he has become a free
agent, [however] destroys that objection, and, in addition to his
nativity, affords all necessary evidence of his attachment to the
community.[29]

His third resolution dealt with immigrants to the state
and those not enjoying suffrage under the existing constitution. Campbell proposed a procedure similar to
that of the federal government in the naturalization of
aliens.

A person who becomes an inhabitant of this State, and who
desires to become a citizen . . . goes to the court in the county
in which he resides, and declares his intention of becoming a
permanent resident. Twelve months afterwards, he returns to
the same court, and promises to submit to, and support the
Government of, this Commonwealth.

Is not this, he asked, "the strongest evidence which the
native of any other State can give of his attachment to,
and of his feeling a common interest with, the community?" It must so appear—and here he indulged in a
characteristic bit of sarcasm—to all except those "who
think that virtue, intelligence and patriotism, spring up
out of the soil, and grow like mushrooms upon its surface, after a person has paid a stipulated price for it."[30]

After considering his fourth resolution, which would
have excluded from citizenship all paupers "except such
as have rendered important services to their country,"
all persons of unsound mind, and all persons convicted of
any high crime or misdemeanor, Campbell concluded this

portion of his argument by insisting that his proposals
were reasonable, just, and accordant both with the
"spirit of the age" and the meaning of the Bill of Rights.
He disparaged the doctrine of expediency, to which some
of the members of the opposition had appealed, and
reasserted his own faith in the rights of man. Asking
the pardon of those who believed that "man has no
rights but what the different Governments in the world
please to bestow upon him," he declared: "Believe this
who may, I cannot. He has, in my judgment, certain inherent and inalienable rights, of which he cannot be di-
vested with impunity. Amongst those is the right of a
voice in the Government, to which he is to submit."[31]

After tracing the right of general suffrage back to the
time of Moses, he referred to the impassioned remarks
of John Randolph, a few days before, protesting against
"his majesty *King Numbers*." Far from assuming an
apologetic attitude, Campbell exulted:

King Numbers, Mr. Chairman, is the legitimate sovereign of all
this country. General Jackson, the President of these United
States, is only the representative, the *lawful representative* of
King Numbers. And, whither, Sir, can that gentleman fly from
the government of this King? . . . Except he cross the ocean,
he can put himself under no other King. And whenever he
may please to expatriate himself, he will find beyond the dominions of King Numbers, there is no other monarch, save King
Cypher, King Blood, King Sword, or King Purse. And . . .
there is none of those so august as our King. I love King Numbers; I wish to live, and I hope to die, under the government
of this majestic personage. He is, Sir, a wise, benevolent, patriotic and powerful prince—the most dignified personage under the canopy of Heaven.

After this eulogy of "King Numbers," Campbell extolled the glories of "the tribunal of *public opinion*."
"This is the supreme tribunal in this extensive country,"
he said. "All our acts must be judged by it, and I rejoice to live in a country in which this is the supreme
law."[32]

Once more, as in the close of his earlier address, he asserted that this amendment would aid the East as much as the West and warned that "when we disfranchise one class of men . . . to secure any property or privilege we possess, we endanger that very property and those very privileges, more by such disfranchisements, than we protect them." He whom we disfranchise becomes bitter and seeks to destroy those rights which are "held at his expense" and the whole system "which degrades him in his own estimation." For the safety and preservation of those very interests, Campbell conceived the extension of the right of suffrage "indispensable."[33]

Following his address the question was put on Campbell's motion and, as the reporter succinctly declared, "It passed in the negative by a very large majority, eleven only rising in the affirmative."[34]

As the debate continued, proponents of a property qualification for voting insisted that freehold suffrage was not "aristocratical" or "oligarchical" since in most counties one could secure enough land to give him the right of suffrage for fifty dollars or less. Only the lazy, therefore, were excluded from the privilege of voting. To which Campbell replied: "No man with due respect to himself and his rights, would stoop to purchase what he had a right to demand."[35] A few moments later another speaker expressed opposition to cutting down the venerable tree planted by his forefathers and planting another in its stead. Campbell declared "the gentleman's alarm about the axe imaginary; it was only a pruning knife to lop off a few aristocratical branches."[36] Various motions were then made and votes taken on the subject of suffrage, most of the decisions going against the West.

Campbell's only other statement or motion on the subject of suffrage came when the house was considering the amendments proposed by the committee of the whole.

After his colleagues Wilson and Doddridge had each failed in similar attempts, he moved to insert into the resolution of the legislative committee the proposal to extend suffrage to all native-born and naturalized free white males on the basis merely of residence and their having paid all taxes assessed against them. In response to the angry remarks of Giles and Henderson, Campbell voiced the familiar western belief that "it was owing to the restraints upon the Right of Suffrage, that Virginia was so far behind some of her neighbors in the culture of her soil, and the progress of general improvement."[37] His amendment was rejected 57 to 36.

Seventeen record votes were taken on the subject of suffrage, on all of which Campbell and the three other delegates from his district agreed. They voted with the majority in regard to most of the modifications proposed to the original recommendations of the legislative committee.[38] But on the crucial issue—the extension of suffrage to all free white males on the basis of residence, and so forth—they were always with the losing minority.

Once again there seem to be no differences between the political conclusions of Campbell, the religious reformer, and the "politicians" from his own district. All espoused and voted for what to their colleagues of the East seemed to be radically republican principles.

Address on the County Court System

The third topic on which Campbell delivered a major address, and another of the most controversial issues of the convention, was the reform of the county court system. He had been a member of the subcommittee on the judiciary which was safely in the control of the conservatives under the chairmanship of John Marshall. When Campbell's proposals to make the county courts more responsible to the people were voted down in committee, he later presented the same proposals as a minority report to the convention on October 24.

The committee resolutions left the county court system practically untouched with the magistrates retaining power to nominate their own successors. As soon as discussion was in order on this subject, Thomas M. Bayly, of Accomack, one of the few strongholds of liberalism in the Tidewater section, moved to amend the first resolution by striking out the words "and in the county courts"—the effect of which would have been to eliminate the county courts as constitutional courts. Chief Justice Marshall arose to oppose this change in the basic character of the county court system. The debate on this issue carried over to the following day, December 1, when Campbell addressed himself to the subject at hand.

The issue was one of crucial importance to Campbell because more of our happiness depends upon the government of the county than upon either the state or federal government, "not merely, because it is nigher home, but because we have more to do with it, or under its jurisdiction."[39]

The basic objection which he leveled against the existing system was that the county courts were not responsible to the people. He suggested a threefold treatment of the topic which he failed to follow in any systematic fashion: "the *manner* in which they are created, . . . their incompetency to discharge those duties assigned them, and the consequent evil influence which they may exercise over the destinies of a county."[40]

His basic criticism was that "the citizens of any county in this Commonwealth, have no more control over these tribunals, than they have over the Government of France or England. . . . We live under a Government not amenable to us, not *responsible* to us; because not created by us."

Some four or five justices are assigned to the bench of [a] new county and the county assigned to them. These justices are to nominate their *successors forever*. Thus the county is . . . signed, sealed, and delivered over to the four or five magistrates first appointed and their successors, as far as all the offices of trust, honor, and profit, as far as the public concerns and interests, as far as the public levies and their appropriations are concerned, or assignable.[41]

Under these circumstances the county is subordinated to three sorts of pride—religious, family, and political. Campbell imagined the first group of justices as being of one religious creed, and showed that they had it in their power to choose their successors from their own particular sect. Here, as in his address on the "basis question," Campbell recognized the dangers of power, the weaknesses of human nature, and the necessity for checks and balances in the structure of government. It was not necessary for him to prove that justices always misused their appointive powers for sectarian ends, he contended. It was only necessary "to show, that they will have the opportunity to do so, to prove the system to be a bad one."[42]

In the same way, if the first justices were all of one family, they had the power of keeping the succession in their own family. If two or three families were involved, they might enter into an understanding by which the office would rotate between the different families so as to "secure to themselves the dominion of the county for ages." The first set of magistrates might be "of one political creed, or of another, and thus an undue preponderance is given to that which is placed upon the bench without the hope of removal."[43]

Although he did not specifically refer to it, Campbell was obviously, in this portion of his address, measuring the existing county court system by the yardstick of the second article of the Bill of Rights, which declared "that all power is vested in, and consequently derived from, the people; that magistrates are their trustees and servants and at all times amenable to them." When he did refer to this article later on, he asked, "When did the justices of the peace derive their power from the people; and how, or in what sense are they responsible or *amenable* to them?''[44]

He proceeded next to show that the county court system violated the principle of separation of powers and functions set forth in the fifth article of the Bill of Rights. ''The variety of powers and functions which are lodged in the same hands, and their incompatibility with each other,'' he said, ''have been for a long time an object of serious and just complaint.'' After listing a few of the specific powers which county court justices exercised, Campbell declared that they ''unite in their own persons all sorts of powers, Legislative, Executive, Judicial, military; and if all these can be safely lodged in the same hands, and at the same time, then . . . all the doctrines on which our political system is founded are erroneous and fallacious.''[45]

The system, he inferred, violated a provision of the sixth article of the Bill of Rights against taxation without representation. ''Do not the magistrates composing the county courts tax us, and deprive us of our property for public uses without our consent, or that of our Representatives?'' The system also virtually repudiated the provision of the fourth article of the Bill of Rights by conferring *''exclusive* privileges, without, and anterior to any public services'' and by tending to make the magistracy *''hereditary.''*[46]

After having tried the county court system by the second, fifth, sixth, and fourth articles of the Bill of Rights, in that order, and found it wanting, Campbell finally quoted the third article of the existing constitution of Virginia which declared that ''the Legislative, Executive, and Judiciary Departments of Government, shall be separate and distinct, so that neither exercises the powers properly belonging to the other; nor shall ever any person exercise the powers of more than one of them.'' The very fact that the founding fathers, after having laid down this principle, went on to make an ex-

ception in the case of the county court justices, by permitting them to sit in either house of the assembly, shows
that this is "not compatible with the doctrine of the
framers of the old Constitution." There may have been
some excuse for this exception at the time of the Revolution when capable leaders were few, but Campbell insisted that the time had now come to get back to the
original principle of the separation of powers. He
quoted Montesquieu on this point and then went on to
ask: "If ... one body of Judges may appoint their own
successors, why may not another body? Why not then
permit the Judges of the ... Court of Appeals, to appoint
their own successors?" With mounting irony he suggested that if these magistrates were so wise they ought
to be given the power "of filling all vacancies in the Legislative Assemblies" and "the right to elect all our
Representatives"![47]

In all seriousness he reminded his hearers that already
the corporate towns in the commonwealth (Richmond,
Petersburg, Norfolk, and others) were electing their
magistrates. These, in his judgment, were as well qualified as any judges in the state. "Why the counties of
Ohio, and Brooke ... cannot do the same," he could not
understand. "I am for reposing the greatest confidence
in the people. The power is safely lodged in their hands;
more safely, I am sure, than in a few privileged ones,
whom they never appointed their *trustees*."[48]

He repeated that he was no enemy of county courts,
but that he wished to "leave them in the power, and subject to the wisdom of legislation" instead of binding
them "irrevocably and unalterably upon posterity by
Constitutional provision." He urged the convention to
go on record as favoring *a* system of county courts rather
than *the* county courts, for "*a* Court of Appeals will admit of Legislative provision, but *the* County Courts will
not."[49]

At the conclusion of this address, Bayly's motion to eliminate the constitutional provision for these courts was defeated. Campbell then moved to strike out the word "the" so as to let the clause read "and in County Courts." With Marshall's support, his motion carried by a vote of 48 to 42—the only significant motion by Campbell to be adopted by the convention. The next morning the action was reconsidered and the "the" restored!

On December 10 the committee returned to the report on the judiciary, and Campbell moved a substitute for the fifth resolution to permit some popular voice in the nominating of magistrates of county courts. When that was rejected, he suggested bitterly "that neither Governor nor Council ought to be troubled in the case at all. Let the County Court who now recommend, have power also to appoint: for there it ended at last."[50]

In its action upon the recommendations of the committee of the whole the convention took twenty record votes on judicial matters. Campbell voted with the majority only nine times and with the losing minority eleven times.[51] Again he followed the reform line of the West. Here for the first time we find some division in the votes of the four delegates from his district, but it was on relatively minor points and reveals no significant pattern of divergence.

VIEWS ON OTHER SUBJECTS

A fourth major problem of the convention dealt with the office of the governor, his election and powers, and the continuance or discontinuance of the executive council. Campbell made no address on this subject; in fact, he made no comment in connection with the extended debates upon it. Still his opinions can be discovered from his votes when the issues came before the convention as a whole.

The report of the subcommittee on the executive department made certain concessions to the liberal viewpoint. Its third resolution declared, "That the Executive Council, as at present organized, ought to be abolished, and that it is inexpedient to provide any other Executive Council."[52] It also provided for the popular election of sheriffs in the different counties. On the other hand, it recomended no change in the method of electing the governor, which in the existing constitution was by the General Assembly.

In the committee of the whole, two efforts to provide for the popular election of the governor were defeated. It was voted instead that he should be elected by the legislature for a three-year term and then be ineligible for the next three years. The elimination of the executive council was approved.

When matters pertaining to the executive branch finally came before the house and record votes were taken, Campbell voted in favor of the popular election of the governor, and for abolishing the executive council.[53]

Again his votes were in agreement with those of the other delegates from his district. The interesting thing is that his opinions on the executive branch were more popular than his views on legislative and judicial matters, for here he voted on the winning side more often than on the losing.

The report of the subcommittee on the legislative department introduced what were perhaps the two major issues of the convention—the basis of representation and suffrage. Certain other recommendations of this committee were of considerable importance to Campbell and called forth minor statements.

Shortly after his address on suffrage, the delegates took up the remaining resolutions of the legislative committee, passing quickly to the ninth on religious liberty. After declaring that "no man shall be compelled to frequent or support any religious worship, place, or ministry whatsover," and that "the Legislature shall have no power to prescribe any religious test whatever, nor to ... confer any peculiar privileges or advantages on any one sect or denomination, over others," it concluded with this proviso: "Provided, however, that the foregoing clauses shall not be so construed, as to permit any minister of the gospel, or priest of any denomination, to be eligible to either House of the General Assembly."[54]

When this resolution came before the house, Richard Henderson moved to strike out the proviso which disqualified ministers from holding seats. In opposition to this motion it was argued that ministers were a peculiar and privileged order by virtue of their being licensed to preach and exempted from military duty, and should not be eligible to the General Assembly. At this Campbell arose to say that these objections applied with equal force to justices of the peace, and nobody contended for excluding them![55] For all of his insistence upon the separation of church and state, Campbell was one of fourteen voting for the elimination of this proviso and in behalf of making ministers eligible for seats in the General Assembly.[56] In this vote his viewpoint was shared by Doddridge and Morgan from his district, although Wilson voted to retain the proviso.

The subject of religious incorporation or religious charters was next brought before the committee of the whole. William H. Broadnax moved that the legislature, which then possessed the power to incorporate seminaries and other religious institutions, have power to review and repeal those charters or acts of incorporation whenever they deemed it expedient. It was inevitable that Campbell should arise to express his opposition to this motion and, in fact, to all incorporations of religious institutions.[57] The amendment was defeated with only twelve voting in its favor. When the convention came to this point in its deliberations as the house, Campbell moved the amendment, "That no incorporation for any eccelesiastical or religious purpose, shall ever be granted, or have validity in this Commonwealth.''[58]   His remarks in this connection were similar to those earlier in the committee of the whole; his motion was "indefinitely postponed" by a vote of 77 to 19.   His colleagues from his district all voted for the motion.[59]

After the house had gone over all of the recommendations of the committee of the whole and had submitted its actions to a subcommittee to prepare a draft of the proposed constitution, there was a lull in which numerous proposals were presented.   Among them was a resolution by Campbell on public education which is significant because it pointed toward his growing interest in the subject.[60]   It was received and ordered printed, but when he moved later for its consideration, the reporter noted: "The question being put . . . the House refused to consider it."[61]

Shortly after Campbell had presented his resolution on education, Archibald Stuart, Jr., proposed one in regard to dueling.   This would have given the legislature power to provide by law "that no person shall be capable of holding or being elected to any post of profit, trust or emolument, civil or military, under the Government of this Commonwealth, who shall hereafter fight a duel, or send or accept a challenge to fight a duel."   It provided further that, before any person could be elected or appointed to office, he must take such an oath as might be prescribed by law declaring that he had not violated the provisions of the constitution in this regard.[62]

This motion set off a heated debate to which Campbell contributed a few remarks explaining why he would vote in favor of the resolution.   He would do so as a means of preventing "one of the most barbarous crimes of the age."[63]   In the four votes taken on this resolution, Campbell favored one to strike out the part pertaining to the oath, but voted against every effort to block the resolution itself.   The delegates from his district divided on each of these four votes, but there seems to be no special pattern or significance in their division. After they had deleted the portion dealing with the oath, the convention approved the resolution 71 to 22.

The frequency of legislative sessions was an issue which divided East and West, the West favoring fewer and shorter sessions with the funds saved going into internal improvements. Campbell joined Morgan and Wilson in voting for a resolution which provided that the legislature should meet only once in two years, unless called into special session; Doddridge opposed. This resolution, which was defeated 26 to 69, is of interest because later, in his discussion of education, Campbell was to make the suggestion that there be fewer sessions of the General Assembly, with the money saved being used to help finance a program of public education.

RESULTS AND CONCLUSIONS

The amount of western dissatisfaction with the constitution as drafted is indicated by two votes taken by the house, one on a motion to prepare an official copy of the new constitution, which Campbell, Morgan, and Wilson opposed—Doddridge being ill and unable to vote. This passed by a vote of only 53 to 42. The subsequent motion on the question, "Shall this constitution pass?" was also opposed by Campbell and the other two voting from his district. The constitution was approved by the convention—but by the relatively narrow margin of 55 to 40.

When it was submitted to the people of the state for their ratification, the constitution was accepted by a majority of 26,055 to 15,563. Of the counties west of the Alleghenies only two voted for it. Most of the others voted overwhelmingly against it. Before the vote was taken in his own county of Brooke, Campbell addressed the people, outlined the main features of the proposed constitution, and expressed the hope that they would reject it on account of the "anti-republican principles" upon which it was based.[64] His remarks apparently had considerable effect, for when the voting was over all 371 of Brooke County's votes had been registered against ratification. This was the only county in the state to vote unanimously in opposition.

Far from satisfying the trans-Allegheny regions, the constitution made the people of this section more bitter than ever before. They had gone into the reform movement of the 1820's with relatively few grievances, but they came out deserted by their allies of the Valley and with no hope of attaining redress. There was a wave of reaction in the West, including many threats of secession. The center of sectional agitation now shifted from the Shenandoah Valley to the trans-Allegheny, and became largely a contest between the areas which are today West Virginia and Virginia proper.

The so-called "Reform Convention" of 1850-51 adopted most of the progressive measures for which Campbell had stood in 1829-30. It eliminated the property qualification for suffrage; abolished the mixed basis of representation; granted the popular election of governor, lieutenant governor, and many other officers; and overhauled the county court system by providing for the popular election of the justices. Even this did not reconcile the trans-Allegheny. With the intensification of debate over slavery and the coming of the Civil War, this section separated from Virginia in 1861. It is amazing that Campbell took no notice as an editor of either the Convention of 1850-51 or the measures leading to the secession of West Virginia. At the time of the Reform Convention he was busy urging the Christian duty of obedience to the Fugitive Slave Law. By 1861 he was weakened by age and lacked his earlier alertness to public issues.[65]

Campbell's performance at the Virginia Constitutional Convention points to two conclusions: First, that he was a consistent "reformer" in the terms of Ambler's analysis of the political theories represented there. It is of more than passing significance that Ambler frequently quotes Campbell's statements as typifying the reformer point of view. Within the framework of national political trends, a study of Merriam's profile of Jacksonian political theory shows Campbell, in the main, following the trend of the times or, in his own phrase, "the spirit of the age."

A second conclusion, based upon a comparison of Campbell's attitudes and votes with those of his colleagues from the same district, is that his left-wing religious position did not lead him to espouse any different political theories or policies than those of the "politicians" from his district. When he came to help formulate a governmental compact, he turned from the Bible to natural law and found his norms where other Americans of his time found them—in the Bill of Rights and the supporting philosophy of Locke, Montesquieu, Jefferson, and others.

CHAPTER VII

THEORY OF GOVERNMENT

NOWHERE did Alexander Campbell give a comprehensive and systematic statement of his theory of government. Still in the light of his addresses and actions at the Virginia Convention and certain of his writings it will be possible to set forth, in rather systematic fashion, his leading ideas concerning the social compact and the ends, elements, and forms of government.

THE SOCIAL COMPACT

Like Locke, Beattie, and others of the natural rights school, Campbell occasionally pictured man in the state of nature. In addition to the parable of the forming of a social compact in his address before the Virginia Convention, he alluded to the subject again in 1843 in the debate with Rice.[1] He believed that the stuff out of which society is made is an aggregation of free and independent individuals.

There are certain forces which impel man toward society. One is his own nature. "Man is a social animal. . . . Alone and solitary, he is like the owl in the desert, and pelican in the wilderness."[2] From the very constitution of his nature, man's happiness will always be incomplete if he is deprived of society. There are clear echoes of Beattie in Campbell's suggestion that diversities of interest and ability help give rise to society and government. "If all minds were equal," he declared, "there would be no government in the world. But it might need none."[3] The other major factor in impelling men toward government is what Locke and Beattie characterized as the "inconveniences" or "inconveniencies" of the state of nature—the invasion of each other's rights and the threat of attack from other societies.[4]

Motivated by their own social natures and by the utilitarian desire to escape the inconveniences of the state of nature, men enter into society. Campbell insisted that this requires a compact or agreement of some sort. In his debate with Owen he declared: "A society without a social compact, to me is unintelligible. Society is not a number of persons covering a certain piece of ground like the trees in our forests. They must congregate upon some stipulations express or implied."[5]

Like Locke before him, Campbell was not too clear in discriminating between the social and governmental compacts. That he made room for such a distinction is clear from his Independence Day oration in 1830 in which he treated history in four "chapters," the first of which (down to the time of the flood) he characterized as "society without civil government."[6] Generally, however, he seemed to equate the social and civil compacts. This was true of all his remarks on the subject at the Virginia Convention. It also seems to have been the implication of a passage in the debate with Rice where, after describing man in the state of nature, he continued:

At last, tired of his wandering over nature's wilds, [man] courts society, and would fondly purchase it at some price. He is asked to surrender so many of his assumed natural and inalienable rights and liberties, for the sake of other advantages found in the fellowship and intercommunication of co-ordinate beings. He agrees to sell so many rights for so many privileges. The bargain is now closed, and is called a *constitution*.[7]

ENDS OF GOVERNMENT

Campbell's fullest statement on the ends of government was made in an address on "Common Schools" in 1841.

The chief end of government is not to preserve itself, build up its own fortunes, and aggrandize itself; but to develope a nation's resources, direct its energies, provide for its exigencies, and protect it from intestine rivalries and animosities, as well as from extrinsic encroachments from foreign power; or, in one sentence, to protect the people in the full enjoyment of all their rights.[8]

This and other similar statements suggest that the chief ends of government are welfare, order, justice, defense, and freedom.

From his characterization of the inconveniences of the state of nature Campbell could be expected to look upon government as a means of defense against aggression from without and from disorder and injustice within. This he did, sometimes by explicit statement, sometimes by implication. "The first aim of all communities," he declared in 1833, "is to get up an efficient system of defence against the infractions of other societies, and to defend the individual members of it from the inroads and frauds of their fellow-citizens."[9] Yet he had no profound sense of the evil in human nature or of the need for restraint. Generally speaking, he shared the optimistic view of human nature characteristic of the Enlightenment. An evidence of this is the fact that he looked upon government as required only for the unregenerate and as a temporary expedient.

In addition to these ends of defense, order, and justice, Campbell also thought of government as a means of making more secure the "rights of man"—both natural and conventional. Although this was one of the fundamental purposes of government, he was not too sanguine about its accomplishment. He often seems to have looked upon government as more of a threat to freedom than as a means of preserving it. One indication of this was his emphasis upon the Bill of Rights at the Virginia Convention.

There is little room for doubt that for Campbell the chief end of government is welfare. Starting out, in the passage quoted above, with the premise that "the chief end of government is not to preserve itself . . . but to develope a nation's resources,'' he went on to say that ''mind'' is a significant part of a nation's wealth. Therefore, ''the intellectual and moral improvement of all the mind belonging to the State is the first concern of every intelligent, just, and patriotic government.''[10] But this was not the only welfare function of government which he recognized. He also gave government a large role in facilitating the economic development of the nation[11] and, after being involved in a railroad accident, took occasion to urge civil action to safeguard travelers.[12]

As his thought matured, some changes took place in the relative importance which he attached to these different ends of government. Actually, defense never occupied a large place in his thinking—due perhaps to the relative security of the nation from outside attack. Justice was always important, as will be seen from his concern for the Cherokee Indians, the sanctity of business debts, the property rights of the South in their slaves, and many other instances. Freedom was one of his greatest rallying cries in the period through 1830 and beyond, although as soon as he began to take a more constructive attitude toward church and public affairs, his emphasis shifted increasingly from freedom to order. Welfare remained a constant emphasis throughout his life.

ELEMENTS OF GOVERNMENT

Campbell's most systematic discussion of the elements of government occurred in a supplement to the *Millennial Harbinger* for August, 1834, on ''The Kingdom of Heaven''—one of the numerous *Extras* which he issued from time to time. His primary concern in this document was the kingdom within the church, but as an analogy and introduction he set forth certain portions of his political theory which were detailed nowhere else.

The essential elements of a kingdom are five: ''King, Constitution, Subjects, Laws, and Territory.'' ''In *forming a state,"* he declared, "the essential elements are people and country." The "people" at this stage of development includes both the king or president, and the citizens or subjects. The undifferentiated people "make a constitution, and this makes a President or a King, citizens or subjects, and everything else belonging to a state."[13]

It is the constitution which differentiates the king or president from the citizens or subjects: ". . . it makes one man a king and the rest subjects." It is the constitution, also, which determines the form of government. As he states it: "It is . . . the relation into which the people resolve themselves, which makes it a republic, an aristocracy, a monarchy." If they choose a monarchy, "they first make the constitution, and this places one upon the throne—makes them subjects."[14]

The last element of a kingdom—laws—derives from the king: ". . . and he gives them laws." Campbell here conceived of law as being the expression of the will of the sovereign. In a republic law is the expression of the will of the sovereign people as registered through their representatives. He once referred to law as "the authoritative will of the majority," and again spoke of "that species of common consent called law."[15]

Consistent with his view of the constitution as making king and subjects, or governor and citizens, he elsewhere insisted that the civil compact is made among the equal and independent people rather than between a sovereign and his subjects. Much confusion on this point, he believed, arises from taking the covenant of Israel as typical. Actually this constitution was unique. It emanated not from the people but "from him who stood in a relation towards the governed in which no other being stood, or ever could stand."[16] With Beattie, Campbell argued that the Jewish government provides no justification for the divine right of kings.

While a *constitution* is a compact made among the people, *government* involves mutual obligations as between the people and those in authority. In the debate with Owen, Campbell declared that in every society "the people and the magistracy . . . are mutually accountable to each other."[17] He later spoke of a constitution as involving "an agreement on certain principles between the government and the citizens."[18]

RIGHTS OF MAN UNDER CIVIL GOVERNMENT

Attention has already been drawn to Campbell's view that when man enters into a social or civil compact he "sells" certain of the rights which he enjoyed in the state of nature. "In entering into society man surrenders a part of his natural liberty for other benefits, which he could not enjoy as a hermit," he declared in the debate with Owen.[19] In the Rice debate he specified the rights which have been sold: "The law-giving power, with the power of judging and government, he has sold; and therefore, he can, of right, use these functions no more, unless they are granted to him by the persons with whom he has identified his fortunes."[20]

There are some rights which man has received from his Creator, which he is "bound by the relation in which he stands to the *donor,* and by the laws of his own constitution to preserve." These "natural rights" belong to man "merely because he exists," and are therefore equal rights. They are "underived . . . as respects human society," and may not be abridged when he enters into society. "To preserve life, to pursue happiness, or to seek food and entertainment for mind and body, is the right and duty of all men."[21] In his debate with Rice, Campbell included among man's "natural rights" freedom of movement upon the earth, ownership of a part of "Mother Earth," and freedom of speech.[22]

For all of his emphasis upon the "rights of man," it
is obvious that this concept of certain rights having been
"sold" might lead to a rather conservative political theory. Campbell did tend in this direction in his later
years. Yet he never forgot or denied that supreme political power resides always in the people, and that government rests upon the consent of the governed. Even
those rights which have been "sold" or entrusted to the
various organs of government may be taken back by the
people if their magistrates fail to fulfill the conditions
of the civil compact or rule contrary to the will of the
majority. "The members of every state, not governed
according to the maxims of reason and justice," he affirmed, " have a right inalienable to effect a revolution
by all *lawful* means, or to emigrate."[23]

Like Locke, Campbell seems to have ruled out individual resistance or revolution. Only the majority of the
people have a right to effect revolution, or to resist the
commands of government. This point was most clearly
made in connection with the discussion of the Fugitive
Slave Law in 1851. He roundly criticized those who advised or countenanced resistance to a law which "merely
represents and reflects the will of the sovereign people."
In response to the argument "that we the sovereign people ... have all power in our hands ... and ... are responsible to no superiors, only to our own good sense, our
consciences, and our God," he said:

On a little calm reflection, we all concede that we cannot retain
and delegate the same power. . . . We cannot, simultaneously,
represent ourselves and be represented by others. When, therefore, our representatives have made laws, we cannot ourselves,
individually, annul them. This is not our form of government. The power that creates, is the only power that can
destroy. The power that gives the law, is the only power that
can annul it.[24]

The word "individually" in this passage is of key
importance. The individual or even a small minority
cannot annul laws made by the representatives of all

the people. ''The power that creates'' is the whole people acting through their elected representatives. Only the people as a whole can annul a law or effect a revolution. In accordance with this principle, Campbell pointed out that, if a particular law is unpopular and unacceptable, the people have ''the power to elect new representatives, and have it repealed.''[25]

FORMS OF GOVERNMENT

Many of Campbell's remarks concerning the forms of government *after* the Virginia Convention seem strangely inconsistent with his earlier enthusiasm for the American government and his devotion to the Bill of Rights. For his customary conclusion was that monarchy is the *ideal* form of government. Here he showed his indebtedness to Beattie rather than Locke.

''History testifies,'' according to Campbell in his *Extra on The Kingdom,* ''that Republics are better adapted to peace than war.'' As he put it later, even republicans concede ''that a kingdom is better adapted to a state of war, than a republic.'' Republics are ''forced and unnatural organizations of society,'' monarchy being ''the only form of government . . . which nature recognizes,'' and the most rational.

The most approved theory of human nature and of human government now current wherever the English language is spoken, either in the Old World or in the New, is, that a monarchy would be always the best government, because the cheapest, the most efficient, and the most dignified; provided only, that the crown was placed on the wisest head and sceptre wielded by the purest hands. Could we always secure this we would all be monarchists; because we cannot, we are all republicans.[26]

Although they are not the most natural or the most rational forms of government, still ''in these last days of degeneracy Republics are great blessings to mankind,'' Campbell maintained. ''While men are . . . so degenerate, and while selfishness and injustice are so rampant in society, republican officers are better than kings—because we can get rid of them sooner." His disillusionment with "republican officers" is strikingly revealed in this phrase and in the sentence which follows. "They are, indeed, kings under another name, with a short-leased authority; and our experience fully demonstrates that in these degenerate days the reigns of our republican kings are nearly long enough." There is a world of disillusionment also in his next sentence:

Till the King of kings comes, we Christians ought to be good republicans, under the conviction that human governments seldom grow better, and that the popular doctrine of our country is true—that political authority generally makes a man worse, and public favors almost invariably corrupt the heart.

Although Campbell elsewhere offered an implied criticism of the spoils system, there was at least this to be said for it:

Rapid rotation in office is the practical influence of the republican theory; and the experiment proves that, brief as republican authority is, it is sometimes too long for republican virtue to sustain without deterioration.[27]

The period of the *Extra on The Kingdom of Heaven* represents perhaps the low point in Campbell's pessimism regarding democracy. It was the period of his greatest disillusionment with American political life. At the same time some of his seeming enthusiasm for monarchy in this *Extra* is due to the analogy he was seeking to establish for his discussion of the church; for the church, on his premises, must be a monarchy. Still there can be no denying that this represents a considerable recession from his exuberant, ultra-republicanism of the previous decade and shows how deep an influence Beattie had upon his thinking.

In his addresses before the Virginia Convention Campbell had shown a realistic recognition that power feeds upon itself. "Men love power, and in proportion as they possess it, does that love increase." He therefore applauded all republican checks upon that power—the system of checks and balances, constitutional and legal limitations upon political power, and the ballot box, which makes officials responsive to the will of the people. His mature thought on the matter, as stated in 1857, was that

> It is the vices of man invested with a little brief authority, that has made our form of government the very best in this world of vices and vicious men. . . . We choose a *democratic* or *republican* form of government, because we can thus hold in abeyance the avarice and ambition of a tyrant "clothed with a little brief authority." . . . Had we in every king a David or a Solomon, we should all be monarchists. As it is, we are all democrats or republicans, because we, the people, can best govern our governors, and rule our rulers out of place and power of encroachment upon our reserved rights and privileges.[28]

Campbell often observed that "God having prescribed no one form of political government, has equally sanctioned every form which society chooses to assume."[29] The Bible "prescribes no form of human government, because no one form of government would suit all the countries, climes, and people of the earth."[30] "That Government," therefore, "is best for any people that is best adapted to their views, wants, wishes, and even prejudices."[31]

Part Three

Problems of Practical Christian

Citizenship

CHAPTER VIII

DENOMINATIONAL ELEMENTS IN
CAMPBELL'S LATER THOUGHT

A GAINST the background of this study of Alexander
Campbell's left-wing, sect-type religious orientation
and of the right-wing, natural law elements in his political theory, it is now possible to examine the manner in
which these somewhat contradictory factors interacted
in his views and actions as a Christian citizen.

A clue is found in the fact that from about 1831 to the
middle of the following decade Campbell's conception of
the church underwent a gradual transformation from
that of the radical sect form to that of the characteristic
American church form—the denomination. In the same
manner—although beginning at a later date, and in a
more limited and tentative manner—his political ethics
approached that of the denominational form.

MATURING VIEWS ON CHURCH ORGANIZATION

When he and his followers were pushed out of the
Baptist fold, Campbell began to take a more positive and
constructive attitude toward church organization. The
first step in this direction was his advocacy of cooperation among local congregations. In his *Christian Baptist*
days Campbell had been so obsessed with the "perfect
independency of the church" that any *association* of
churches was taboo. But in 1831, in discussing the

"means" by which Christians might seek to reform the world, he affirmed that "a church can do what an individual disciple cannot, and so can a district of churches do what a single congregation cannot." After examining the situation in apostolic times, he concluded: "The primitive churches in certain districts did co-operate in *choosing* certain persons for the work of the Lord, and these persons when chosen were called the '*Messengers of the Churches.*' "[1]

In the months that followed, Campbell frequently urged cooperation of the churches in a particular region for purposes of evangelization. As a beginning he suggested that the six churches in the county of Brooke "unite their energies for the conversion of their fellow citizens. Those in Washington, Pa. and those in every other county, ought to do likewise." He proposed a general county meeting once each year at which reports would be made "of the moral condition of every vicinity in the county." The meeting would then "select some seven or fourteen stations in the county, to be supplied once every week by some member of these communities, as their agent."[2]

This general plan was adopted rather widely, and soon almost every issue of the *Millennial Harbinger* carried notices of such meetings. In reporting the action of one of these Campbell admitted that there is no express *command* for this procedure in the New Testament, but neither is there for printing the Scriptures, for publishing, or for building houses of worship. There is ample *precedent*, however, in The Book of Acts.[3]

Later he called attention to the need for some authority beyond the local congregation to which persons excommunicated by a local church might appeal and by which offending congregations might be tried.[4]

In 1838 he began to turn his attention to the problems of order and organization within local congregations and to oppose with increasing frequency and growing vigor what he called the "fierce democracy" or "mobocracy" of ultra-independency. Abandoning the extreme congregationalism of his radical Baptist period, he sought some sort of middle ground between the Baptist and Presbyterian systems.

In an article on "The Senatorial Government of the Church," in March, 1838, he set forth "two or three axiomatic truths" on the subject of the eldership, concluding that *"the church of Christ is a community that needs government, and that her Founder and Head has communicated authority for this purpose"*—to the elders. He further declared: "There are extremes of Congregationalism and monarchial despotism. . . . Mobocracy may become as tyrannical as unlimited monarchy. Both are to be eschewed."[5] The following year he made the blunt assertion:

I, for one, do not believe that all men are equal. Equally intelligent, learned, prudent, wise, moral, Christian, they are not. I, for one, believe that "the younger should submit to the elder," in experience, judgment, piety. I do not think that the will, caprice, intelligence, or vote of Master John, my youngest brother in the church, should balance or neutralize mine. This may be called aristocracy: if so, I am aristocratic, and I do not care who knows it.[6]

In a subsequent article he opposed the system which allowed minors and *"females"* to swing the vote and decide an issue in a congregation. He also suggested "weighing" as well as "counting" the votes, and rejected the system which allows "President Numbers" to triumph over "Presidents Age, Experience, and Moral Excellence."[7] This stands in striking contrast to his eulogy of "King Numbers" at the Virginia Convention.

Campbell returned to the subject of church government at intervals throughout the remainder of his life. In 1844 he reminded his readers that while authority in the church is derived not from the pope but from the people, yet

No community ever did or ever can accomplish any thing by latent authority. Men will as soon set the ocean on fire by its latent caloric, as govern themselves by latent authority. This latent authority must be disengaged, and concentrated in deacons, evangelists, pastors, overseers. . . . But when constitutionally communicated, it must be submitted to. It cannot both be communicated and retained.[8]

This was quite in line with his views of the social compact and apparently represents a modification of his extreme left-wing views under the influence of the natural rights philosophy and the changing church situation.

A third sign of evolving churchmanship was Campbell's growing emphasis upon a trained and adequately paid ministry. In 1843 he declared: "The proper education of young men devoted to the ministry of the Word . . . is on all hands confessed to be [a matter] of unspeakable importance." At the same time he seems to have either forgotten his earlier attacks upon a "hireling clergy" or else underestimated the influence of his words, for he went on to express surprise "that the churches seem to take so little interest in raising up well qualified young men to plead the cause of Bible Christianity."[9]

In October, 1849, the first national convention of the Disciples of Christ was held in Cincinnati, and the American Christian Missionary Society organized. Campbell was elected president of both. He and the religious body of which he was the recognized leader had come a long way from the early sect days when he had put such extreme emphasis upon "the perfect independency of the [local] church."

INTERDENOMINATIONAL COOPERATION

The denominational character of Campbell's later views is even more clearly revealed in his growing ecumenical spirit during the decade of the 1840's and his eager cooperation with Christians of other religious bodies in Bible distribution and other cooperative enterprises. There was a foreshadowing of this in his famous "Lunenberg Letter" of 1837 in which he recognized the existence of genuine "Christians among the [Protestant] sects."[10]

The first clear indication of this spirit appeared the year after S. S. Schmucker offered his well-known "Plan for Protestant Union." In 1839 Campbell expressed satisfaction at the widespread interest being shown in other circles in what had ever been with him "a darling theme"—the subject of Christian union. He then went on to make his own proposals for a congress of all Protestant bodies with representation apportioned according to the number of their constituents, the union to be based upon their common understandings and agreements in matters of faith, piety, and morality. This proposal was removed from the realm of practicability by his further insistence that churches entering this congress pledge themselves to abandon all tenets, forms, and usages not admitted of divine authority by all Christendom.[11] This latter provision, quite similar to Chillingworth's plan for union, shows that Campbell had not completely abandoned his New Testament primitivism.

He also showed great interest in the Evangelical Alliance established in London in 1846 which he characterized as one of the "great initiatory institutions" toward the union of all Christians.[12]

In 1842 he urged support of the American and Foreign Bible Society as an agency of evangelization, and later was one of the vice-presidents of the American Bible Union which broke away from the parent body in 1849. In his address before the Bible Union Convention in 1852 he declared that "in order . . . to pray, or to preach, or to labor *for a millennium,* we must have a Bible that is most explicit on this great subject" of immersion as the scriptural mode of baptism.[13] While this insistence upon scriptural correctness has a sectarian ring, an indication of Campbell's denominational trend is seen in the fact that he was willing to cooperate with those of other denominations in a project of Bible translation and distribution, and also in the fact that he actually opposed the organization of a Disciple Bible society, urging that Disciples of Christ cooperate instead with the American Bible Union.

His enthusiastic support of the American Protestant Association, the American Sunday School Association, and other interdenominational enterprises further illustrates his transition from an exclusive sect attitude to a more irenic denominational spirit.

DENOMINATIONAL TRENDS IN HIS POLITICAL ETHICS

As Campbell moved from the extreme left toward the middle in his views of the church, he also moved, though somewhat more haltingly, in the direction of a denominational attitude in regard to the state and political affairs. Another way of putting it is to say that he moved toward a synthesis of the sect elements and the natural law elements which had existed side by side in his thought from the beginning. This trend is seen in three particulars: an indirect rationalization of his use of both biblical and natural law norms, a more positive attitude toward the state, and an increasing emphasis upon order and obedience to "the powers that be." Each of these developments brought him closer to the social and political ethics of Calvin.

RELATION OF NATURAL LAW AND REVEALED ETHICS

As a New Testament primitivist Campbell turned to the Bible for the norms of religious and moral action. At the same time he got many of his basic ethical and political concepts from Locke and Beattie in the natural law tradition. Upon occasion he spoke of "moral precepts . . . more or less discernible . . . merely by the light of nature."[14]

His problem in reconciling these two diverse elements was not unlike a problem of Locke's. The British philosopher's psychology left no room for the existence of innate ideas, since he insisted that all knowledge comes as the result of reflection upon data derived through sense experience. But in the area of politics he believed in the existence of innate principles, discernible by reason, to which political relationships must be made to conform. Locke never resolved this difficulty—if in fact he ever faced it frankly.

Campbell dealt with the problem in an address, "Is Moral Philosophy an Inductive Science?" before the Charlottesville Lyceum in 1840. What he said there about ethics in general presumably applies to political ethics. The five points of primary importance in moral philosophy, he said, are: *"the origin, the nature, the relations, the obligations, and the destiny of man."* He then set forth as his thesis: "the perfect impotency of philosophy and human reason, however cultivated, possessing only the mere light of nature to decide and enforce any one of these five cardinal points."[15] Fastening upon a remark of Socrates, "There is much ground to hope that death is good . . . according to *what we are told,*" he concluded that:

Tradition, then, and not induction, originated in the minds of the Socratic school all the light of the origin, moral obligations, and destiny of man, which this school and the Grecian and the Roman world from it enjoyed.

Building upon this foundation, Campbell went on to show the relationship between natural and revealed ethics as follows:

The history of the whole matter is this:—The Romans borrowed from the Greeks, the Greeks stole from the Egyptians and Phenicians, while they borrowed from the Chaldeans and Assyrians, who stole from the Abrahamic family all their notions [of God and morality].[16]

While his object in this address was to show the inadequacy of natural ethics, he implied that such good as there is in natural ethics is ultimately derived from revelation, which gives something of a synthesis between revealed and natural ethics. The correlation, to be sure, was at the level of the patriarchal, rather than Christian, dispensation. That distinctively Christian norms have also entered into tradition and helped shape the ethical concepts of "natural man" can be assumed. In an early issue of the *Christian Baptist* he contrasted the "natural man" of today with the "natural man" of the Apostle's time, and concluded that "our natural man's ear has heard . . . in some way or other, the things which were revealed by the Holy Spirit unto the Apostles."[17] In the debate with Owen he charged that his opponent's benevolence sprang not from his materialistic philosophy or natural reason but from Christian roots. "I must again remind you," Campbell told his audience, "that Mr. Owen's system, as far as it has any peculiar benevolence proposed in it, or stamped upon it, is a plagiarism from christian society."[18]

In addition to the involved rationalization of his address on Moral Philosophy, there was a simpler and perhaps more convincing theory of the interrelations of "nature, reason, and religion." Campbell assumed that these are all in harmony since all are expressions of one creative will. Once he attempted to establish the will of God not only on the basis of his revealed word, but also by means of the constitution he has given the human race as reason may discern it. In opposing Owen's repudiation of marriage, he declared:

God *said*, it is not good for man to be alone! He then *created* a help meet for him. . . . Polygamy was denounced in the creation of but one woman for man; and the equal distribution of the sexes since has shewn, that every man ought to have his own wife, and every woman her own husband.[19]

Here Campbell showed his indebtedness to Thomas Reid's "common-sense" philosophy. Not only did he use Reid's illustration, but he was obviously following Reid's second fundamental axiom: "As far as the intention of nature appears in the constitution of man, we ought to comply with that intention."[20]

Campbell was sure that reason, properly used, points in the same direction as revelation. He once said that "man was created and made to walk by faith and reason, not separately, but conjointly."[21] In his denominational phase he frequently used revelation and "reason" (or natural law) "conjointly" in his search for the Christian solution to political problems. In fact, more often than he realized "reason" seems to have guided him to the Scriptures which supported her own conclusions!

In his more mature period he did not discriminate too closely between the three levels of his dispensational ethics. In writing on slavery, the Fugitive Slave Law, capital punishment, and economic ethics, he made frequent use of Old Testament passages from both the Jewish and patriarchal periods. This practice can be explained by his working principle of reverting to an earlier dispensation to fill in gaps in the New Testament ethic. But at times it seems to have come from a desire to find scriptural justification, from whatever dispensation, for views and judgments arrived at on other grounds.

Actually Campbell turned to both New and Old Testament and natural law sources for his political norms without ever having formulated and stated a satisfactory theory to justify his practice. His predicament was that of the typical denomination-type Christian who can accept neither the rigorous New Testament primitivism of sect-type Christianity nor the all-out natural law philosophy of church-type Christianity.

MORE POSITIVE ATTITUDE TOWARD THE STATE

In his *Christian Baptist* days Campbell was concerned largely with preserving the rights of citizens and paid little attention to the responsibilities of citizenship. Even his participation in the Virginia Convention can be interpreted as part of an attempt to secure to the people of western Virginia their full rights and privileges as citizens. In the early 1830's, during the period of his great disillusionment, he shifted from a merely negative attitude toward the state to one of actual withdrawal, going so far, during the late 1830's and 1840's, as to discourage Christians not only from seeking political office but also from voting.

Even as he was giving this advice, Campbell began to reveal a more positive, characteristically denominational interest in the practical problems of citizenship. His concern over the Roman Catholic issue, which came to a head in the debate with Bishop Purcell in 1837, might be interpreted as merely a new phase of his left-wing fear of an established church, but his evangelistic passion for public education as a bulwark of democracy, which came to a focus in the address on "Common Schools" in 1841, represents a far more constructive concern for the foundations of democracy. His treatment of the ethics of economic life from 1838 to 1843, and his essay on "Capital Punishment" in 1846 mark further milestones in the emergence of a denominational attitude toward public problems. Although he had shown a vital concern for slavery from 1829 to 1831, never in that earlier period did he attack the institution as aggressively as he did in 1849 in his "Tract for the People of Kentucky." His treatment of the Fugitive Slave Law in 1851 and his defense of law and order and the integrity of the union reveal a spirit and attitude which is a far cry from the sectarian's unconcern over the politics of this world.

In a word, the remaining chapters of this book comprise one extended commentary on Campbell's more positive attitude toward the concerns of public life.

EMPHASIS UPON ORDER AND OBEDIENCE TO "THE POWERS THAT BE"

A third indication of an emerging denominational position on political matters is to be seen in Campbell's increasing emphasis upon order and obedience to "the powers that be." Here more than anywhere else, is a genuine synthesis of left- and right-wing elements. His position on this point was, if anything, right of center—that is, closer to the ecclesiastical body than to the sect position.

Left-wing elements in this synthesis include an Acts-Epistles primitivism, which led to a Pauline-Petrine attitude of obedience to the powers that be, and a preoccupation with a millennial churchmanship, which paved the way for an attitude of patient and passive obedience in the interim before the millennium dawns. Right-wing elements include a Lockean love of order, and the doctrine that the individual must yield to the will of the majority as expressed through their properly constituted representatives. Another factor was Campbell's own rather conservative, if not "aristocratic," temperament.[22] All of these factors—left-wing, right-wing, and temperamental—combined to lead him to an increasingly strong emphasis upon order and subordination.

Campbell's growing stress upon the inequalities within the church and the duty of all to submit to those whom God, through the voice of his people, had chosen to be elders, had its counterpart in his political views, as he began to emphasize the inequalities of citizens and their duty to submit to "the powers that be" as "ordained of God."

An indication of this trend, and of the interrelationship between his ecclesiastical and political views, is to

be found in a discussion of church order and discipline
in 1840. In his *Christian Baptist* days Campbell had
frequently emphasized the Baptist contribution to American democracy. Now he ridiculed the idea that Jefferson "got his *beau ideal* of the American Republic from
a visit which, in his youth, he is said to have made to a
Saturday meeting in a case of discipline" in a Baptist
church in the neighborhood. With the ironical statement that "the meeting of the late Congress might be
appealed to as a proof of it," he went on to point out that

there is no Senate in the Baptist Church, and therefore it is
preposterous to assume that the sage of Monticello learned the
frame-work of our government from a hundred and ten men,
women, and children, meeting to try a delinquent for an offence
against the Lord.[23]

As Campbell began to stress the "presbyterial" elements
in the New Testament church, he emphasized also the
principles of order and subordination in the state.

There were foreshadowings of this note as early as the
first volume of the *Christian Baptist*. There he published a statement by Alexander Carson which declared
that "as a subject of civil government" the Christian

is called to unreserved, unequivocal obedience, without waiting
to inquire into its nature or quality, or even the legitimacy of the
title of those in power. . . . In Britain he will submit to monarchy; in America to a republic; and in France he will obey,
without puzzling himself in determining whether Buonaparte is
a legal governor, or a usurper.

In a footnote Campbell insisted that American citizens
have the right to effect a revolution—under certain circumstances and "by lawful means." But in general he
concurred with Carson as to the responsibility of the
Christian to submit to "the constituted authorities."[24]

When he dealt with the subject of slavery in 1845, he
took the position that so long as "any political arrangement, institution, or law" is not "in contravention of
any precept or consecrated usage in the apostolic writ-

ings, . . . it is not to be violently assaulted or resisted by any law-abiding Christian.'' This holds true even though, ''in our abstract reasonings . . . we think it on the whole inexpedient and politically injurious.'' The Christian ''must 'be subject to every ordinance of man,' and to 'the powers that be, because they are ordained of God,' as saith the eternal and almighty King.''[25]

If the state demand of the Christian action that is ''in contravention of'' the apostolic writings or ''reprobated by the Bible,'' then the situation is different. Then he has three alternatives. He may seek to change the law. He may remove himself from the sway of the law—in the case of slavery, by freeing his slaves or by migrating to another state.[26] If neither of these alternatives is feasible, he *must* obey God rather than man, for ''a Christian man cannot hesitate a moment whether he ought to obey man rather than God, or God rather than man.''[27] This last remained largely a theoretical alternative for Campbell, given his temperament and his views of slavery as a scripturally sanctioned institution. Nor did his pacifism bring him into conflict with the state, as it might have done if he had lived in a time of total war and conscription.

His most extreme statements on the duty of obedience were made in 1851 in connection with discussions of the Fugitive Slave Law. Having demonstrated to his own satisfaction that that law was not immoral, he quoted Romans 13:1-7 and 1 Peter 2:13-18, and then concluded that it was a ''moral, and even religious'' duty for the Christian to obey this law, ''because political government is an ordinance of God'' and is ''to be obeyed, for conscience's sake.''[28]

In a discussion of capital punishment he affirmed that:

Though neither Cesar nor Napoleon, neither Nicholas nor Victoria, were, ''*by the grace of God,*'' king, emperor, or queen; still the civil throne, the civil magistrate, and, therefore, civil government, are, *by the grace of God,* bestowed upon the world.[29]

The view of government as divinely ordained also carries with it the duty of rulers to rule according to God's law.

The Bible is of right, and it ought to be, just as much a law to kings, and governors, and presidents, as it is to masters and servants, to husbands and wives, to parents and children. Those magistrates, therefore, who will not be governed and guided by it in the faithful execution of God's laws, God himself, in his own proper person, will judge and reward.[30]

These statements sound strongly Calvinist, and illustrate Campbell's emphasis upon the obligation of Christians to obey "the powers that be," and of citizens and rulers alike to obey the law of God.

Chapter IX

AMERICA AND HER PARTIES

ALEXANDER CAMPBELL's political views cannot be fully understood without taking into account his attitudes and feelings as an American citizen and his political alignments and affinities.

Early Enthusiasm for the American Republic

His first reaction to America was one of joyous release from the restrictions and oppressions of the Old World. His biographer has described the impression made upon Campbell by this new land as he first made his way across Pennsylvania toward his new home. On the first evening out of Philadelphia, after arrangements had been made for the night, and all had eaten, Campbell went for a stroll in the woods. Richardson has attempted to portray the emotions with which he

trod upon the soil of a new world—the land of liberty and of Washington, whose liberal institutions had long been the object of his admiration. All nature around him seemed to sympathize with his emotions. The balmy air, fresh from the wild mountain slopes, the new varieties of birds, which from almost every tree seemed, to his fancy, to chant their evening song in praise of the freedom of their native woods, the approaching shades of evening, veiling the distant landscape in a gentle haze,—all seemed to speak of liberty, security and peace.[1]

On December 28, 1815, in a letter to his Uncle Archibald, in Newry, he exclaimed:

I cannot speak too highly of the advantages that the people in this country enjoy in being delivered from a proud and lordly aristocracy . . . I would not exchange the honor and privilege of being an American citizen for the position of your king.[2]

When he came to write the preface to the seventh volume of the *Christian Baptist* on July 4, 1829, Campbell took note of the date as "the day on which this nation was born, and . . . on which Thomas Jefferson and John Adams died." With this introduction he went on to write a rather lengthy essay on "the *rights of men,*" more than half of which was devoted to discussing and extolling the "*natural* and *unalienable*" political rights for which this government stands.[3]

On Monday, July 5, 1830, the members of the church in Pittsburgh, Pennsylvania, held a celebration "*in honor of the fourth of July,* 1776," at which Campbell delivered the oration. He spoke in fulsome terms of the government of "this most favored of all lands." "The praises of a Washington, a Franklin, and a Jefferson," he declared, "will long resound through the hills and vallies of this spacious country."[4]

Another indication of his enthusiasm for American democracy may be seen in his frequent use of naturalization into citizenship as an analogy for the process of initiation into the church.[5]

DISILLUSIONMENT AND DESPAIR

Campbell's republican ardor cooled considerably in the early 1830's. One of the most important factors in bringing about this change was his experience at the Virginia Convention where he saw firsthand the power and recalcitrance of vested political interests. Of the "aristocrats in the late Virginia Convention," he wrote in 1830:

Orpheus could, by his music, as easily have caused the oaks to follow him, as could the republicans, by their arguments and demonstrations, have caused the oligarchs in power to consent to extend equal rights and immunities to the proscribed casts in this commonwealth.[6]

A short time later, in referring to his proposals for a program of popular education at the convention, he declared: "There were few ears in that body disposed to hear a word upon the subject. It was a scramble for power."[7]

There followed a series of political events which tended still further to disillusion him with regard to American democracy. In the first number of the *Millennial Harbinger* he protested against Georgia's violation of the rights of the Cherokee Indians. The issue, he declared, was this:

Have treaties any sanction, any validity, any faith? . . . Or is it the right of the strong always to plunder the property and insult the person of the weak? . . . All this . . . is assumed by Georgia in reference to the Cherokee Indians.

He went on to express the hope that

there is yet so much justice, so much pure republicanism, so much regard to truth and national faith, in the bosoms of the American people and of their representatives in congress, as will not permit them to give up an innocent and harmless nation to the cupidity of a few capitalists in Georgia or anywhere else.[8]

Another development much closer home had an even more profound effect upon his thought—the failure of the Virginia legislature to act on the slave issue following the Southampton or Nat Turner Insurrection. Much space in the January and February issues of the *Millennial Harbinger* for 1832 was given to the story of this insurrection and to editorial reactions to the incident in the public press. The February issue carried a long editorial by Campbell advocating the colonization of slaves either in Africa or in some remote part of this continent. In April he reviewed the actions of the Assembly to date, and in May bitterly noted the failure of the legislature to take any constructive action.

The last Assembly of Virginia has rendered itself memorable by many eloquent speeches which were made on the subject of slavery . . . but arose without passing a single law on the subject. The *Marylanders*, without making a single speech, passed a law appropriating 200,000 dollars for the colonization of free people of color in Liberia. The Virginians for *eloquence* and the Marylanders for *action*.[9]

In addition to these particular critical incidents of the opening years of the decade, there were certain continuing trends which played their part in diminishing Campbell's faith in the American form of government. One was the increasing intensity of partisan strife in connection with political campaigns. After the presidential election of 1828 he asked "whether any nation or any people are more rapidly degenerating than the good citizens of the American Republics." Men, he said, "seem to think no sacrifice is so acceptable to the idol of their party, as the good name of his competitor."[10]

The "spoils system" introduced by Andrew Jackson also came in for mention as a sign of political degeneracy.

Men are now basking in the full blaze of presidential patronage, whose fortune would have been quite the reverse had they been less skilled in political divination. But . . . there will arise a king who knew not Joseph. . . . Then comes the crash of the old nobility and the induction of the new.[11]

It is not surprising to find Campbell in 1833 discussing the morphology of all human institutions and declaring that "all the great states are in their dotage." Even "under our own political and religious institutions we see what an amount of ignorance, crime, and misery exist." It was here that he concluded with his peroration of despair: "What then is to be done? Wait the coming of the Lord . . . or shall we fight on . . . in the firm persuasion that our labor in the Lord shall not be fruitless?"[12] This—October, 1833—represents perhaps the lowest point on the curve of Campbell's enthusiasm for American democracy, although it was not to rise appreciably for some time to come. It is significant that the *Extra on The Kingdom of Heaven,* in which

appear some of his most critical remarks concerning
democracy, was issued less than a year later, in August,
1834.

The menace of slavery continued to grow on Campbell's horizon, and in February, 1835, he declared that
slavery was one of two great issues threatening the perpetuity of republican institutions. The other, and one
to which he devoted increasing attention in the next few
years, was that of Roman Catholicism. In an article on
education he declared that there was

much reason for alarm, and to doubt the long continuance of
privileges of which it appears we are unworthy. The Roman
hierarchy and Negro slavery, or the former by means of the
latter, may, and in all probability will, dash the American ship
upon a rock, and engulf us all in one common ruin.[13]

Other factors besides political ones contributed to his
despair. Among them was an increasing "love for titles
in this reformed republican country." "The English
statesman," he said, "is not more perplexed to find out
new subjects of taxation, than the good people of this
country to find out and obtain honorable titles."[14]

Another ominous trend was the growing spirit of insubordination on the part of the young. In reporting a
student uprising at the University of Alabama in 1837,
he declared that such incidents, which were becoming
more and more common in the South and Southwest, are

ominous of the momentary duration of all our State governments: for as certain as the seasons of the year revolve, . . . so
certain it is that insubordination to parents and teachers is
wholly incompatible with subordination to civil authority.[15]

A third social trend which filled him with fear for the
future was the growth of violence and the tendency for
men to take the law into their own hands. When Joseph
Smith and his brother were killed, Campbell greeted the
news of their death with a curious reaction. On the one
hand, he noted that they had been "providentially [sic!]
cut off in the midst of their diabolical career." On the

other hand, he was alarmed that they were put to death so "lawlessly and mobocratically." "One of the ante-diluvian signs of the times," he reminded his readers, "was, that 'the earth was filled with violence.'" Yet now "from Boston and Philadelphia to New Orleans this land is filled with violence; and, analogically reasoning, some great catastrophe is coming upon the world."[16]

RETURNING ENTHUSIASM

A distinct change in Campbell's attitude toward the American republic became noticeable in 1847 after he had visited the Old World and seen anew the contrasts between American and European society.

Even the prospect of his visit to the British Isles—or perhaps it was the sea air, for he wrote this message on the Atlantic Ocean east of the Banks of Newfoundland—led him, in his Baccalaureate Address of 1847, to eulogize "the greatest nation and the happiest community on the earth" in language reminiscent of his Fourth of July address in 1830. In this address, read in his absence by the vice-president of the college, Campbell extolled the United States for the size of its territory, the amplitude of its resources, the enterprise of its people, its population, commerce, and education. In his peroration he referred to our government as "the least expensive," and our civil institutions as "the most rational, equitable, and free, ever vouchsafed to man."[17]

His letters from Europe give unmistakable evidence of a revived appreciation for American democracy. In language not unlike that of Thomas Paine, he described the evils of the British system, which permitted a few aristocrats to live in pomp and luxury amid the "squalid poverty and wretchedness" of the poor. He wrote of the evils and the inequity of the law of primogeniture, by which twelve of the sons of a nobleman "must be comparatively poor that one of the thirteen may be exuberantly rich.''[18] In the cities, especially London, he reported seeing

thousands of little children in the streets, bearing all the insignia of squalid, wretched poverty. . . . No school for them—no table—no bed—no book—no teacher. . . . For every *Prince,* and *Lord,* and *Nobleman,* there are likely thousands of these. For every palace there are multitudes without a cottage, a hut, or a home. I ask myself, Is this the price of a splendid monarchy! Are these the conditions on which royal palaces are reared! . . . If so, then let me have a land without palaces, a country without splendid parks and gardens, cities without Gothic temples, a nation without Lords, and a community without beggars, starvation, and pestilence![19]

In another letter, Campbell wrote his daughter:

I . . . often think of the hills around Bethany, and the enviable lot of those I left behind me, compared with that of the millions through which I am passing in this Old World. . . . May the Lord in his mercy watch over the destiny of your native country, and long preserve it from the vices and follies [of Europe].[20]

In the course of his stay in England he visited Parliament and was delighted by the addresses of the Duke of Wellington and others, including Lord Brougham, whose writings he had long followed and quoted with approval. After reporting these addresses and describing the British system of government, he concluded: ''The whole House of Lords, Bishops, and all, apart from their titles . . . are in no intellectual endowments superior to a Virginia House of Delegates, an Ohio Senate, or any other deliberative body elected by any sovereign State of the Amercian Union.''[21]

After visiting France, he wrote that the United States had risen ''one hundred per cent'' in his esteem above any country he had seen since he left. He went on to express the hope that the people of his adopted country would ''never sell for a mess of pottage their birthrights.''[22]

Soon after his return to America, Campbell made a trip to Baltimore and Washington. In the notes on this tour he compared the physical aspects of Washington with those of the Old World capitals, concluding that

our capitol in Washington, and our President's palace, transcend in beauty, in fine taste, if not in real grandeur, any capitol, parliament house, court, or legislative hall, in Europe. . . . If they have not around them all that antique hoary Gothic magnificence [of the Old World edifices], they have more real beauty, more republican simplicity and grandeur.

While in the city he also visited the Senate chamber, "so replete with wisdom and eloquence, viewing and hearing the great men of the day." Some of them, he said, were "indeed, the greatest statesmen of the world."[23] This was quite a different reaction from that which he had shown when he visited Washington a decade earlier and was impressed only by the atmosphere of politics which he had found so "antipodal" to the spirit of the gospel.

On December 11, 1849, Campbell addressed the Young Men's Mercantile Library Association, of Cincinnati, on "The Anglo-Saxon Language—Its Origin, Character and Destiny." Tracing the Anglo-Saxon people back to the descendants of Japheth, he discussed their character as reflected in their language, pointed up the role that Protestantism had played in shaping this character, and then gave a glowing picture of the destiny of the Anglo-Saxons. "The spread of the Anglo-Saxon tongue all over the world" he was sure would bring with it the golden age of peace.[24]

Campbell spoke more specifically of "The Destiny of Our Country" in an address before the Philo-Literary Society, of Canonsburg College, Pennsylvania, in 1852. There was a note of warmth and devotion in his first reference to "our divinely favored and beloved country," after which he drew a poetic and moving picture of the blessings and progress of the American people in the seventy-five years of their existence. He described the beauty of the "thousand hills and vallies, waving in rich harvests, or covered with green pastures, overspread with bleating flocks of sheep or lowing herds of cattle, interspersed with beautiful villas and romantic hamlets." He extolled the courage of the pioneer who opened up the West, "grubbing the virgin earth in quest of his daily bread," and the enterprise of the sons and daughters of the pioneers who had erected "thrones of justice, solemn temples, stately residences, colleges, male and female seminaries [which] every where attest their good taste, their liberality, patriotism, and genuine philanthropy."[25] After speaking more particularly of the progress made in education he concluded by saying that while patriotism "has no special place in the Christian Religion" it may become a channel by which we can communicate to others blessings which otherwise "no Christian man could bestow upon his species."[26] The spirit of this address is a far cry from the pessimistic, critical attitude which Campbell showed toward the American union in the decade of the 1830's and in the early 1840's.

Another thing which contributed to this new enthusiasm for the Union was the increasing fear he felt for her continued existence. His devotion to the Union seems to have increased in proportion to his fear for her future as a result of the Roman Catholic and slavery threats. No one can read his addresses on "The Anglo-Saxon Language," "The Destiny of our Country," or the Baccalaureate Address of 1847, without noticing how closely interwoven were his fears of Catholicism and his devotion to American democracy. Two other passages suggest the relationship between the deepening slavery crisis and his renewed devotion to the Union.

In discussing "Our Position to American Slavery" in 1845, Campbell appealed to the love of the Union as a motive for preventing any breach between Christians of the South and of the North. "Every man who loves the American Union," he declared, "as well as every man who desires a constitutional end of American slavery, is bound to prevent, as far as possible, any breach of communion between Christians at the South and at the North."[27]

In 1851, when he was pleading for support of the Fugitive Slave Law as a means of preserving the Union, one of his most able correspondents and critics noticed this new concern and asked why he had not shown a similar interest earlier when "disunion meetings were held all over the south, and the Nashville Convention assembled." "Why all this alarm *now*," his critic asked, "when there is a simple refusal, on the part of many conscientious persons in the north, to obey what they regard as *unrighteous* requirements?"[28] Campbell made no attempt to answer this criticism. The charge is significant because it shows that some of his readers saw a correlation between his returning concern for the Union and the threat of its impending disruption over the slavery issue.

Campbell's revived enthusiasm for American democracy was thus born partly of love and partly of fear— partly from seeing democracy in a new light against the background of European society, and partly from the fear that, with all its shortcomings, it might be destroyed and worse evils follow.

Party Alignments and Political Affinities

In an editorial on the "Impartiality of the Editor" in 1846, Campbell affirmed: "As for politics, no one could ever say, from any thing inscribed upon our pages, whether we had any partizan politics at all, or whether we belonged to any political party in our nation." He went on to report that on a recent tour in Missouri he was asked by a "constant reader" to which political party he belonged. The reader "confessed he never could decide from the Harbinger whether I was Whig or

Democrat."[29] There seems, however, to be some evidence that in the late 1820's Campbell was essentially a Jacksonian Democrat, but that by 1840 he had become a Whig.

In an address at the Virginia Convention Campbell listed General Jackson among the great men whose talents and skill made them "as useful to the State, as a whole district of mere slave-holders."[30] In all his addresses and votes at the convention and in other actions throughout his *Christian Baptist* period he rather consistently supported a stronger executive directly responsible to the people, general suffrage, the elimination of property qualifications for voting and holding office, rotation in office, the democratization of the judiciary, anti-Sabbatarianism, and other elements of Jacksonian democracy. He was also in general agreement with Jackson in opposing the Bank of the United States and supporting general laws of incorporation in place of legislative charters. As a *Christian,* though not as a *politician,* Campbell supported Jackson's moderate tariff policies. It is significant to note in this connection that Campbell's county of Brooke gave its support to Jackson in the presidential election of 1824 and again in 1828.

Campbell's references to Jackson and Jacksonian policies became increasingly critical with the passing of the years. After Jackson's death a memorial sermon, preached at Harrodsburg, Kentucky, by James Shannon, became the occasion for an extended and heated discussion in the *Millennial Harbinger.* A communication was printed from Thomas M. Henley which decried the prostitution of the Bible by using its texts as the basis for eulogies of such characters as Jackson. In introducing this letter Campbell admitted that Jackson was a true patriot, a great general, and a gentleman, but denied that he ever "exhibited any of the characteristic excellencies of a Christian. . . . On the contrary, he was characteristically profane, irreverent, and enslaved to passion."[31] In a subsequent issue a communication appeared which criticized both Henley and Campbell and eulogized the late President. Campbell denied any partisanship in the issue and pointed to his willingness to publish this tribute to Jackson as evidence of his impartiality. Still one cannot help sensing in Campbell's remarks and handling of the incident a critical attitude toward the late President.

In his later years he also took a stand against certain practices and policies associated with Jacksonian democracy. His criticism of the spoils system has already been noticed. At a much later date he referred to the veto, which first came to prominence during Jackson's administration, as a sign of monarchial power. Our presidents, he said, "either constitutionally have, or assume to have, a more absolute power than has ever been exercised by any of the present dynasty of English sovereigns,—not one of whom ever presumed to veto a law passed by the two houses of Parliament."[32]

Alongside of Campbell's critical attitude toward Jackson as a person, and toward certain characteristic emphases of his administration, may be placed his references to two religious leaders prominently associated with Jacksonian democracy: O. B. Brown and Abner Kneeland. The former was denounced as a "political reverend" and the leading example of that type of "political scavenger and brawling demagogue," in an article by Charles Hammond, which Campbell published in 1835 and commended to the attention "of some of our own brethren."[33] Abner Kneeland he referred to in criticizing the infidelity and politics of Portage County, Ohio. The columns of the *Ohio Watchman,* he said, were enriched "by occasional drafts on the sophistical and filthy columns of the apostate Kneeland, now of the 'Boston Investigator,' who has boxed the compass of all errors, from the extreme of hypercalvinism to the extreme of ultra atheism."[34]

Campbell's references to subsequent presidents and presidential candidates were few. In his "Notes on a Tour to the Northeast," in 1836, he revealed the characteristic Whig propaganda bias against Van Buren as a man of wealth by referring to the "Patrician church" in Albany where "Mr. Martin Van Buren and Governor Marcy hold pews."[35] This same Whig fiction of Van Buren as a patrician, who later converted the White House into a palace, was reflected in 1839 in some notes in connection with a visit to Washington. "The President's house, the navy yard, and the capitol, are all rising in worldly promp and splendor. Indeed, every thing appears less and less Christian and Republicun" since "we last visited the Metropolitan City."[36]

In 1840 the Whig candidate for the presidency was William Henry Harrison. During the campaign period, Campbell is reported to have asked John Rudolph which of the candidates he thought would get the Ohio vote. Rudolph replied: "General Harrison," to which Campbell responded: "I hope it may be so. I will vote for him myself, as he is a personal friend and I approve his policy."[37]

As early as 1836, then, in his references to Van Buren, Campbell revealed definite Whig leanings, and in 1840, he was a supporter of the Whig candidate for president.

Political Affinities

In his middle and later years he grew increasingly critical of the more radically republican writers like Paine and Jefferson, and more enthusiastic about those with a more aristocratic spirit, like Webster, Macaulay, and Brougham. In July, 1836, he began to reprint from the *Christian Observer* a series of critical sketches of the life of Thomas Paine. Two decades later he expressed surprise and regret at the increasing "celebration of the birth of one who lived and died a reviler of the Author and Founder of all the true rights, honors, and dignities of man.''[38]

In 1839, in reporting a visit to Monticello, he commented on ''the patchwork appearance of the edifice standing on a sterile and exhausted farm.'' This, he said,

gives to the whole the appearance of a splendid failure, and betokens that the proprietor was rather ideal and imaginative than practical and sound in his views and undertakings. Of the wisdom of his other theories, it is to be hoped that time, that great interpreter of all human efforts, will speak more favorably.[39]

Jefferson's ''godlessness'' came in for attack in 1856.[40]

Another indication of Campbell's political affinities is to be found in his enthusiastic endorsement of Daniel Webster in 1860. In commending ''Daniel Webster's Confession of Faith,'' he expressed the belief that Webster was unquestionably ''one of the most profound lawyers, and one of the greatest statesmen in our country.''[41] The American writers on constitutional law whom he commended, and whose *Commentaries* were used as texts at Bethany College, were both political conservatives—James Kent and Joseph Story.

In 1860 he quoted a letter from T. B. Macauley, setting forth the latter's rather aristocratic political views. In introducing the excerpt Campbell cautioned his readers against supposing that ''we are disposed to turn politician, because of our republishing a letter from the pen of one of England's giant men.'' But he believed Macauley's views to be ''worth as much as those of any other man of his day and generation.'' The passage quoted was outspokenly critical of Jefferson's democratic philosophy.[42] Another political writer whom Campbell greatly admired and quoted upon many occasions was Henry Brougham. The editor of this British Lord's *Opinions* says that while Brougham was a ''consistent Liberal, and a sincere friend to the people,'' he was "far from being, a Democrat." In fact, Brougham declared his "most unequivocal opposition to . . . Universal Suffrage."[43]

All these signs point to the fact that in politics, as in religion, Campbell became more conservative as he grew older.

"Moderate" Democracy

In the midst of this unmistakable trend toward conservatism, two elements remained constant in Campbell —a strong Jeffersonianism and an essentially aristocratic temperament, the latter strengthened in his later years by association with followers of higher social status.

Despite his criticisms of Jefferson, Campbell remained to the end essentially a Jeffersonian democrat. Like the Sage of Monticello, the Sage of Bethany was a thoroughgoing agrarian, with a distrust of the city, an idealization of the gentleman farmer, and a view of society as constituted by independent and relatively equal yeomen.

His attitude toward the city was typical of the country gentleman and frontiersman. After a trip to the East in 1843, Campbell reported that "the American cities, like all other cities, are not favorable to the [prevalence] of pure religious influences." It is a "grand and pernicious mistake," he declared, to suppose,

because the inhabitants of cities understand trade, politics, and fashionable dress, better than farmers, and other country people, that they . . . [possess] superior Christian science and piety, and higher intellectual and moral attainments! . . . [On the contrary] they are generally neither so intelligent in the scriptures, nor so pious as the people of the country.[44]

In addressing the graduates of Bethany College in 1844, he set forth a typically Jeffersonian viewpoint. Asserting, as he frequently did in his middle and later years, that "educated men must rule the world," he urged his hearers to lay their "scenes of earthly enjoyment in the more innocent walks of rural life." Among

the advantages which would accrue are "leisure for . . .
personal improvement," independence, and the opportunity for "communion with God and Nature." Yet in
his eulogy of the farmer's life Campbell was no escapist,
for he pointed out that a farmer's estate gives him "a
theatre . . . from which, if he have any gift that society
needs, . . . he may send his mind abroad on errands of
philanthropy."[45]   Like many another philosopher before and since, Campbell universalized his own particular situation and experience.

He shared not only Jefferson's agrarianism but also
the political philosophy based upon it.   The distinction
between the Jeffersonian and Jacksonian versions of
democracy centers in their differing concepts of "the
people."   For Jefferson "the people" in whose hands
political power was to be vested were, in the main, farmers and residents of villages and small towns.   The prop-
erty-less city masses were not yet a factor in national
politics.   But in the Jacksonian version of democracy
"the people" included, as an important element, the
urban workers, many of whom were untutored and without property.

Many of the classic catalogs of political forms include
two variant forms of democracy—one good and the other
bad.   The first is moderate democracy or "polity," and
the second, its corruption, "fierce democracy" or "mobocracy."   Both of these latter terms were used repeat-
edly by Campbell in his middle and later years as he
denounced excesses both in the church and in the state.
If he had attempted to analyze the situation carefully,
from his maturing Whig point of view, Jeffersonian
democracy—with its more aristocratic, agrarian character—would have come under the classification of moderate democracy, and Jacksonian democracy—with its
lower-class, urban character—under the second.   But not
analyzing the situation carefully, and opposing certain
aspects of democracy as it evolved under Jackson, Camp-

bell tended to react against "democracy" in general. It is significant that his criticisms of democracy did not begin to appear until the Jeffersonian form had been thoroughly supplanted by the more extreme Jacksonian type.

HIS "ARISTOCRATIC" TEMPERAMENT

Throughout his life Campbell revealed signs of the aristocratic temperament which has traditionally been associated with "moderate" forms of democracy. Montesquieu, whom he continued to respect as one of the great political philosophers, referred to the republican form of government as a "conflation" of aristocracy and democracy. Jefferson, though repudiating an "artificial aristocracy," admitted the existence of a "natural aristocracy," and insisted that government must provide for "a pure selection of these natural *aristoi* into the offices of government."[46]   From Milton, Campbell may have acquired his ideas of the "aristocracy of genius," and from Plato the thought that the educated must rule.

He was in this philosophic tradition, then, when he said, as he was constantly saying in his baccalaureate addresses, that "educated mind [or men] must rule." This was also the burden of his address on "The Responsibilities of Men of Genius," at Miami University in 1844, where, after noting that the sun governs the movements of lesser masses in the solar system, he declared that "educated mind must as certainly govern uneducated mind, and the more vigorous and talented the less favored . . . It is Heaven's own law."[47]

He often revealed a condescending, even contemptuous, attitude toward the untutored masses. In the *Christian Baptist* he spoke of "the unchartered ignoramuses which constitute the fearful majority" of the populace.[48] He frequently referred to Roman Catholic immigrants in such terms as "illiterate, degraded, superstitious Romanists" and a "mass of degraded and debased hu-

manity.''⁴⁹ In one baccalaureate address he called attention to "the improvident, thriftless, dissipated tatter-
demalions . . . with a numerous retinue of ragged,
squalid, ill-fed, and untaught children" who must be
educated.⁵⁰

Campbell believed strongly in the duty of minors to
obey their elders and of "juniors" to show proper respect for their seniors—both in the home and in the
church. In 1844 he had a rather "touchy" editorial
about "juniors" addressing their seniors in the field of
religious journalism without proper deference and re-
spect.⁵¹ He later declared: "It is as revolting to reason
as to good taste, to change the order of nature, by setting the young and uneducated to teach and rule over
the more aged and experienced members of any community, civil or religious.''⁵²

In the same spirit he felt that woman should acknowledge the superiority of man in both church and state.
His objection to the Baptist "mobocracy" which allowed
"*females*" to exercise the balance of power in a local
church has already been noticed. He also opposed
woman suffrage in the political sphere. Although there
were indications of his views earlier, he did not deal
directly with the subject until after the so-called "Mob
Convention" of the woman's rights advocates in New
York in 1853. His opposition to woman suffrage was
based upon Scripture and reason. Adam was formed
before Eve; therefore man and woman are "neither
equal in rank nor in age." Woman was created to be
"a *help meet* for man," and her authority is "only house
wide." "If Paul would not have a woman to pray *un-
veiled* in a Christian church," it would be most unseemly
for a woman to "mount the rostrum" and, in the eyes
of the "ogling" crowd, discuss matters that are outside
her competence. On the grounds that woman is "constitutionally, legally and religiously, modest and retir-
ing, in the presence of him whom God made first," Camp-

bell concluded gallantly that "it would be cruel, tyrannical, and unmanly, to do violence to female modesty,
by forcing her to . . . figure in broils and battles in the
forum, in the Senate . . . or in the battle field."[53]

Another insight into his temperament is to be seen in
his fear of change and criticism of existing institutions.
In face of the abolitionist agitation, he spoke in 1845 of
the "doubtful and dangerous tendency" which a nation
institutes when it "guarantees to every citizen 'liberty,
of thought, liberty of speech, and liberty of action.'"
Specifically, he was alarmed at the "spirit of free discussion" which had "gone abroad through all this land"
and which nothing apparently could stop.   He was obviously fearful of "his Majesty FREE DISCUSSION"
in this instance, as he was later when the institution of
capital punishment was called in question.[54]

With his "aristocratic" temperament Campbell was
quite naturally more at home among Whigs than among
Jacksonian Democrats.

RISING SOCIAL STATUS OF HIS FOLLOWERS

An influence not to be minimized in accounting for
the political attitudes and affinities of Campbell's later
years is the social status of those who joined the religious movement of which he was the acknowledged
leader.   From the beginning the movement appealed
particularly to the middle classes in the villages and
towns.   As the years went by, Campbell's own personality and ability, together with the spirit of the movement itself, drew into it many prominent men and women
from all parts of the nation.   After the launching of
Bethany College in 1840, Campbell necessarily had to
seek out and cultivate men and women of means in order
to secure the funds necessary to operate and endow the
college.   As a result he hobnobbed more and more with
social, business, and political leaders—especially of the

South and West. These contacts inevitably strengthened the aristocratic elements already present in his personality and political philosophy.

The *Christian Baptist* for September, 1828, made mention of the occupational status of one hundred and eighteen persons baptized in a three-week period by Jeremiah Vardeman in Cincinnati. These "were collected from almost all the grades and occupations in society—doctors, lawyers, judges, clerks, auditors, merchants, mechanics, and laborers."[55] Some months later, when D. S. Burnet reported the immersion of "William R. Cole, Esq. of Wilmington," Campbell said in an editorial footnote:

Brother Cole is not the only respectable member of the bar who has recently bowed to the sceptre of the mighty Lord; Father [Thomas] Campbell, a few weeks since, immersed four members of the bar of high standing, in Somerset County, Pennsylvania, together with several other persons of the same place, of much influence in society.[56]

In the years that followed, notes like these appeared with increasing frequency in the department of "News from the Churches":

The families of two Doctors and two Merchants have obeyed; we have one Lawyer, the Clerks of the county, Circuit and Chancery Courts, with their families . . . Also . . . the Jailor and all his household, the wife of the Post-Master, the wife and daughter of the Sheriff of the county.[57]

Within the last few days we have received thirty-six of the principal citizens of this county.[58]

In 1845, in his "Notes on a Tour to the South," Campbell characterized a member of the Disciples of Christ, in Augusta, Georgia, as "one of the best Mayors" he had known. He also reported forming "some very interesting acquaintances with sundry highly distinguished persons" on that tour, among them the "ex-governors Schley and Hammond."[59] By 1850 Governor Wright of Indiana had become a member of Disciples of Christ.

On a tour of the South that same year Campbell observed that the members of sixteen Christian churches in Madison County, Kentucky, "possess some two-thirds of its entire wealth, in taxable property."[60] By 1851 almost every issue of the *Millennial Harbinger* gave additional evidence of the rising social status of the movement as a whole.

Campbell's own prestige is seen in the fact that he was asked to preach before Congress on Sunday, June 2, 1850, to pray before the Indiana Constitutional Convention on November 11, 1850, and to address the Missouri Legislature in 1853. When he preached in the Baptist Church in Washington late in 1857, he was "honored with the presence of the President, and a majority of his Cabinet, and a good representation of both houses of Congress." Upon this occasion he reported enjoying "the generous hospitalities of Judge Black and family, now Attorney General of the Union."[61] President James Buchanan also received him at the White House. Campbell counted among his close personal friends Henry Clay, Robert E. Lee, James A. Garfield and others prominent in the political life of his time, many of whom visited his home in Bethany.

This increasing association with the "great" probably strengthened still further Campbell's natural affinities for "moderate" rather than radical democracy.

CHAPTER X

THE ROMAN CATHOLIC QUESTION

ONE OF THE special problems with political impli- cations which agitated the Protestant churches in America during the lifetime of Alexander Campbell was that of Roman Catholicism. It was inevitable that he should give attention to this issue which came to a focus for him in the debate with Bishop John D. Purcell in 1837.

THE BACKGROUND OF HIS CONCERN

Ray Allen Billington, in his *Protestant Crusade,* points out that one of the roots of anti-Catholicism in America was the English fear and hatred of Roman Catholics which the colonists brought with them to this country.[1] One of the roots of Campbell's fear and distrust of Ca- tholicism is certainly to be found in his Scotch-Irish background. Tension existed in Ireland from the mo- ment the Ulster Scots settled in a land already occupied by a native population largely Roman Catholic. Peri- odically this tension flared into open conflict, as in the rebellion of 1641 when the native Catholics robbed, stripped, and massacred many of the Protestant intrud- ers.

Campbell's own contacts with Catholics as a boy and youth led him to look upon them as, on the whole, "an ignorant, priest-ridden, superstitious people." His friend, Robert Richardson, reports that he early con- ceived an abhorrence for the whole system of Roman Catholicism "in its superstitions, its ceremonies, its spirit and its practical effects." When the ship on which

Campbell first set sail for America in 1808 was dashed
upon a sunken rock, he was impressed by the terror and
fear which seemed to grip the Catholic passengers more
than any others. Later as he journeyed through the
forests of central Pennsylvania toward his new home,
he reflected one night on the fact that the inn at which
he was stopping was without lock or bolt on the door.
"Why," he asked himself, "are residents of this land
so free from fears of robbery or attack?" On the basis
of his experience in the Old World, he credited it to the
absence of Catholicism.[2]

Although he brought to this country a strong prejudice against Catholicism, and although the "no-popery"
cry was raised in many quarters in the decade of the
twenties, Campbell had almost nothing to say about the
subject during this period. At this time his attention
was preoccupied with the threat of one of the "daughters" of Rome. In this period when he spoke of "popery" it was usually the prelude to an attack upon the
"popish" spirit in Presbyterianism. An insight into
the workings of his mind is found in a statement regarding his publication plans in 1829. "The present," he
declared, "is a momentous crisis. . . . Catholic and Protestant Popery are plodding and plotting for the supremacy. The little and the great Popes are on tiptoe."[3]
Here "Popery" was used in a generic sense. As a radical left-wing Protestant, Campbell was as fearful of the
"little Popes" of Protestantism as of the "great Pope"
in Rome.

In the *Christian Baptist* he paid no attention to Catholic immigration, the Papal Jubilee of Leo XII in 1827,
the sessions of the Provincial Council of Catholicity in
Baltimore in 1829, or the controversy over trusteeism.
Although many items were reprinted from other religious journals, none came from those which in this period were outspokenly anti-Catholic.

In one significant regard Campbell was definitely out of step with those forces which were setting the stage for "the nativistic drama." He was untouched by the wave of revivalism which had built up in certain groups and individuals a reservoir of emotional energies requiring release in some sort of crusade. This has significance not only for Campbell's reserve in the anti-Catholic crusade but also for his opposition to abolitionism, the temperance movement, and all of the other "causes" —except peace—which in this period were being advanced on tides of emotional fervor flowing from revivalism. Campbell had neither the temperament nor the theological viewpoint for a crusader of the emotional type.

CONFRONTING THE ISSUE

He first dealt with the Catholic issue in the *Millennial Harbinger* for August, 1832, when he reprinted a sketch of the history of the Jesuits "taken from a late edition of Pascal's letters." In introducing this material Campbell expressed the belief that "the Jesuits have meditated the establishment of the Catholic religion in these United States, and that their plan is now in progress."[4] This statement appeared in the year in which the New York Protestant Association, formed in 1831, was revived by W. C. Brownlee, and public meetings on the issue in New York City resulted in a minor riot in the month of May. Campbell made no reference to any of these events. The following June, in a brief notice of the "Roman Catholic and Protestant Controversy," he referred to the discussions between John Hughes and John Breckenridge, which had begun in the eastern press in January, 1833, and those between Brownlee and the priests in New York City.[5]

November, 1833, saw him launch a series of articles on the "Catholic Controversy," which he characterized as "one of the most important controversies of this con-

troversial age," important in its bearings both upon
religion and "upon the political destinies of this nation,
involving the fundamental principles of free government." It therefore "demands the attention of all political men." "The varied, ingenious, persevering, and
bold efforts of the Romanists to gain the political ascendancy in this country" were not so "chimerical" as many
supposed.[6]

Already, he alleged, 40,000 Jesuits "are silently and
secretly at work in the bosom of our country." "Large
sums of money have been advanced from the coffers of
St. Peter to found schools, colleges, and churches in these
United States"—schools which have become so attrac-
tive to our "fashionable Protestants and philosophic
Sceptics, that they prefer them to any Protestant schools
for the education of their children." Other ominous
signs were the flood of Catholic immigrants crowding
our shores in the ratio of three Catholics to one Protestant, the boldness with which the Catholic priesthood of
New York and Philadelphia "provoke controversy, and
. . . challenge the investigation of their principles," and
the recent proposal "to have various presses established
in America for the purpose of making proselytes to the
Catholic faith."[7]

With this introduction Campbell proceeded to discuss
the Breckenridge-Hughes controversy, to which he returned in the early months of 1834. His comments on
this debate show that he was writing not just as a Protestant but as a *left-wing* Protestant. He advised Breckenridge, for example, that he ought to begin at Jerusalem
rather than at Geneva if he wanted successfully to as-
sail the pretensions of Rome. After quoting extensively
from Breckenridge's exposé of the Inquisition and the
persecuting spirit of Catholicism, he gave equal recognition to Hughes's references to the cruelty of Presbyterian persecution and proscription. In spite of his
growing awareness of the Catholic threat, Campbell had

not closed his eyes to what he regarded as "popish" tendencies within Protestantism itself. The issue had not become one of Protestantism versus Catholicism, but remained one of left-wing sect versus right-wing church theories.

By 1835, when the religious leaders of America were generally engaged in "saving the West from the Pope," Campbell began to reflect elements of the nativist argument, although he dealt with many of the alleged "facts" in a rather critical spirit. In February he quoted an item from the *Cross and Baptist Journal* on "Roman Catholicism in the Valley" and then went on to register dissent from certain measures widely advocated for the defense of Protestantism and democracy.

Admitting the danger to American institutions from the torrent of Catholic immigration into the Mississippi Valley, he asked, "What is to be done; or what would those panic-stricken sectarians, that fear this mammoth sect, have to be done in this crisis?" First he took up the suggestion that immigration be stopped and laid it aside with the remark: "Then down goes our temple of equal rights and our boasted indifference to all political concern in religion. We cannot place Catholics under disabilities." Campbell could not follow Locke in the latter's denial of civil rights to Catholics. Nor did he approve the policy of those alarmists who "raise such a cry against the Papists." "Why arouse their jealousy?" he asked. "Why tell them that we fear them . . . ? Is not this bad policy . . . ?" Why create a panic which cannot be allayed?[8]

Yet "there is an ark of safety which might be reared," Campbell affirmed. "That ark is UNIVERSAL EDUCATION—education patronized, sustained, guarded, and controlled by the State." With this he went on to advocate "state funds, state teachers, state schools, and state laws compelling all to be enlightened." "An enlightened community," he declared, "cannot be enslaved

—an ignorant and uneducated society cannot be free.''
He advised those who feared ''a Catholic ascendancy''
to remember that the ''Catholic bloodhounds of the dark
ages'' were ignorant persons who never had been able
to read.[9]

A month later he characterized the spirit of popery
as ''naturally, necessarily, and essentially despotic,
cruel, and implacable.'' Still he made it clear that he
spoke of ''*the system* of Popery'' and not every individual Catholic in his private capacity. Occasionally, he
admitted, ''the man triumphs over the system.''[10]

The first direct evidence of Campbell's indebtedness to
the anti-Catholic press of the time is his publication of
an excerpt from the *New York Observer* in March, 1835.
The passage charged that ''popery'' threatens both the
political and religious liberties of the American people.
Six months later he quoted from the *Observer* materials
which set forth the S. F. B. Morse thesis that the Leopold
Association's missionary efforts in the United States
were part of a plot of the Holy Alliance to save the monarchies of Europe by ''destroying the influence of our
republic on the progress of liberal principles in the Old
World.'' Campbell agreed with his ''Presbyterian
friends'' that it was quite possible and entirely probable
''that the Pope contemplates the establishment of the
'true faith' in the Valley of the Mississippi.''

We must, however, dissent from the hue and cry of bitter denunciation with which the Mother Church has been assailed by
her ungrateful progeny. . . . If there be a plot on hand . . . to
supplant Protestantism and free government in our country,
the fierce denunciatory and vindictive spirit with which it is
met, is not in keeping with the philosophy of religion, morality,
or sound policy.[11]

It is apparent from these remarks and from Campbell's subsequent practice that he did not swallow whole
the charges and insinuations of the more rabid anti-
Catholics. Nor did he at any time join in purveying the

sensational "disclosures" of the immoralities which purportedly went on in Catholic convents. Instead his arguments were always pitched on a plane of reason and Scripture and consisted for the most part in pointing up discrepancies between the spirit of the Catholic system and the New Testament, or the conflicting tendencies of Catholicism and democracy.

THE PURCELL DEBATE

In October, 1836, Campbell attended the sessions of the Western Literary Institute and College of Professional Teachers, in Cincinnati, Ohio, to deliver an address on "The Importance of Uniting the Moral with the Intellectual Culture of the Mind." A previous speaker, Joshua L. Wilson, had recommended the use of the Bible as a reading book in the schools. This was objected to by the Catholic Bishop of Cincinnati and one of his priests.

Campbell approved Wilson's suggestion and in the introduction to his address ascribed the cultural superiority of the English-speaking people, "whether in the Old World or in the New," to the Protestant Reformation, whose maxim was that "Man by nature is, and of right ought to be, a *thinking* being," and that "he ought not only to think, but *to think for himself.*"[12] Campbell here showed his indebtedness to Thomas S. Grimke, from whose address on "The Character and Objects of Science" he had quoted in the *Millennial Harbinger* in 1833. The cultural effects of the Protestant Reformation he was to discuss many times through the years.

To the assumption of Campbell's introduction Bishop Purcell objected, asserting rather that the Protestant Reformation was the cause of all the contention and infidelity in the world. Both amplified their views in public addresses apart from the sessions of the College of Teachers with the result that Campbell was urged by

some citizens of Cincinnati to develop his position in a
series of lectures. He replied that it would be impossible
for him to do so at that time because of other commit-
ments but offered to meet any of the "Catholic priesthood" in a free and full discussion of the matter after
the beginning of the new year. Bishop Purcell finally accepted this challenge, and the debate opened at the Syca-
more Street Meeting House on January 13, 1837.

The propositions which Campbell was to defend had
by this time been reduced to seven—the last of which
read:

The Roman Catholic religion, if infallible and unsusceptible
of reformation, as alleged, is essentially anti-American, being
opposed to the genius of all free institutions, and positively
subversive of them, opposing the general reading of the scriptures, and the diffusion of useful knowledge among the whole
community, so essential to liberty and the permanency of good
government.[13]

In Campbell's original arrangement of the propositions
this stood first.

Most of the debate under the first six points is irrele-
vant to this study. It may be noted, however, that in
the course of the discussion, Campbell rejected the right-
wing conception of a church "as wide as the human
race,"[14] traced the true succession not through the line
of the popes but through the sects,[15] and referred to
England as "the cradle of all political freedom."[16]

To the fifth proposition—the immoral tendency of the
Roman Catholic system and its injuriousness to the well-
being of society—he gave considerable attention, quoting
from Catholic sources to show the church's lax attitude
toward moral sins and the ease with which these might
be atoned for. It was in this connection that he got into
one of his most heated exchanges with Purcell, on the
question of clerical concubinage, and in so doing came
as near as he ever did to joining in the popular charges
of immorality on the part of Catholic priests and nuns.

The decrees of the church councils, said Campbell, attest "that these priests have not been such immaculate purities. . . . Half their legislation is about the specks and blemishes of this virgin priesthood." As an illustration of the immoralities which are the product of Catholic insistence upon a celibate clergy and also of the essential immorality of the system which seeks to rate sins as lesser and greater, he referred to a passage from a Catholic authority, Liguori, to the effect that "If a priest should keep a *niece* [concubine], it is a very expiable and trifling offense; but should he marry a wife, he must be excommunicated forever."[17] Purcell immediately insisted that no such passage appeared in Liguori's works. Campbell was unable to produce the evidence at the time, but in the Appendix to the published debate gave a page reference with various certificates of disinterested persons attesting the accuracy of his quotation.

CATHOLICISM ANTI-AMERICAN

Campbell brought the discussion around at last to the seventh proposition—that the Roman Catholic religion is "essentially anti-American." He felt that his opponent was shying away from this subject and, on the afternoon of January 20, challenged the Bishop to face the issue. "This concerns him and his party more, than any other one of the seven," he said.

The community expect him to discuss this subject above all others. They are much excited and interested on this point. Many who have no antipathy against Roman Catholics have some fears of them. I belong to that class. . . . I do sincerely believe and think, that Roman Catholicism, in any country, is detrimental to its interests and prosperity: and in a republic, directly and positively tending every moment to its subversion.[18]

In upholding his side of the argument Campbell decried the undemocratic structure of the Catholic church, its restrictions upon freedom of thought and speech, its

view of the state as subservient to the church, and the
oath by which priests are bound to support a foreign
prince.

He objected first to the monarchial nature of the Catholic church in which the pope is judge, executive, and
lawgiver. In the case of a controversy between the
church and a heretic or a reformer, "who is supreme
judge of both? One of the parties, indeed, the church
herself!... What a splendid picture of a republican president or judge have we got in the Roman church!" When
the Bishop argued from Deuteronomy 17 that it is quite
proper to place legislative, judicial, and executive powers in the same hands, Campbell reminded his opponent
that in the Jewish theocracy "God himself was lawgiver—the priests kept and expounded the law—the
judges and kings executed it. Where, then, were all
these powers accumulated in one and the same dynasty?"
He concluded that Purcell had not only misapplied the
Scripture, but revealed his ignorance of the nature of
political government. "The very elements of a just and
pure government will be found in separating these powers; the very essence of a despotism in uniting them in
one and the same person."[19]

In the second place he argued that Catholicism is a
system of "spiritual despotism," which keeps Catholics
in mental slavery and ignorance.[20] It puts the Bible
"under a bushel,"[21] forbids the reading of it, and thus
makes the Catholic population "abject slaves to their
priests, bishops, and popes." Nor is this "benumbing
and paralyzing influence" limited to religion. The
hierarchy

has always opposed freedom of thought, of speech, and of action, whether in literature, politics, or religion. Such are the
laws of mind . . . that if in religion the mind be enslaved . . .
[this tends to] disqualify a person for the relish and enjoyment of political liberty. For . . . religious liberty is the cause,
and political liberty an effect of that cause, without which it
never had been found.[22]

Later Campbell referred to the evil consequences of the Catholic practice of proscribing books and denying liberty of the press.[23]

A third anti-American element which he discerned in Catholicism is its theory "that *God has made the political government subject to the spiritual.*" This point he illustrated with several instances from history in which popes had deprived kings and rulers of their dominions, absolved subjects from their oaths of allegiance, and forbidden them to pay any obedience to their kings. "Is this the genius of our government?" he asked—to have

kings hurled from their thrones, and subjects released from their allegiance, without ceremony, by the vicars of Christ and the head of the church! Who is this that sets aside oaths, and religious obligations, in the name of the Lord?[24]

This argument was quickly picked up by Purcell and turned against Campbell in a very embarrassing manner. "Suppose you had been living at the time of the American Revolution," Purcell asked,

when the spirit of a mighty and numerous people was roused by excess of wrong, to make one vast effort for freedom. Under these circumstances, the General in chief, the officers, and the army, the revenue department, and postmasters, all of whom had taken an oath of allegiance to . . . king [George], appeal to you, inquiring, what is to be done? Asking you if the oath was binding. What would be your reply?[25]

Campbell answered: "If they had taken a solemn oath, they should not break it." To which Bishop Purcell rejoined: "Then was George Washington a perjurer, and all the officers of the army and navy, all the signers of the Declaration of Independence, and all the subjects of the king of Great Britain were perjurers!" Campbell insisted that this did not necessarily follow. When the Bishop asked what he would have had persons do who had taken the oath of allegiance, Campbell replied lamely: " 'It is better not to vow, than to vow and

not pay'—as saith the good Book." "We should always
do our duty, and leave consequences to God." He continued, in the spirit of Calvin, "When he [God] intends
the deliverance of a people, he will effect for them re-
demption, as he did for his people out of Egypt."[26]
Purcell made the most of Campbell's embarrassment.
Turning to the audience, he exclaimed:

You see the dilemma to which the gentleman has been reduced
. . . While Catholics are reproached for their slavish tenets, he
himself teaches the whole doctrine of passive obedience, and
condemns the very principle of the American Revolution.[27]

The next morning Campbell returned to the subject—
this time armed with the Lockean argument for revolution. He affirmed that in Protestant doctrine "no circumstance or contingency, can ever absolve a person
from the obligation of an oath, into which he has intelli-
gently and voluntarily entered"—but

if . . . an oath has in it the nature of a covenant, then one of
the parties failing, so far vacates the covenant as to set the
other free from his oath: but this is not absolution for break-
ing it; it is a simple annulling of its conditions.

So it was, he concluded, in the case of the American Revolution.

The king of England was generally allowed to have receded
from the conditions on which that oath was taken by the persons who renounced allegiance to him; he having failed to protect and cherish his American subjects, according to the tenor
of the charter given, they were freed from the obligations of
allegiance.[28]

A fourth consideration with Campbell was the oath
which all bishops take to obey the pope and to persecute
and destroy heretics and schismatics. After quoting the
oath he insisted that it alone sustains his seventh proposition and proves "that the genius of the Latin church
is anti-American and essentially opposed to the existence of all free institutions."[29] To show its incompatibility with full allegiance to the government of the

United States, he also quoted the oath of naturalization which calls upon a new citizen to "renounce forever, all allegiance and fidelity, to any foreign Prince, Potentate, State or Sovereignty, whatsoever." "Such are the oaths and laws of naturalization," he said.

Now, as the pope of Rome is a foreign prince—at this very moment a prince temporal as well as spiritual . . . and claiming allegiance in temporals as well as spirituals, throughout the whole Roman Catholic world; I ask, can anyone who has sworn "to *increase* and *advance his authority*" . . . *take* or *keep* the oath of citizenship in this country without perjury?! In my most deliberate judgment, it is impossible.[30]

Another feature of the oath is that bishops must swear to "*persecute* and *oppose* . . . heretics and schismatics," which clearly conflicts with the constitutional guarantees of religious liberty. On this point Campbell quoted, from the *Encyclopedia of Religious Knowledge,* a passage which he said showed that Catholicism,

chameleon like, first accommodates itself to the customs of every country, and seems to inhale and exhale the popular atmosphere until it reaches its end . . . and so soon as it gains the fulcrum of popular opinion and the lever of the majority, it builds up an empire, after the model of the Prince Metternich. This has hitherto been its history, in every climate, and country, and age.[31]

Other items of interest in connection with the closing portion of the debate include Campbell's reference to Lyman Beecher's *Plea for the West,* which, he declared, "ought to be in every family, and read by every adult in the great valley, who feels any interest in the preservation of our free and happy institutions."[32] A moment later, in contrast to his earlier practice of referring to our government as "secular" or "infidel," he implied that the United States is a Protestant country. Comparing his own relationship to this nation to that of his opponent, he said:

Although . . . we both may be called foreigners; yet, we are not foreigners in the same sense. I claim a very intimate relation

with the Protestant family. . . . It was then my family, that first
settled this country. The bishop's family settled Roman Catholic America. He is a foreigner here, as I would be a foreigner
in Mexico or South America.[33]

In his concluding statement Campbell denied that the
participation of Catholic soldiers in the Revolutionary
War was any evidence of "Roman Catholic love of either
civil or religious liberty." Their action was dictated more
by "hatred of *Protestant* England" than by "love of
rational liberty," he asserted.[34]

Feeling ran high in Cincinnati during the debate. The
editor of the *Gazette* pictured Campbell in the role of
one waging war upon Catholicism and declared his efforts a failure even before the discussions were finished.
At the conclusion of the debate a meeting of citizens
passed resolutions declaring it to be their unanimous
opinion "that the cause of Protestantism has been fully
sustained."

The *Millennial Harbinger* for the early months of
1837 carried numerous items dealing with Catholicism,
most of them related to the debate. In one, Campbell
dealt rather bitterly with the "Jesuitical maneuverings"
of Purcell and his associates in attempting to supplement and strengthen the Bishop's speeches for the published volume.[35]

LATER TREATMENT OF THE CATHOLIC QUESTION

During the next ten years Campbell had little to say
on the Catholic issue except as he made brief comments
upon materials reprinted from others or upon events in
the news.

In April, 1843, he noted with satisfaction the organization of the American Protestant Association. "Such
an association I have long thought the peculiar signs
of the times loudly called for," he added. In fact, about
the time of his debate with Purcell, he had

proposed to Dr. Beecher . . . and some others . . . to have such
an association got up in the valley of the Mississippi, . . . but
the Doctor thought that in the openings of Providence the time
was not yet come; or that it would make too great a draft on
ministerial time and services.[36]

With the story of the organization of the association,
Campbell reprinted its constitution and the list of its
officers. The next month he began publication of an "Address" of its Board of Managers and in August discussed this statement and expressed his wholehearted
support of the association's program.

Having referred to the Champlain book-burning incident in the *Millennial Harbinger* for April, 1843, Campbell took note of the Philadelphia riot of May, 1844, the
following September. Instead of lamenting the action
of the Protestant mob, he used the incident to illustrate
the lack of veracity on the part of Catholic priests whenever their "loyalty to the Pope and the church is concerned."[37]

His visit to Ireland in the summer of 1847 led Campbell to speak again with new conviction of the contrasting
cultural effects of Catholicism and Protestantism—as he
did, for example, in his addresses on "The Anglo-Saxon
Language," in 1849, "The Destiny of our Country," in
1853, and "Colleges," in 1854. He and many of his followers had been concerned about the plight of the Irish
following the famine of 1845-46. Notes in the *Millennial
Harbinger* for April and May, 1847, indicate that the
church at Bethany was collecting funds for Irish relief.
Some of this money was taken to Ireland by Campbell on
his trip to the British Isles. A year after his return he
reported:

Nothing so impressed my mind, as the testimony in favor of
Protestantism, given by the North, or the province of Ulster,
in bold contrast with Romanism, as developed in its influences
upon the other three provinces of Munster, Leinster, and Con-
naught.

The Catholic provinces had the richest soil, and yet "the wretchedness of the people and the country stands in fearful and ominous contrast with that of the North" or Protestant portion. "During the famine and pestilence of 1847," he continued,

the North suffered very little more than in some other years. It exported some six or seven millions sterling worth of produce to England during that year, while we were sending money and bread from America, to relieve the south and west of the Island! What a comment on the tendencies of these two systems! Roman Catholicism enervates, while Protestantism energizes and invigorates the minds of the people.[38]

In a similar vein he later reported the contrast between the Protestant and Catholic portions of Canada when he visited that country in 1855.[39]

By 1850 the anti-Catholic movement in America had largely spent itself. Campbell continued to show some interest in the subject for two or three years more— largely in the form of an occasional item quoted from another periodical. The most vigorous statement from his own pen in these later years came in 1851 as he expressed alarm at the "encroaching policy of haughty Rome, and the supple sycophancy of American politicians." The occasion was the return of Bishop John Hughes from Rome where he had gone "to kiss the hand or the toe . . . of nine times pious Pius, and to woo a cardinal's cap." No sooner did the newly elevated archbishop return than

a fatted ox is killed, a puncheon of wine ordered, Chief Justice Taney, Senator Webster and Senator Clay, with all the pillars of the papacy of our great American emporium, are invited to grace the banquet, and to welcome, with all forensic and rhetorical eloquence, the safe arrival of this great Americanized ambassador of Christ's Vicar.

Campbell took little comfort from the fact that "from great prudence, uncontrollable circumstances forbade the attendance of these chief political dignitaries of our land," for "Senatorial letters, apologetic, were read

from them to the assembled guests, full of flattery and
full of welcome, ingeniously adapted to the well educated
ear of Archbishop Hughes!!'' ''I think I see great break-
ers ahead,'' he concluded.[40]

From this survey it is clear that Campbell took a vigorous stand against Roman Catholicism as an enemy
both to the Christian religion and to American democracy. Although he was influenced to a considerable extent by the prevailing currents of American nativism,
he maintained a critical attitude toward most of the
''facts'' and documents of the nativist movement. He
did not go ''all out'' on the subject like many of his
contemporaries—partly because he was not the emotional ''crusading type,'' and partly because he retained
enough of his left-wing spirit to cause him to divide his
fire between Roman Catholicism and right-wing Protestantism. Even more important, perhaps, is the fact that
his energies were quite largely absorbed in more constructive efforts to meet the Catholic problem—public
education, Bible translation, and preparing teachers and
preachers for the West.

CHAPTER XI

EDUCATION IN
A REPUBLIC

APART from his influence as a churchman, Alexander Campbell's chief contribution to American democracy was undoubtedly in the field of public education. His vigorous advocacy of free public schools sets him off from the narrow sectarian who withdraws from the world of public affairs and marks him rather as a citizen with a broad sense of responsibility to the community. As a faithful disciple of Locke and Beattie, Campbell never ceased to stress the importance of education in a republic.

Education was one of his lifelong concerns. As a boy in his teens in Ireland he taught in his father's academy at Rich Hill. In 1818 he started an academy of his own, Buffalo Seminary, which he carried on for about five years. He was the moving spirit in the incorporation of Bethany College in 1840, and from that time practically to the end of his life he served as its president and one of its professors.

Campbell was a perennial advocate of free public schools, which he looked upon as the chief bulwark of religion, morality, and representative government. His interest in public education antedated his major concern with the problem of Roman Catholicism, but after the midthirties the two issues were closely interrelated in his thinking—as can be seen from his prescription of universal education as the ''ark of safety'' for the Mississippi Valley in face of the inflowing tides of Roman Catholicism.

The interdependence of Protestantism, public schools, and democracy was clearly set forth in the Baccalaureate

Address for 1853, in which he bluntly declared that it is to Protestantism that "we, as a people and a nation, owe the common school system of education, which [in turn] is one of the chief bulwarks of religion, morality, and representative government." It is because of the strategic importance of the common school system, he continued, that the Roman church is seeking to crush and annihilate it. "Of this fact you either are, or ought to be, fully apprized, and also amply prepared to maintain and sustain the common school system . . . in the face of all opposition."[1]

The right of suffrage, he argued, "can be exercised with safety to all interests only by an intelligent, moral, and virtuous people." This necessitates "schools, Bibles and teachers," without which "such a population cannot be created." The common school is "a political institution, in which the whole community are deeply and essentially interested." He went on to stress the place of "the Bible in every school," which was the special target of Roman Catholic attack.[2] This relatively late address points up his two major emphases in connection with the subject—the role of free public schools in a republic and of the Bible as a textbook in those schools.

THE NECESSITY FOR FREE PUBLIC SCHOOLS

The battle for public education in the United States was fought largely in the quarter century between 1825 and 1850. Ellwood P. Cubberley distinguishes seven phases of the struggle: for tax support, to eliminate the pauper-school idea, to make the schools entirely free, to establish school supervision, to eliminate sectarianism, to establish the American high school, and to establish the state university as the crown to the whole system.[3] Campbell seems to have been chiefly interested in the first three and fifth of these subjects.

In view of the fact that the Lancastrian monitorial system of instruction, introduced into the United States in 1806, did much to awaken sentiment for free schools, it is significant that Campbell, in his Virginia Convention address on the basis of representation, referred to Joseph Lancaster as another of those great public benefactors "as useful to the State, as a whole district of mere slave-holders." Social, political, and economic influences which helped arouse people to the need for free schools included the extension of suffrage, and the increase in the number of paupers and criminals which accompanied the growth of cities and the rise of manufacturing. Both of these figured prominently in Campbell's concern.

EARLY VIEWS

A few months after the Virginia Convention he elaborated in the *Millennial Harbinger* the proposals on public education which he had there offered. Taking for granted that "ignorance is the parent of idleness . . . immorality and crime of every gradation" and that "to *prevent* crime is much wiser than to *punish* it," he maintained that it is one of the duties of a wise government to devote its energies to the education of its citizens. He advocated levying such taxes as will be "sufficient to educate well every child born within the commonwealth," maintaining "as many common schools as will make it convenient for all the children in every vicinity, to attend," and one state university whose function would be, "besides affording a liberal education to all who attend it, . . . to furnish teachers for the common schools."[4]

The chief objection to such a plan, he anticipated, would be its expense. Yet it could easily be shown that any state in the Union could support such a system without additional taxes. He proposed a reduction in the number of legislators and fewer meetings of the General Assembly, so that the funds saved thereby might be used to finance a system of public education.

A second objection would come from the rich who felt it was no concern of theirs to help educate the children of "the indolent and vicious poor." He advised the rich that it would be better to expend a little on the education of the children of the poor, than to spend so much for laws which

make themselves no safer, and the vicious poor no better. More money is now paid by the virtuous and industrious part of the community on account of this vicious mass of ignorance, idleness, and crime, without relieving the community from it, or improving it in the least, than would be sufficient to banish it out of the land altogether, by the proper means.[5]

As he had done upon more than one occasion at the Virginia Convention, he then asked his opponents to consider their own children's stake in the matter. Even though a man may be able to educate his own children, and considers himself oppressed when he has to pay for the education of the poor, he should remember that he is thereby accomplishing two great objects:

First, he is defending his offspring from the infractions of ignorance and crime by removing them out of the country; and in the second place, all he pays annually, under such a system, would be only paid in advance for his own poor descendants.

In two or three generations his own descendants, in all probability, would "sink to poverty and ignorance; but under this system they would not so likely become poor; and if poor, they could not be deprived of education."[6]

On a tour to the Northeast in 1836 Campbell visited the Auburn Penitentiary. This impressed him as a "valuable . . . school for the unfortunate and vicious of society." After paying tribute to its success in reforming many inmates, he went on to point out that "the great mass of the convicts are persons who were neglected in their early education, and thrown into society with little literary and less moral instruction."[7]

Early in 1837 he reprinted, from the *American Pres-byterian,* an enthusiastic account of the Prussian system of education—an article which incorporated long passages from an address by Calvin E. Stowe. In introducing this item Campbell expressed the hope that the American people "shall be stirred up by the example of *Protestant Prussia* . . . to commence a new era on this the most vital of all the interests of our country and of human-kind."[8]

The following year he admitted that while he might be "too sensitive on the subject of education," he regarded his fellowcitizens as

generally too remiss in this great matter. If I had a thousand votes in the State they should all go for *universal education* at public expense. I would make the literary and moral education of every child born on the territory of the commonwealth the first and paramount duty of the State.[9]

THE ADDRESS ON COMMON SCHOOLS

Campbell's most systematic discussion of the role of public education in a democracy came in his address on "Common Schools," prepared for an educational convention at Clarksburg, Virginia, on September 8 and 9, 1841.

A divergence of educational interest had become apparent in Virginia as early as 1816 when residents of the western part of the state insisted that the total income from the "literary fund" be used to establish free schools. Charles H. Ambler points out that the vote on Campbell's resolution on education at the Virginia Convention was a sectional vote.[10] The people of eastern Virginia relied upon private schools for elementary education and sought to divert as much as possible of the literary fund to the state university in which they took great pride. In the western part of the state, schools for the poor were maintained out of an appropriation from the literary fund. Since there were a dearth of good private schools there and an absence of social distinctions, children of all classes attended these schools, although they were originally established and maintained for the poor whites.

During the 1830's a movement to transform these pauper schools into free common schools gained momentum. The Governor, a resident of the southwestern part of the state, raised his voice in behalf of common schools in 1838. The result was a series of educational conventions, the first and most important of which was that held in Clarksburg in 1841, attended by 130 delegates from the northwestern part of the state and the Shenandoah Valley and also by educators from Ohio and Pennsylvania. According to Ambler, "Rousing addresses were made; elaborate plans for a free-school system were submitted; and enthusiastic communications were read from many of the most prominent citizens of the west."[11]

One was the "Address" submitted by Alexander Campbell. Starting out with the "oft-repeated maxim that a representative government depends not merely for its prosperity and perpetuity, but for its very existence, on the intelligence and virtue of its citizens," he dealt with the subject under two headings. First: "What sort of an education is adapted to the common wants of the whole community, to the happiness and prosperity of the State?"[12] In this portion of his address he discussed the content and character of education—a subject which is not especially relevant to this study. It may be noted in passing that for Campbell the scope of education was broader than the traditional "three R's" and included other useful arts and sciences as well as the study of the Bible and the basic facts of our "common Christianity."

The second division of the address dealt with the question: *"How shall such a system be established and made commensurate with the wants of the whole community?"*

He recognized that the biggest problem lay in the conflict of interest between the eastern and western parts
of the state.   The aristocrats of eastern Virginia "are
more disposed to patronize Colleges and one great Eastern University, than to extend education throughout the
length and breadth of the land," whereas western Virginia wants free common schools for all.   Campbell cautioned against setting up a rival monopoly of common
schools in the West over against a monopoly of the university in the East.   The West as well as the East, he
said, "must have colleges, or normal schools, to supply
teachers."[13]

He warned against a class system in education—

colleges for the rich and common schools for the poor. . . . We
want colleges for those who by Nature's moulding and forma-
tion have more appetite, taste, and capacity than the common
standard; and we want common schools for all.[14]

He also rejected the idea of "gratuitous instruction for
paupers [only] . . . we want schools for all at the expense
of all."   The worthy poor, who most deserve education,
would not accept it under such "humiliating conditions"
as must prevail if two classes of pupils were to be
brought together in the same school—"one class educated at the public expense, and another at their own."
"To avoid all this," he said, "is one of the objects of
common schools."[15]

In comparing the educational philosophies of East and
West, Campbell made some observations regarding the
role of economic and geographical factors in helping determine political forms.   He noted the correlation between aristocracy and wealth, on the one hand, and democracy and relative poverty (or equality) on the other.   In
the eastern part of the state, he said, "they have two
sorts of population of great political disparity."   Common schools and aristocracy do not go together, for a
patrician believes that "it would undignify his son to

learn out of the same grammar, under the same teacher, and in the same school-room with the son of a plebian." On the other hand, the people of the West "are generally too poor—that is, too democratical for such notions."[16]

As for the influence of geography, he said: "It is . . . problematical whether aristocracy ever did thrive in a region so high and rough as ours. It is rather indigenous to extended plains, great cities, and level countries." In western Virginia farms were smaller, and children did not have to walk "from the centre of a thousand acre parallelogram" to visit a neighbor or go to school.

The propinquity of less patrician inheritances is our happier lot; and, therefore, not merely equality of fortune, but propinquity of residence, are signs in our zodiac favorable to . . . the introduction of a common school system.[17]

The last portion of his address dealt with the steps which he believed should be taken to establish a system of public education—use of lecturers and the periodical press to awaken the public to the importance of the issue, getting up petitions and addresses to the legislature seeking a fair distribution of the annual income from the literary fund, asking from the Assembly power for counties to levy taxes for school purposes, dividing the counties into school districts, erecting one good schoolhouse in each, and setting up a school committee and treasurer in each district to be responsible for employing competent instructors and supervising the schools. "Here are five practicable means," he said, "which . . . can be adopted and made very efficient to establish and sustain a county, or a large district, of common schools."[18]

In his conclusion Campbell referred once more to the importance of education, spoke of the appalling amount of illiteracy, declared that the state itself was responsible for it, and suggested that education ought to be made a qualification for voting. With regard to this last suggestion, he reported that in one county there were 2,100 persons of mature age and reason who could neither read nor write. Still they had the franchise, and

their illiterate vote must, in our government, outweigh the vote of two thousand and ninety-nine Solomons, could they be found. Is this rational? Is this right? . . . If we must have universal suffrage, let us have universal education. I would limit the one by the other. . . . The right of suffrage in the hands of such voters, uneducated in morals and literature, is like a razor in an infant's hand, or a flambeaux in the hands of a drunkard in a magazine of gunpowder.

Campbell did not believe in measuring or counting votes by cash, nor did he deny that the poor man's vote might be as good as that of "Monsieur Girard or that of Baron Rothchild." Yet it was "preposterous" to him that "ignorance should neutralize intelligence, or that two thousand uneducated persons should decide the election of a state or the fate of a nation."[19]

Education continued to be a major concern with Campbell. He participated quite regularly in the meetings of the Western Literary Institute and College of Professional Teachers, one of the most effective propaganda agencies for public education in the West. He was aware of educational developments in other parts of the country, for in his Baccalaureate Address of 1846 he paid indirect tribute to the work of Horace Mann and Henry Barnard.[20] He continued to treat education at frequent intervals in the *Millennial Harbinger,* and many of his addresses in later years dealt with this subject. In addition to those which have been preserved in this periodical, Campbell refers to another "on the great subject of Education" before the Missouri legislature in 1853.[21]

The Bible and Religion in the Schools

In the light of his extreme views on separation of church and state, it is somewhat surprising to hear

Campbell in 1835 urge governors to decree reading and study of the Bible in the schools as a means of defense against papal tyranny. "Let the Bible, as a school-book, be taught and read from the same policy, and by the same authority," he said, "which administers oaths before civil tribunals" and suspends legal processes and courts of justice on Sundays. He would

let no squeamishness on the subject of a state religion, prevent the reading and teaching of the Bible. . . . The Bible is the shield of the nation; and if it be not read and universally taught from Dan even to Beersheba, the Catholics will take away our place and nation just as certain as the waters of the Ohio descend into the Mississippi.[22]

In his address on "The Importance of Uniting the Moral with the Intellectual Culture of the Mind," before the College of Teachers in 1836, he examined the view that "religion and morality are matters of private and individual concern, and that it belongs to parents and ministers of religion, rather than to the . . . schools and colleges, to take charge of such concerns." What, he asked, "shall become of those who have irreligious and immoral parents, and no ministers of religion!" It was the "melancholy fact" that

to prevent rival ascendancies, we make a decree that it shall be unfair . . . in any teacher . . . to make a single suggestion on the whole subject of religion, lest in so doing his party should gain some advantage, or its rival some loss by the operation. . . . [Thus] all the grand vital impulses to morality are taken away from schools and teachers.[23]

After thus implying that religion, as well as the Bible, should be introduced into the public schools, he went on to explain that Protestants have "a common religion." While they may not be able to agree on the theories of religious belief, they can and do agree upon the simple facts. "The evidences, the absolute certainty and divine authority of the Christian religion, of the Old and New

Testaments," can and should be taught "in every high school in christendom."[24]

In 1837 he discussed further the *"common Christianity"* which should be taught in the schools, and "against which no intelligent Protestant could object." This includes:

The evidences of the Christian religion—the arguments that prove the divine person and mission of the common Saviour—the reasons why he is to be accredited and received as the only Saviour of the world—the necessity of faith in him—of repentance towards God—of a new heart and life—of supreme devotion to his will—the value of his death as a sin-offering—the necessity of his resurrection, and the certainty of his coming to judge and retribute the living and the dead according to their works. These great cardinal points, in which all Christians agree [Campbell affirmed], ought to be taught in every Seminary in the length and breadth of the land.[25]

Later that year he referred to a resolution passed at the October meeting of the College of Teachers, "That, in the judgment of the College, the Bible should be introduced into every school, from the lowest to the highest, as a school-book; *only without denominational or sectarian comment.*" The italicized portion, he noted, was his amendment and was unanimously adopted.[26] This was the same formula which Horace Mann had established in the Massachusetts public schools.[27]

"Why the Pantheon and Pagan mythology should be introduced into any school, high or low, and the Bible excluded," was to Campbell "an insoluble problem."[28] In 1854 he said it was important to have Bible chairs in the colleges so that teachers could be adequately trained to handle these subjects in the schools.[29] He later stated his "capital position" as follows:

That the Holy Bible must be in every school worthy of a Christian public patronage, and not in the library only, but daily in the hand of teacher and pupil, professor and student. . . . The Bible and the school master are God's two great instrumentalities to enlighten, to civilize, and to aggrandize man.[30]

This stress upon the Bible as a textbook in the public schools grew out of his conviction that in a democracy the electorate must be virtuous as well as intelligent, and that the only sound morality or virtue must be founded on the Bible. It was probably also in part a reaction to the Catholic effort to keep the Bible away from the people. It clearly represents a softening of his earlier fear of anything that might lead to a church-state alliance.

In his views on public education Campbell followed in the main the "western line" as set forth by Ambler and Merle E. Curti.[31] He was in harmony with "the spirit of the age" in the battle for free state schools as outlined by Cubberley.

Chapter XII

ETHICS OF ECONOMIC LIFE

ALEXANDER CAMPBELL'S economic ethics furnish one of the best examples of his merging of sect and ecclesiastical body elements into a rather consistent denominational synthesis. Major attention was given to this subject in the period from 1838 to 1843.

His economic views reflect his own geographical and economic status. A western gentleman farmer and editor, he had little sympathy for traders or speculators, and little awareness of the problems of the industrialist or urban worker. In 1814, shortly after his marriage, he received his father-in-law's farm as a gift. His extensive publishing business—periodicals, the volumes of his debates, his edition of the New Testament, hymnbook, and other works—must have added measurably to his income. He early increased his land holdings in and around Bethany and later invested quite extensively in unimproved lands in Ohio and Illinois. His will included bequests of some $29,000 besides 1,550 acres of farmland in Brooke County and town property in Bethany. Benjamin Lyon Smith declares that Campbell "died the richest man in West Virginia."[1]

The period from 1800 to 1815 saw the introduction into America of new breeds of fine-wooled sheep, especially the Merino. This greatly stimulated sheep husbandry and wool manufacturing in the West, particularly in the tristate area of western Pennsylvania, the panhandle of Virginia, and southeastern Ohio. The center of this development was about 20 miles from Bethany in the vicinity of Steubenville, Ohio. Campbell's enterprising spirit is shown by the fact that he was one of the first farmers in his area to import these improved breeds of sheep. This economic interest in wool, on the part of Campbell and his western Virginia neighbors, was one of the factors leading to their devotion to the "American system" of Henry Clay with its emphasis upon the protective tariff.

Since most of the more significant economic developments of the period took place in connection with the rising industrialism of the East, fewer correlations are to be found between Campbell's remarks on economic matters and the economic trends dealt with in standard histories of the subject than is the case with the other topics with which he dealt. Still he maintained a lively interest in economic theory and for several years taught political economy at Bethany College, using Francis Wayland's *Elements of Political Economy* as his text.[2]

THE RIGHT OF PRIVATE PROPERTY

Campbell everywhere assumed the inviolable right of private property although he nowhere took the trouble, like Locke and Beattie, to demonstrate that it is a natural right. He dealt with this subject only indirectly as he denied that the communism of the early church was binding upon Christians of his day.

In an article on "Restoration of the Ancient Order of Things," in the *Christian Baptist* in 1825, he insisted that although the early church's practice of weekly communion is binding upon the church of later centuries, its communism is not. The Jerusalem Christians shared their goods only because their extreme poverty required it, and this "precedent" is binding only upon such as may find themselves in similar circumstances. If a society of Christians were "absolutely so poor that they could live in no other way than by the selling of the possessions of some of the brethren, it would be an indispensable duty to do so." Yet Campbell reminded his readers that "even in Jerusalem at this time the selling of houses and lands was a voluntary act . . . without any command from the Apostles."[3] Thus summarily did he dispose of an apostolic precedent when it conflicted with his views of natural right!

More penetrating were his later remarks distinguishing between "a 'common stock' church, and a common participation of goods as every one has need." "The idea of a common stock for creating either wealth or the means of subsistence," he said, "is an idea essentially different from that of a common distribution of joint or particular donations according to the wants of the brotherhood." For the latter there is ample precedent in Scripture, but not for the former.[4]

In his debate with Robert Owen, Campbell implied that man and society cannot exist without private property. In reference to his opponent's socialistic proposals, he said: "Sooner will he cause the rivers to flow backwards to their sources; sooner can he reverse the decrees of gravitation, than abolish . . . private property."[5]

As might be expected, Campbell had little sympathy for the various communistic enterprises which were thriving in America in his day. To be sure the members of the Brush Run church voted, on June 8, 1814, to migrate and establish a colony outside of Zanesville, Ohio, and Campbell was a member of the committee of five which visited various sites and brought back this recommendation. But apart from a school the plan seems to have contemplated none of the characteristic features of a "communistic village" of cooperation. When his father-in-law offered him his farm a short time later and Campbell accepted it, the church abandoned its plans for the colony. In 1845 Campbell expressed the opinion that Christians should not enter "associations, communities, or phalanxes." "I regard all such schemes as more or less utopian, unnatural, and inexpedient," he said.[6]

REACTION TO PANIC AND GOVERNMENT POLICIES

The economy of the United States suffered a stagger-ing blow in the panic of 1837, and the nation's first major depression followed—brought on largely by overexpan-sion and speculation in land and transportation facilities. The crop failures of 1835 and 1837 were contributing factors, and Jackson's financial policies the precipitating cause.

In June, 1837, Campbell noted the

various trials and difficulties which have in some places occurred . . . the paralyzing influence of the fortune-hunting schemes, which, like Jonah's gourd, seem to have grown up in a night, and . . . the deficits of the harvest of the last season.[7]

Early in 1838 he spoke once more of the disastrous effects of the panic upon the finances of the country as a whole and of the *Millennial Harbinger* in particular.[8]

He had nothing specific to say about the bank question, although one or two earlier remarks seem to indicate that his sympathies were with state or local banks against the Bank of the United States—a typically west-ern reaction. In the *Christian Baptist* for January, 1828, he had declared: "The Mammoth Bank of these United States is not more formidable to the little county corporations, than is the moral authority, or the capital stock of influence, of the leading sects, to the small patri-mony of the Sabbatarian or the Covenanter."[9]

He said nothing definite on the currency issue, although there were hints that he recognized the need for some more adequate system of federal control. In 1843 he compared the difficulties of establishing a college to those of regulating "the currency of twenty-six sovereign and independent States, sometimes wayward and whim-sical withal, although professing to be under a Federal Constitution."[10]

He made no comment upon labor unions, the shorter working day, or the abolition of imprisonment for debt—

issues which were coming to the fore in the larger
centers of population as part of the Jacksonian ferment.
Nor did he express any preference between legislative
charters or general laws of incorporation as the basis for
industrial or commercial enterprise, although some
earlier remarks, in connection with the subject of colleges, seem to suggest more opposition to charters than
to the system of incorporation.

OPPOSITION TO UNCHRISTIAN ECONOMIC PRACTICES

In spite of the fact that he had little if anything to
say on these particular economic issues, Campbell did
have much to say, in the years 1838-40, about the prevailing spirit of Mammon-worship, the problems of Christian
vocation, and the ethics of speculation and sharp commercial practices.

In January, 1838, he began a series of articles on the
"Morality of Christians." After the first eight essays
this series settled down to a sustained and systematic
discussion of the ethics of economic life.

"Mammon never had, in the same number of people, a
larger class of devoted worshippers," he said in the ninth
article, "than are found at this hour in England
and America." Even the Christian church has fallen
under this influence, as "the spirit of American enterprise, aggrandizement, and national improvement has
seized all classes of this community, and greatly aug-
mented and confirmed the love of this world in the minds
of men."[11] Later he gave this description of the way in
which individuals fall into the worship of Mammon: The
first step is

immersion into debt; then, to meet their covenanted vows and
promises, immense struggles become necessary. These sometimes fail; then their promises totter and fall; and with them
sicken and die all . . . delicacy of feeling . . . honorable sensibility and conscientiousness. . . . Truly, then, may it be
said, that "*the love* of [money] is the root of all evil."[12]

At the same time Campbell had a more-or-less typical Calvinist-Puritan view of the duty of labor. There were strong overtones of John Wesley in an earlier article where, in an entirely different setting, he quoted Ephesians 4:28, and declared: "Christians ought to be industrious, frugal, economical, in order to have more than they want for themselves that they may be rich in good works, liberal, and communicative to the necessities of the saints and to the exigencies of society."[13]

Next he took up the morality of "callings in society which are exceedingly inimical to, if not actually and positively subversive of, the morality of the gospel"— for example, "the manufacture of the stiletto, dirk, Bowie knife, and other instruments of assassination." As proof of the immoral nature of such a calling, he said: "The maker and the vender of such barbarous and savage instruments surely cannot pray for a blessing upon their labors and profession."[14]

In the same class he placed those who earn their living by the manufacture or sale of "ardent spirits." The test was the same: How can a Christian distiller, seeing the havoc which alcohol wreaks in the lives of men, "lift up his eyes to heaven, and in the presence of his God and his own household, say in the words of the saints of another age, 'Bless, O Lord, the work of my hands:' 'the labor of our hands, O Lord, do thou establish it!' " Such a person cannot even pray for "his daily bread" without praying for success in his calling, and that means "praying for the poverty, distress, and ruin of his customers—for the widowhood and orphanage of his neighbor's wife and family!"[15]

Campbell had no room for the logic of the distiller who once denied that he manufactured ardent spirits to kill or ruin anyone and said he did not know of anyone ruined by his distillery. Campbell replied: "What your intentions are, or what your knowledge of the effects of

your profession may be, I do not need to know to convict
you of the immorality of your calling.'' Chiding him
for trying to ''shuffle the matter upon the shoulders of
the retailers,'' Campbell declared: ''If you did not
furnish the article, they could not sell it. You are the
cistern of their iniquities—the reservoir of all their
crime, infamy, and ruin.''[16] Later he observed:

Some men would be the janitors of Pandemonium for a living.
They would invent machines for cursing, perjury, and blasphemy, if they could find a ready market for them; and would
flatter themselves that neither the inventor, nor the manufac-
turer, nor the vender, but the operator who uses them, is
culpable.[17]

The sins of speculation and sharp business practice
next received attention. This subject was introduced by
the story of two speculators who were hastening through
the country buying up an important product which they
knew was about to go up in price. Thanks to their inside
information they were able to pocket forty per cent on
every transaction. No Christian who believes in the
Golden Rule can justify himself in such dealings, Campbell declared. Speculation must therefore be counted
''amongst those callings and professions which are either
directly or indirectly contrary to the morality of Christianity.''[18]

The ''*trade* of speculation'' he subsequently defined
as ''the art of living upon nothing, or the art of making
a fortune by cunning.'' The speculator can best be understood by contrasting him with

those of other callings . . . [who] do something for society—
give value for value received. They create, new-modify, trans-
fer, transport, or minister something for man; while the speculator does none of these. . . . His whole business is to buy
cheap and sell dear—to consult no one's interest but his own.
He aims not to change the quality, position, or place of any thing
he buys; but simply its price.

Campbell went on at some length to contrast the true
merchant and the speculator, and finally declared that

the trade of speculation, "in all its branches, is but sheer
selfishness at work to enrich itself on the labors of others
. . . and is wholly incompatible with the genius of Christian morality."[19]

After devoting the next article in this series to
slavery, Campbell turned to the discussion of sharp trade
practices. The conduct of many professing Christians
"in their commercial transactions" was, to him, "gross
immorality and unrighteousness." He illustrated by
recounting a conversation "between a father and his
son, both members of the same church," who were plotting the sale of a good-looking but nearly blind horse
they had just got. Christians who have been "reared
and hackneyed in the ways of the world," Campbell said,
"are not always capable of appreciating the difference
between the spirit of the morality of the world and that
of Jesus Christ." "The very atmosphere of the trading
world is contaminating. . . . Many of its maxims . . .
are not reconcileable to the benevolent spirit and precepts
of the gospel."[20] A man can ordinarily rise to success in
business, he believed, only by "the sacrifice of his moral
feelings, conscience, and religious character."[21]

In contrast to this spirit of trade stands the command
of "the Christian Lawgiver [who] says, 'Look not on
your own wealth, but also on that of one another.'"
Said Campbell: "The man who obeys this principle in
our religion, will never seek to advance his fortune one
dollar, by invading the rights of another to the value of
one cent."[22]

QUALIFIED APPROVAL OF INTEREST

In all his discussions of the evils of Mammon-worship,
unchristian vocations, speculation, and sharp commercial
practices, Campbell reacted like a typical sectarian
moralist whose roots were in the soil. But in one respect
he was in harmony with the forces moving in the direc-

tion of large-scale industrial enterprise: he approved lending money at interest for business purposes.

In the *Millennial Harbinger* for 1842 he discussed a sermon on Romans 13:8—"Owe No Man Anything"—by one "D. L." He agreed with the object of the sermon, which was to warn Christians against recklessly going into debt. But he did not accept the view that *all* lending or borrowing is wrong. Indeed he believed that the preacher had not "exactly used his text as Paul intended," for "Paul spake of *paying* debts, while these good friends are thinking and writing of *contracting* debts." Reminding his readers of the precept, "Him that would borrow of thee turn not away," Campbell asked: "Would the Lord make it a sin to borrow, and a virtue to lend!" The context of Paul's words explains their meaning:

'Render to all their dues,' or 'Pay off all your debts'—'Owe no man any thing'—'Pay the last farthing to every human being' —'Feel no obligation to any man but that of good will.' Most certainly this is Paul's own contextual interpretation of the precept.

Nevertheless, Campbell regretted that "many of the Christian profession are not more cautious in contracting, nor more exemplary in discharging their debts, than other persons."[23]

In his comment upon D. L.'s sermon on debt, Campbell stressed the obligation of the Christian to pay his debts. Like most Protestants of his time, he had a very strict sense of the obligation not to default on a contract. No amount of prayers and alms deeds can make up for a man's failure to fulfill his business obligations. To pay one's debts is "a point of the highest honor, as well as of eternal obligation. All the statutes, laws, and ordinances of all human tribunals under heaven, never can free a Christian man from any debt whatever which he owes to God or man."[24]

In this spirit he declared in 1853 that a Christian may not avail himself of the bankruptcy laws of the state.

The obligation to pay a just debt can never be canceled by man. It is founded on the moral law promulged on Sinai, by God himself . . . It is farther developed, sanctioned, and re-enacted by the Author and Founder of the Christian institution.

His proof text for the latter statement was the familiar "OWE NO MAN ANYTHING but *love.*" This single exception makes it obligatory for the Christian to pay all his other debts in full, unless "for love or sympathy" they are "canceled on the part of the creditor." If in mercy a creditor forgives a debt, and can pay his own debts without it, "he may do it to his own honor and praise. But no one can, by law, exact mercy from his fellow-man."[25]

For Campbell it was "abhorrent to every principle of law, and justice, and honor, for any man to betake himself to the refuge of a bankrupt law to discharge a debt, which, by a rigid economy, industry and frugality, he may, at some time, be able to pay." He made room for only one exception: "Persons of a high sense of Christian integrity and honor, may, in certain cases, be justified in availing themselves of the advantages of a bankrupt law," if by so doing they may eventually "be enabled to pay all their debts." But in other instances "a man who pays off his debts by a notice of his insolvency, or through the operations of a bankrupt law, is, in the sight of God, as dishonest as he who violently seizes his neighbor's property and appropriates it to himself."[26] Campbell went on to imply that churches should exclude from membership any who used the machinery of the bankruptcy law to evade their just debts.

In 1843, in response to persistent inquiries, Campbell published an article on "Usury." On the basis of its etymology, he noted that "*use* is the parent of *usury;* and, therefore, that any price paid for *the use* of goods or chattels, lands or tenements, or money, may be called

usury." If then "*usury* simply means *premium* or *hire*
paid for the use of money," he asked why it is that we
justify usury "in every other case, save in the single case
of *money.*" After reference to the definitions of Bentham, Selden, and Blackstone, he proceeded to examine
the Scriptures on the subject. He noted that in Deuteronomy 23:19f loans and interest are specifically approved in the case of strangers or aliens, and prohibited
only in the case of a "brother." Furthermore, the proscription against loans to brothers applies only to "a
poor brother," because "such only, in the time of Moses,
among that nation, were borrowers of money, victuals,
or other necessary goods." This, he said, "is clearly
taught" in Exodus 22:25 and Leviticus 25:35. As for
the New Testament he felt that the parables of the talents
and the pounds "would seem to indicate that the receiving of interest for money loaned is altogether right, else
the Lord could not have represented himself as receiving
it."[27]

From these Scriptures two conclusions follow:

1st. Interest for the use of money ought never to be exacted,
or even received when proffered, from a poor brother, who
borrows, for food, raiment, or any of the indispensables of life.
To such, a Jewish saint or a Christian must not only lend
without interest, but even *give* without the desire or expecta-
tion of any return, either of the principal or of interest. . . .

2d. A Christian man may loan money or any sort of property
on interest, to any one who borrows not for immediate wants
. . . but for the purpose of trade, commerce, or speculation.[28]

Having reached these conclusions as to the cases in
which the Christian may lend money, Campbell next took
up the question of legitimate *rates* of interest. He had
earlier noticed Bentham's distinction between the *political* or *legal* definition of usury—"the taking of a greater
interest than the law allows of"—and the *moral* definition—"the taking of a greater interest than it is usual
for men to give and take."[29]

In the present context he began by declaring that "a Christian man can in no case transcend the lawful or customary interest of the country and time in which he lives." In the absence of a law on the subject, "then the practice of the majority is the custom; and that may be called the law of custom, to which a good man . . . will always conform." But in this community "there is a law; and that law is the authoritative will of the majority." This law is "obligatory on every subject of Christ's government. [For] The law of Christ enacts submission to 'every ordinance of man' . . . in all questions and matters that pertain to this life."[30]

A little further on he declared:

The premium or interest on money, lands, and other commodities, differs in various countries, and is wholly a matter of political arrangement. . . . Hence if the law says six, seven, or eight per cent. (as the case is in different States) then any thing more is in the sight of God and man *unjust*.[31]

In a word he felt that there is no room for "abstract views of justice" in this matter. The positive law of the state determines what is just.

In principle Campbell also supported government fixing of prices on other commodities besides money, for he declared: "I presume not to question the right, nor to explore the reasons, why the governments of the civilized world have fixed the value of money rather than of merchandise or any article of trade. They have had good reason for it, no doubt."[32] Presumably, if the government had "good reason" for fixing the prices of other articles of trade, every Christian would have to acknowledge that right and obey these regulations also as a *Christian* duty.

His views on usury Campbell summarized later as follows:

As to *usury*, . . . no Christian man can take interest, simple or compound, for money lent to sustain the widow, the orphan, or him that is famishing for bread or apparel. But when men borrow money in order to make money out of it, I see neither law nor reason, human or Divine, against receiving for it a consideration called *interest*, any more than in receiving hire for a horse, or rent for a farm, or any other species of property, placed in our hands by its proper owner, for a definite time and at a definite and legal value—whether that shall be, in the judgment of umpires or lawgivers, one, three or seven percent. affects not the principle—the value of money is fixed by that species of common consent called law, and what in this respect is called lawful and right does not appear to me condemnable either in the law or the gospel dispensation.

But he that exacts from any man according to his necessity or distress, whether it be five or ten per cent., or any thing beyond what common consent makes the current value of money or any thing loaned or rented, is an oppressor or a tyrant, and stands condemned both by the letter and spirit of our religion.[33]

ROLE OF GOVERNMENT IN ECONOMIC LIFE

Campbell agreed with Locke that one of the primary functions of government is "to protect the life, liberty, reputation, and *property,* of every citizen in the community."[34] Accordingly he gave his approval to the action of government in issuing deeds to property and urged churches to secure deeds to their real estate.[35] In 1851, when a pirated edition of his *Christian Hymnbook* had been put on the market, he made use of the copyright laws for the protection of his property rights in the book.[36] *As a citizen,* he supported governmental action to protect native enterprise by means of a protective tariff.[37] As has already been noted Campbell also had definite ideas regarding the responsibility of government to regulate currency, set interest rates and, if the occasion should warrant, establish fair prices for other commodities as well. Yet no governmental enactment could relieve the individual Christian from his obligation to pay his just debts.

This survey makes it clear that Campbell's economic ethics were quite similar to those of Calvin and followed the general pattern of American Protestantism at the time as Max Weber characterizes it in his essay, ''The Protestant Sects and the Spirit of Capitalism.''[38]   It presents the best example of Campbell's merging of sect and church-type traditions into a more-or-less typical denominational synthesis. His acceptance of the right of private property was a right-wing natural law element. His opposition to Mammonism, unchristian vocations, and unchristian economic practices was clearly a left-wing sect element. His qualified approval of interest united a left-wing insistence upon lending without interest to the poor and needy, with a right-wing approval of interest on other loans made for business purposes.

Campbell was obviously indebted for many of his economic views to Locke, Beattie, and other natural law writers. The scripture texts he used were drawn largely from the Old Testament, with only a selective use of New Testament passages. He brought government into the picture for purposes of protecting private property, regulating economic practices, and facilitating the economic development of the nation. His discussion of interest rates furnishes the first and perhaps only instance in which he made the positive law of the state *the* moral law which the Christian must obey or ''forfeit his character as a law-abiding disciple of Christ.''

CHAPTER XIII

THE SLAVERY ISSUE

THE MORAL issue upon which Alexander Campbell wrote most extensively and over which he was most often on the defensive is that of slavery. He held to a rather consistent colonizationist antislavery line throughout, but his emphasis underwent several marked shifts in response to the changing situation within the country and his own evolving churchmanship.

He took a vigorous stand against the institution of slavery in the early 1830's. In his reactions against abolitionism after 1835, and in his efforts to preserve the unity of the church in 1845, he tended to defend the master-slave relationship. Both his concern for unity and his opposition to the rigorous, exclusive moralism of the abolitionists will be recognized as characteristic denominational elements. Once the danger to the unity of the church was past, he issued a ''Tract for the People of Kentucky'' in 1849 which revealed as vigorous an antislavery stand as he had taken even in his earliest sect days. In 1851 in the midst of widespread resistance to the Fugitive Slave Law, he took up his pen in defense of law and order and appeared once more as a defender of slavery.

In a different connection Campbell said of himself: ''I was once so straight, that, like the Indian's tree, I leaned a little the other way.''[1] The same may be said of him in regard to slavery. When he was trying to dissociate himself from abolitionism, to preserve the unity of the church, or to uphold obedience to law, he sometimes "leaned a little the other way" and appeared as a proslavery advocate. But when he felt free to speak his mind on the evils of slavery as such, his opponents at least felt that he leaned too far toward abolitionism. He was, in fact, often charged with being both proslavery and abolitionist at one and the same time. Curiously enough when he dealt with slavery from the point of view of Scripture he generally approved it—due to his extremely verbalistic Acts-Epistles primitivism. But when he wrote or spoke as a "politician" or citizen, he opposed it.

He was "in the middle" on the question from the point of view of geography. In 1840 he said of his village: In relation to "the unfortunate controversy between slavery and antislavery, we are, perhaps, on the most neutral ground, as a county, that could well be imagined. We are in a slave state, it is true; but almost literally without slaves."[2]

COLONIZATIONIST ANTISLAVERY STAND

His early antislavery views were revealed in the opening article of the first issue of the *Christian Baptist* in which he listed some of the inconsistencies between "Apostolic Christianity" and current practices. The most glaring, he said, was presented by

those christians, who are daily extoling the blessings of civil and religious liberty, and at the same time, by a system of the most cruel oppression, separating the wife from the embraces of her husband, and the mother from her tender offspring . . . because *might* gives *right*, and . . . [the slave's] skin is a shade darker than the standard color of the times.[3]

This represents a typically sect reaction uncorrupted by his later scriptural and other rationalizations.

It has already been observed that one of Campbell's chief reasons for seeking a seat in the Virginia Conven-

tion was his desire to submit a plan for ''the final abolition of slavery in this state.'' As he explained later,
he did not do so because

in the more matured judgment of many members of that convention . . . who were as alive to this subject as we could be, it
was thought impolitic and inexpedient at that time to urge
this subject further than to guard against the insertion of a
single word in the constitution recognizing the existence of this
evil.[4]

In 1849 he spoke of having ''attended one caucus . . . on
the question of general emancipation, while the Convention was in session.''[5]

The first issue of the *Millennial Harbinger* in 1830,
as of the *Christian Baptist* in 1823, carried a strong antislavery statement—this one reprinted from the *Wheeling
Compiler*. The article reported an address by Henry
Clay before the Colonization Society at Frankfort urging
the rooting out of slavery from Kentucky. Campbell's
views on the subject were always quite close to those of
Clay.

The first extended treatment of the slave question from
Campbell's own pen came in an article entitled ''Emancipation of White Slaves,'' in March, 1830. It was occa-
sioned by another editor's having ''cautioned his slaveholding readers . . . against admitting [the *Harbinger*]
into their territory'' on the grounds that it might ''bring
ruin to their interests in their slaves.'' After disclaim-
ing any intention of turning slaves against their masters,
Campbell called upon owners to abolish slavery in order
to free themselves from slavery to fear. ''It is masters
I wish to emancipate,'' he declared. ''The *fear of your
slaves* in many instances is master over you. You are
in this view the slaves of slaves, while your slaves are
only the servants of masters.'' An evidence of the
servitude of masters was the fact that many slave owners
feared insurrection, had to garrison their houses, and

awakened at midnight in terror of their lives and the lives of their children.[6]

In this same article he took note of a recent effort in the Virginia Assembly to make it illegal to teach either free Negroes, mulattoes, or slaves to read or write. He was convinced that this would have violated both freedom of press and liberty of conscience. For *"freedom of the press"* means more than "the working of a machine upon type. . . . To prohibit teaching or learning the art of reading is the most effectual destruction of the liberty of the press which I can imagine." Then, too, as long as there are persons in the commonwealth of Virginia "who feel any obligation arising from religion to teach such persons . . . to read the scriptures of truth," such a law would be "a direct infringement upon that liberty and rights of conscience which our Bill of Rights and Constitution secure to all persons in the commonwealth."[7]

The following month a letter from a subscriber in Essex, Virginia, expressed concern at the antislavery tone of the *Millennial Harbinger*. The correspondent, who claimed to be interested in Campbell's good name and the success of the "reformation," reported that his antislavery attitudes were being used to inflame people against him in eastern Virginia.

I have thought it my duty to inform you that your readers are not pleased with your touching the subject of *slavery* any further than the New Testament authorizes you to teach the duty of servants and masters to each other. This is a delicate question among *us*. . . . it will be best to say as little as possible upon [the] subject.

Campbell's reply was clear and forthright. "I never was deterred from doing what I conceived my duty, because of a patronage promised for not doing it; or threatened to be withdrawn if I did it. Such a character has not marked my course."[8]

After this flurry of interest in the early months of 1830, nothing further was said upon the subject until 1832.

The slave issue came to a head in the state of Virginia with the Nat Turner or Southampton Insurrection of August 22, 1831, in which more than a hundred whites were killed. The East thenceforth sought to secure itself against similar outbreaks, and the West to rid the state completely of slavery. The burden of the western antislavery argument was that slavery was an economic evil, that it was ruinous to the whites, retarded improvements, rooted out the industrious portion of the population, and banished yeomanry from the country. "Moral issues," according to Charles H. Ambler, "influenced only a few of the Virginia abolitionists of 1832." Marshall is quoted as saying: "Our solicitations to the slaveholder . . . are founded but little on the miseries of the blacks."[9] Campbell's remarks in this period reflected most of these antislavery arguments and, he, too, was more concerned about the effects of slavery upon the whites and upon the community at large than upon the slaves.

After keeping silent on the subject for eighteen months, he devoted several pages in both the January and February, 1832, issues to "the crisis" which "has made all men think upon a question from which the philanthropist and the christian often turn away in portentous indecision and trembling anticipation." He was glad that the Assembly had been called to consider the matter and hoped that that body would not be content with such half measures as merely "exiling from the state the free people of color."[10]

While "the christian is governed by one class of principles and the politician by another; yet sometimes . . . these principles act in *conjunction*." The present, he believed, was such a time. Voicing the typical economic arguments of the people of the western part of the state,

Campbell affirmed that "slave labor has . . . wasted the
real estate and destroyed the lands of Eastern Virginia;
and . . . now it is *dearer* and less productive than any
other sort of labor." "Unless an end be put to this all-
prostrating evil," he predicted, Virginia "will become a
wilderness, with a few scattering inhabitants," and the
Old Dominion will again become "hunting grounds."
These were arguments which he believed would "speak
powerfully to the *conscience* of the rich."[11]

Now, he wrote, *"It is in the power of Virginia . . . to
free herself from this evil without loss of property."*
He assured the East that

whatever the legislature can do to deliver us and our brethren
in the East from all the curses, direct and indirect, which are
found hanging upon that vine brought from Africa, they will
have the countenance, support, prayers, and thanks of every
Virginian in all the hills and vallies of the West.[12]

The following month he presented his own constructive proposal for getting rid of

Slavery, that largest and blackest blot upon our national escutcheon, that many-headed monster, that Pandora's box, that bitter
root, that blighting and blasting curse under which so fair
and so large a portion of our beloved, country groans—that
deadly Upas, whose breath pollutes and poisons every thing within its influence.[13]

His solution seemed so practicable that he wondered
why it had not occurred to some of the politicians—"or
if it [has] occurred, why it has not been at least proposed
for consideration." The plan was to take the ten million
dollars annually of federal tax money which had formerly
been needed to amortize the national debt—now "as
good as paid"—and apply it toward the purchase and
colonization of slaves. The resolution he suggested
Henry Clay might introduce to give it effect recognized
slavery as a violation of the doctrines of the Bill of
Rights.[14]

Three groups he would colonize by means of federal funds—those already free, slaves whom their masters might be induced to emancipate, and *"female slaves of certain ages"* who might be purchased "from those who would not emancipate." The appropriation of "ten millions per annum, for 15 or 20 years" for this purpose "would rid this land of the curse, and bind the union more firmly than all the railroads, canals, and highways which the treasury of the union could make in half a century."[15]

Three years later he spoke again, and in somewhat more detail, of this proposal. He recognized "the rights of the South to their slaves" as being on a par with "the rights of the North to their land." He would, no more think of "wresting" a slave from his master than he would land from its owner, "without a full and satisfactory consideration."[16] Here his anti-abolitionist apologetic was beginning to appear.

At the same time he would make the issue a national affair—in spite of the "squeamishness" of some—"by showing that this was a question *sui generis* . . . involving in it national existence." So he would "have the nation to act upon this matter . . . and without any constitutional scrupulosity proceed in the most expeditious manner to carry out the will and wishes of the majority." To meet the opposition of states' rights advocates, he declared:

There is one thing the majority can constitutionally do, and that is enough for our purpose. *They can dispose of the surplus revenue to save the life of the nation* . . . Only let it be done judiciously according to vested rights, and our national existence is secured.[17]

He urged the getting up of petitions to Congress from all over the land asking the appropriation of all surplus revenue for years to come for this purpose. He further advised that "all debates, pamphlets, and speeches on the *abstract* questions now debated be suppressed," and that citizens get to work on this practical scheme for doing justice to "South, North, East, and West, to master and to slave."[18]

In this early antislavery period which—except for the further amplification of the colonization plan in December, 1835—may be considered closed in 1832, Campbell was definitely critical of the institution of slavery and aggressively sought its elimination. He opposed particular evils associated with the institution, such as the practice of separating families, and legislative efforts to prohibit teaching slaves to read and write. He opposed the institution itself on the grounds of its economic and social consequences and its inconsistency with the doctrines of the Bill of Rights. In this period, as later, he looked to southerners like Clay to take the lead in ridding the nation of "that deadly Upas." But he urged national action to purchase and colonize the slaves. Actuated more by sympathy for the whites than for the slaves themselves, he looked upon slavery as a misfortune rather than a sin.

Reaction Against Abolitionism

In the period from 1830 to 1832 Campbell himself had been charged with abolitionism. From 1835 to 1840 he reacted vigorously against the new type of abolitionism appearing in the North and began to face charges of being proslavery.

Abolitionism in 1830 and even in 1832 was still in the main a rather vaguely defined philosophy of gradualism. Following the launching of Garrison's *Liberator* in 1831, the organization of the American Antislavery Society in 1833, and the antislavery revival in Ohio under Theodore Weld in 1835, abolitionism became an organized propaganda with the objective of immediate emancipation and the passion of a religious revival. In spite of efforts of men like Lyman Beecher to hold the anti-

slavery movement together, a growing breach developed
between the more gradually minded colonizationists and
the abolitionists. As the lines formed Campbell stuck
to his colonizationist viewpoint and became increasingly
critical of abolitionism.

His first contact with abolitionists as such occurred
some time in December, 1833, when he met with a "dep-
utation of New England abolitionists" in Philadelphia.
He also reported conversations with "leading abolitionists in Ohio during their first meeting at Mount Pleasant."[19] Although his first contact was with abolitionists
of the New England or Garrisonian type, he had more
frequent experience in the West with that represented
by Theodore Weld, the "Lane rebels," the *Philanthropist,* and the American Antislavery Society.

Gilbert H. Barnes has described the evolution of this
antislavery impulse from the Great Revival which began
in western New York in 1826 under the preaching of
Charles G. Finney. "The emotional impulse which Cal-
vinism had concentrated upon a painful quest for a safe
escape from life, Finney . . . turned toward benevolent
activity," with the result that the Great Revival "released a mighty impulse toward social reform."[20] In
1837 a group of Lane seminary students, coached by
Weld, started up and down the state of Ohio as "evangelists of abolitionism." With all the fire and conviction
of typical evangelists, they proclaimed a doctrine of
sin—the sin of slavery—and called for immediate repentance—the freeing of all slaves. They had no room for
the view that slavery was merely an evil; it was a sin!
Nor could they accept such temporizing policies as those
of the American Colonization Society; the slaves must be
freed at once! Subsequently, as the Great Revival
waned, the antislavery impulse itself was altered. By
1839 it

no longer expressed itself in a benevolent effort "to bring all
enslavers to immediate repentance for the sin of slaveholding."

The hope that somehow abolition doctrine would permeate to repentant Southern ears was failing, and in its stead there grew a hatred of the sinner as well as of his sin, a sectional hostility toward slavery and the South.[21]

From 1835 to 1840 Campbell opposed abolitionism in the pages of the *Millennial Harbinger* on three grounds: its premise that slavery was a sin, its program of immediate emancipation, and its spirit of intolerance and bitterness toward the slaveholder and the South.

His attention was first directed to the *spirit* of abolitionism. In July, 1835, he reported an evening spent with "our good brother Dr. *Field,* of emancipation memory." Said Campbell: "He is in body, soul, and spirit opposed to American slavery, and would, if he could, have one American Jubilee, which would leave no room for a second." But Campbell feared that "he loves liberty even to intolerance, and would compel the churches into measures unprecedented in the days of the Apostles."[22] Five years later he characterized another editor of the *Philanthropist,* Gamaliel Bailey, as "a very zealous and spirited writer" who "gets a little snarlish at times." Abolitionists in general he looked upon as "philanthropists who have forgotten that philanthropy includes the love of both master and servant, and contemplates justice and kindness to all."[23]

Taking note of the "feverish excitement, bordering on insanity" which had been aroused on the slavery issue, Campbell was alarmed at those who seemed to have sworn that the question

shall only be discussed by the light of burning palaces, cities, and temples, amidst the roar of cannon, the clangor of trumpets, the shrieks of dying myriads . . . the horrid din and crash of a broken confederacy . . . and the agonizing throes of the last and best republics on earth.[24]

It was as an alternative to these extremist measures that he went on in that article to reiterate his proposal for the use of federal funds to colonize slaves in Africa or elsewhere.

Not until 1840 did he directly attack the basic *premise* of the abolitionists—that slavery is a sin. In March of that year he devoted his article in the series on the "Morality of Christians" to the subject of slavery. He reaffirmed his belief that slavery was "a great evil" and "a great misfortune to the American family," and admitted that he, too, looked forward to the day when it could be eliminated "with the consent of all parties." But he rejected the view

that "*the holding a person as a slave (or in a state of involuntary servitude) is always a sin.*" From this [he said] follows the capital doctrine of *immediate emancipation* as its legitimate consequence; for if it be a sin in every case to hold a slave, it is the duty of all Christians instantly to repent of it and abandon it.[25]

In attacking this position he referred to the text at the head of his article—Colossians 4:1. If the Apostles had viewed the subject as the abolitionists do, he said,

we never would have met with the command, "Masters, render to your servants that which is just and equal." It would have read, "Masters, immediately emancipate your slaves, and pay them wages, or let them go and seek employment elsewhere."

To the charge that American slavery was worse than patriarchal, Jewish, or early Christian slaveholding, Campbell declared it was not—at least when masters obey the Pauline injunctions. Nor could he condemn all slaveholders because some are cruel, or American slavery *per se* because the laws permit cruel or immoral practices. For American Christian slaveholders "are not obliged to treat their slaves as the statute books may allow." It is apparent that Campbell was not facing the total problem of slavery in this discussion. In fact he said he intended "no legal nor political discussion of this question," but wanted only to refute "those abolitionists who make slaveholding in the abstract . . . always and in every case a sin.''[26]

He expressed concern at the way the agitation of the issue was disturbing the fellowship of the church. Complaints were reaching him ''that public ministering brethren, in passing from one state to another, are by brethren viewed with a suspicion and jealousy wholly irreconcilable with Christian candor, good feeling, and cordial co-operation.'' Campbell was convinced that ''men equally distinguished for . . . Christian character . . . are found on both sides of this controversy,'' and insisted that ''as *Christians*, we have nothing to do with political or adventitious excitements.''[27] This concern for the harmony and unity of the church was to grow and become his chief passion five years later.

Before closing this 1840 article he offered a word of advice to slaveholders. The scripture text which he had used to refute the abolitionists he now used to instruct the owners of slaves. The South ''has said much on the patriarchal character of this institution.'' Now let the slaveholders be as considerate of their slaves as were Abraham and other ancient slaveholders, and slavery may become again ''a very happy institution.'' Campbell was sure that ''if the professors of Christ's religion and morality at the South, were to obey the laws of Old and New Testaments, *as masters,* nine-tenths of all abolitionists would hold their peace.''[28]

Campbell's rejection of the *program* of the abolitionists, although implied earlier, was first clearly stated in an article written in 1840 to defend himself from ''the brand of *proslavery*'' fixed upon him by Gamaliel Bailey of the *Philanthropist.* He could not imagine, Campbell said, ''what blessedness either to master or servant, to free states or slave states, could possibly arise from the *immediate* emancipation of all the slaves in these United

States in their present habits, economical and moral.''
Rather this would "be a great injury to master and
servant, and would increase rather than diminish the
grievances and evils, political and moral, so generally
complained of.''[29]

At the same time Campbell could see "immense advantage . . . to the whole community, if 'masters would
render to their servants that which is just and equal;'
and 'if servants would obey in all things their masters
according to the flesh.' " He neither defended American
slavery nor advocated instant and universal emancipation. He favored approaching the ultimate goal of
emancipation "by an inclined plane.'' In the meantime
churches should use their disciplinary powers to insure
that slave owners within their fellowship carried out "all
the injunctions given to them in the New Testament.''[30]

1835-40 represents a transition period in Campbell's
stand on slavery. His antislavery statements were
tempered by the desire to dissociate himself from the
abolitionist doctrine now in the field. While he was still
charged by some with being an abolitionist, by the end of
this period he was more frequently engaged in defending
himself against charges of proslavery.

He was still critical of the institution of slavery, but
a defensive note had crept in. In a "Letter to England''
in 1835 he referred to slavery as a "misfortune'' entailed
upon the American people by their English ancestors.[31]
During a tour of the southern states in 1839 he observed
that slavery was as much an economic and social evil in
South Carolina as in Virginia, but as far as the condition of the slaves was concerned it was "generally
much more mild and comfortable'' than he had imagined.[32] A concern for the unity and harmony of the
church in the face of abolitionist agitation had also appeared, and he had begun to search the Scriptures for
commands regulating the master-slave relationship.

THE SCRIPTURAL DEFENSE OF SLAVERY

After having given considerable attention to the slavery issue in the early 1830's and to a lesser degree at the middle and end of the decade, Campbell allowed the subject to lie dormant until 1845. He was occupied with the launching of Bethany College in 1840, the problems of "Difficulties in the Churches" and "Christian Cooperation" in 1840 and 1841, and discussions of the millennium from 1841 to 1843. He refused to publish an abolitionist circular in 1842 on the grounds that it would be "entirely incompatible with the genius and design of our work to admit any such discussions, involving in them matters much more political, prudential, and local, than either religious or moral." Besides he had "more important matters on hand."[33]

Agitation over the slavery issue increased, particularly in connection with the Texas question and the annexation of 1844. The tension within the churches also grew more serious as the abolitionists became both more numerous and more aggressive. In 1844 Methodists and Baptists alike were in the process of dividing over slavery. This led Campbell to take up the subject again but in an entirely different spirit from that of the early 1830's. Then he had been concerned about what the *continuation* of slavery would do to the South and the nation; now he was concerned about what the *agitation* of the issue in the churches would do to Disciples of Christ. Earlier he had dealt with the issue of slavery *per se;* now he dealt primarily with the issue of church unity. Earlier he had been critical of the *institution* of slavery; now he went to great lengths to defend the *master-slave relationship* and began to reflect many of the proslavery arguments.

There can be no question as to the motive which prompted him to launch his series of essays on "Our Position to American Slavery" in the February, 1845,

Millennial Harbinger. In the opening article he referred to the way the slavery controversy had split the Methodist Episcopal Church along "Mason's and Dixon's line." "Other denominations," he feared, "must be constrained to take the same ground."[34] In May he reported that "the Baptist Board, regulating missions, has recently passed resolutions on this subject indicative of schism," and that "one denomination of Presbyterians has already declared non-fellowship with any and every master of a slave in the whole nation."[35] The "grand object" of his discussion was "to preserve unity of spirit among Christians of the South and of the North."[36] In the concluding article he spoke again of his purpose as "preventing any division amongst us after the manner of some other religious communities."[37]

Campbell proposed to achieve his end by showing that there was no ground for the exclusion or disfellowshiping of slaveholders under the principles upon which the churches of Disciples of Christ were established. "We are the only religious community in the civilized world," he said, "whose principles (unless we abandon them) can preserve us from such an unfortunate predicament" as that in which the other religious bodies found themselves.[38]

The issue which faced the churches, he insisted, was not political or economic, but moral—or, to put it more accurately, biblical.

Our position is not that of a politician, an economist, a mere moralist; but that of a Christian. Our premises are not the Declaration of American Independence, the bills of political rights or wrongs, natural religion, natural conscience, natural liberty; but the Christian Oracles.[39]

In the concluding article Campbell summarized his position in three propositions:

1. That the relation of master and slave is not in itself sinful or immoral.

2. That, nevertheless, slavery as practised in any portion of the civilized world, is *inexpedient*. . .

3. That no Christian community, governed by the Bible . . . can . . . make the simple relation of master and slave a term of Christian fellowship or a subject of discipline.[40]

The first and third of these points received major attention. In fact the second was not discussed at all until the last article and then to defend himself against the charge of being proslavery.

"The doctrine of those properly called *Abolitionists*," he said, "is, that the *relation* of *'Master and Slave'* is, in all cases, morally wrong—a relation not authorized by God—'evil, and only evil, and that continually.' "[41]   In refuting this proposition Campbell reviewed the arguments of Francis Wayland and Richard Fuller, recognized spokesmen for Northern and Southern Baptists respectively.

Wayland admitted that the institution is sanctioned in the Old Testament, and that the New Testament contains no precept prohibiting it. Thus far Campbell agreed. But he denied Wayland's assertion that "the precepts of the New Testament furnish no justification of slavery." On the contrary the Baptist had overlooked one significant passage—1 Corinthians 7:20-24—"Everyone should remain in the state in which he was called, etc." Since it is admitted that there were masters and slaves in the church at Corinth to which Paul was writing, Campbell concluded that this statement justifies *Bible* slavery, although whether it "will justify American slavery as found in our statute books, is," he admitted, "quite another question."[42]

In two succeeding articles he continued this investigation into the teachings of the Bible on the question at issue—"is the simple relation of master and slave necessarily and essentially immoral and unchristian—as that, for example, of the adulterer and adulteress?" Again and again he replied: *"We are clearly and satisfactorily convinced it is not.''*[43] Perhaps the most comprehensive summary of his position appeared at the beginning of the fifth article.

Regarding the relation of Master and Slave, it is not immoral, because existing amongst Patriarchs, Jews, and Christians, regulated by various and numerous divine laws and statutes; and because amongst masters, there were the greatest saints under all dispensations of religion;—Abraham, Isaac, Jacob, Job— the Jews in mass—and the church of Christ among the Gentiles. There is not one verse in the Bible inhibiting it, but many regulating it. It is not, then, we conclude, *immoral.*[44]

From his scriptural defense of the slave relationship, Campbell moved on to the question: *''Whether a master, professing Christianity, must, for the simple and only reason that he is a master,* be debarred from Christian fellowship.''*[45] In the sixth article he brought to this question his distinction between faith and opinion. While the tenets of Campbell and his followers "inculcate a strict adherence to the *faith,* the *precepts,* and *ordinances* of Christ," they "allow to every man the right of private opinion and judgment in all other matters." Thus the churches cannot, "without a renunciation of our tenets, make any man's opinions about the expediency or inexpediency of the continuance, or of the existence of such an institution, on the part of the state, a term of Christian fellowship." With reference to the divisions appearing in other churches, he declared: "It becomes us to recur to first and fundamental principles . . . and to fix our minds upon . . . the ground of union, communion, and co-operation which we have assumed before the universe in our ecclesiastical relations and duties.''[46]

While insisting that the mere possession of slaves was no basis for exclusion from the Christian fellowship, Campbell also stressed, but not so strongly, the importance of the churches using disciplinary measures to see that masters and slaves alike obeyed the divine laws and statutes regulating that relationship. "If . . . all members of churches were to discharge their duties to their servants all over the South," he believed "a happier serving population than they would not be found within the bounds of the American Union."[47]

Not until the eighth article did Campbell qualify what would otherwise have been an almost wholly proslavery position. Quoting Paul—"All things are lawful for me, but all things are not expedient"—he continued: "While, then, I affirm the conviction that the relation of master and slave, by the providence and law of God, is, in certain cases and conditions, morally right, I also affirm the conviction that *in this age and in this country it is not expedient.*" The institution of American slavery he regarded as "not in harmony with the spirit and genius of this age, nor with the peculiar genius of our American population and political institutions" for these reasons: "*because of its abuses and liabilities to abuse —because of its demoralizing influence upon society through these abuses—because of its impoverishing operations upon the states and communities that tolerate its continuance.*"[48]

In his political relations Campbell was, therefore, a candid and fearless advocate of "a state constitutional termination of it by a gradual approach, through an inclined plane approximation, predestinating some ultimate day, when both the master and the slave would be prepared for it." He went on to espouse Jefferson's plan for freeing all slaves born after a certain date—in his case, 1860—when they reach the age of 21.[49]

His own personal example was offered as "the best proof" he could give of the sincerity of these convictions.

Many years since, I advised the emancipation of a number of slaves that would have come to me by inheritance. . . Since that time I have emancipated several, that were bought . . . with the intention to manumit at the proper time. . . So that I have set free from slavery every human being that came in any way under my influence or was my property.

Although he had always remonstrated against abolitionism, he had, as far as was in his power, and at "a considerable sacrifice of property, abolished slavery."[50]

In the concluding article Campbell thus qualified somewhat the proslavery character of this series, but the
reader cannot help feeling that even this failed to do
justice to his real views. Like the "Indian's tree," in
trying to be straight he had leaned a little the other
way! The fact of the matter is that in these articles
Campbell was discussing not the slavery issue but the
church issue. His primary concern was not the rightness
or wrongness of slavery, but the unity of the church.
He insisted throughout that he was dealing with the
moral issue of slavery, but this—in his characteristic
manner—he converted into a *scriptural* issue. His extreme biblicism admitted no other evidence on slavery,
conceived as a moral issue, than an *obiter dictum* of
Scripture, more particularly of the Epistles. It closed
his mind to the humanitarian arguments of some of the
more philosophically inclined abolitionists and antislavery men. He justified Bible slavery, but evaded the
issue of American slavery. This was a source of considerable confusion among his abolitionist readers. In
August, 1846, he replied to those who wanted to use his
pages to show that American slavery was not scriptural:
"AND WHO SAYS THAT IT IS? I never did."[51]

There is sufficient evidence that he knew what he was
doing and chose his course deliberately. In a brief article in June, 1845, he frankly spoke of his position as
one of "expediency" designed to maintain the unity of
the church.[52] Yet he was sincerely convinced that observing the scriptural regulations would ameliorate the
system for those subject to Christian masters. He also
believed that while the church has no direct power or
authority to attempt the reformation of the state, it has
"an immense *indirect* power upon every community by
the reflex light of the gospel through its example."[53]

212 THE POLITICAL ETHICS OF ALEXANDER CAMPBELL

Beyond this he left the social and political problem of slavery outside the purview of the Christian church and seemingly subject to no moral controls.

In his fear of abolitionism and its possible disruption of the church, Campbell was led to the rather strange position that it was proper to oppose slavery as economically unprofitable or socially corrupting, but not as morally wrong! He approved those "political economists and ... *philanthropists*" who favored the emancipation of slaves "not because of the immorality of the relation, but because of the unprofitableness thereof, and because of its bearings upon their domestic peace and comfort and that of their beloved offspring." "But the technically denominated *abolitionist*," he said, "is quite a different personage. . . . He regards slavery as morally wrong in its very essence." Campbell concluded that no "*Christian* . . . could be an abolitionist."[54]

DIFFICULTIES OF THE MIDDLE WAY

Campbell's experiences in the period from 1845 to 1850 reveal the difficulties of the middle way he had chosen. His statement of "Our Position to American Slavery" in the early months of 1845 called forth considerable criticism from abolitionists within and without the fold of Disciples of Christ. In July he reported that several of his subscribers "immediately ordered a discontinuance of the Harbinger." One correspondent, who had received a prospectus urging him to get more subscribers, declined, saying, "All our brethren, who are good punctual paying men, are abolitionists, and they choose to read other papers." He closed with the suggestion, "When you write on slavery again, say *my* position instead of *our* position."[55]

The following year a correspondent from Illinois asked Campbell how he reconciled his statements of 1832—that slavery is the "*largest and blackest spot upon the na-*

tional escutcheon" and *"poisons everything it breathes upon"*—with his statements of 1845. Said Mr. York:

You *seem to* regard slavery in the *concrete, wrong,* though in the *abstract, right* . . . Many . . . say that you denounce that as a *curse,* in 1832, which you advocate as *right,* in 1845. . . They say that "Alexander Campbell, at last, after *all* his labors, settles down that a *'blighting curse' is right,* and can be sustained by the Bible."[56]

Similarly an abolitionist reader in 1848 rejected his theory of slavery while approving his practice. The subscriber applauded the editor's example in freeing his slaves, but declared: "The difference between us is, that your faith and practice are different, whereas mine are agreed; for I wish it abolished because of its tendency to evil, and that continually."[57]

Campbell seemed surprised at the one-sided reaction to his discussion of the issue and in several briefer articles throughout the closing months of 1845 defended himself against abolitionist attacks and tried to restate his position in more acceptable terms.

One of the most dramatic reactions to his views occurred in Scotland. While he was lecturing in Edinburgh in 1847, three men from an antislavery society called and queried him as to his position on slavery. A few hours later placards were posted in the streets of Edinburgh calling upon the citizens to "BEWARE! BEWARE! THE REV. ALEX. CAMPBELL, OF VIRGINIA, U. S. OF AMERICA, *Has Been a Slaveholder Himself and is Still the Defender of Man-Stealers."* Although he had earlier disclaimed any intention of discussing this issue, Campbell found it necessary to set forth his views on the subject. After advancing his usual argument that slavery *per se* is not a sin, he declared that

Christianity *regulated,* but did not annihilate the relation of master and bond servant; and that although I was constitutionally, politically, economically, and morally opposed to all forms of slavery . . . I could not legislate on the subject beyond the passages of scriptures which I read.

Tension ran high during the two-hour address. There were "hisses, cheers, groans, clapping of hands, questions, objections, inquiries, and long continued commotions of mingled feeling."[58] Campbell's views were set forth later in a letter to the editor of the *Edinburgh Journal*.

As he was about to leave Scotland, Campbell was arrested and jailed in Glasgow on September 6. The occasion for his arrest was a damage suit filed against him by James Robertson on the basis of certain allusions to himself in the letter to the *Journal*. Campbell was released after about a week's imprisonment, continued his journey, and was subsequently exonerated of all charges. The experience served to heighten his opposition toward abolitionism, for he took this to be a clear revelation of the spirit of "a certain class of anti-slavery men. My liberty was taken away by liberty men. A reverend declaimer on liberty gave the order—'Take him to jail.' "[59]

In rebuking Gamaliel Bailey for his "snarlish" attitude in 1840, Campbell was not surprised at "the increase of a proslavery spirit at the South." If his own principles on the matter were unsettled, he declared, "such assaults as that before me . . . would have a tendency to drive me into proslavery measures."[60] Although the criticisms of abolitionists did not drive Campbell into proslavery *measures,* they did put him on the defensive and led him to give utterance to some of the characteristic proslavery *arguments* of the South as summarized by Charles E. Merriam.[61]

In addition to his scriptural defense of slavery, he excused the present generation of Southerners from responsibility for the existence of slavery and defended the lot of the slaves as "generally more mild and comfort-able" than he had imagined.

Like others from the South, he felt that "in general the slave toils less and fares better" than many wage earners in the North "who labor twelve hours per diem for the veriest pittance."[62] In one of his "Letters from Europe" he spoke of the complacency of the upper classes in face of the plight of the Manchester poor. "And yet these are among the people who declaim against 'American slavery;' who tell us of 'the half-fed, over-wrought, and uneducated three million of African slaves owned by American Republicans!' "[63]

Campbell also began to reflect the typical southern view that slavery was a matter for state rather than federal action—an obvious shift in emphasis from his earlier insistence that it was a national concern. Upon his return from the British Isles he explained to his American readers that "England and Scotland always speak of American slavery as if it were a constitutional or national affair which a simple congressional majority could any day abolish." He said he had informed his audiences in Edinburgh that "the United States could not abolish slavery in a single state of the Union."[64] This point was reiterated in the "Tract for the People of Kentucky."

He also followed the proslavery line in denying that all men are created free and equal. There are "differ-ences providentially occurring in the circumstances of nativity," he said.

Paul had providential and political rights from being born in Tarsus, which he would not have had, had he been born in Nazareth. To divest him of these rights, would have been to do him wrong. But not to allow them to one not born in Tarsus, would not have been wrong. Therefore, all men are not born free and equal according to political rights.[65]

Later he referred to the cases of Sarah and Hagar. "The child of Sarah he makes free, because his mother was a free woman; the child of Hagar he makes a slave, because her mother was a slave."[66] The doctrine that all men are created free and equal now seemed to him to be "as popular and as senseless a saying as any political aphorism of this age"[67]—although at the Virginia Convention he had assumed this as one of those principles "canonized" in the Bill of Rights.[68]

At this period Campbell insisted that the political status of an individual must be determined by his capacity. "Without intelligence and virtue on the part of the people" the rights granted by the constitution are "dangerous investments."[69] It is doubtful, though, if he would have admitted any inherent inferiority of the Negro, for he had earlier criticized those who denied slaves the opportunities of education and religion and then spoke of them as ignorant and irreligious.[70]

In spite of his acceptance of many of the proslavery arguments Campbell did not follow the advocates of slavery to the conclusion that it was a positive good. If he "leaned a little the other way" in the opening months of 1845 in his scriptural defense of slavery, in the years that followed he recovered some of his earlier critical spirit, occasionally pointing out the evils of the institution as it actually existed in America.

The high-water mark of his later antislavery statements came in 1849. When the Virginia Constitutional Convention was called in 1829, Campbell had seized it as an opportunity to do something about the slave question. Two decades later when the state of Kentucky called a convention for a similar purpose, he issued a tract to his "friends and brethren in Kentucky" urging them that the time was ripe for their state to "demonstrate its love of liberty and right, by extending them to every thing in the form of man that breathes its air or treads its soil."[71]

He was interested in the forthcoming convention and its actions because Kentucky was "a much honored mem-

ber of the great sisterhood of American states," because it was "the worthy daughter of Virginia," and
"because in it the first great impulse was given to the
cause of an evangelical reformation." On the basis of
this interest and these ties Campbell presumed, "as a
philanthropist and a Christian," to "tender . . . a few
thoughts and conclusions on one subject which, more
than any other that can come before them at this time,
demands their most profound and religious consideration and regard."[72] Although he wrote not as a political
economist, nor as a patriot, but as a Christian, he said
in passing: "It is most satisfactorily decided, to my
mind, that slave-labor is the dearest and most painful
labor which a State can employ."[73]

He then proceeded to drive home the responsibility of
each individual Christian in Kentucky. "A time has
come when no citizen of that State can say,—'I can
neither prevent nor perpetuate the indefinite continuance
of Slavery in Kentucky. I did not put it upon the State
nor can I take it off.' " A single clause in the new constitution would put an end to slavery. "The Ruler of
nations" has thus placed responsibility squarely upon
every citizen in the state, by his vote in the matter, to
be indeed "an instituter or annuller of Slavery in Kentucky."[74]

Campbell commended to his readers the plan set forth
by Henry Clay in the "Letter on Emancipation." Just
as he had quoted from a speech by Henry Clay in the
first issue of the *Millennial Harbinger* and looked to
Clay in those days for leadership in the elimination of
slavery, so again in 1849 he associated himself with
Clay's plan for a constitutional provision freeing slaves
born after 1855 or 1860 when they reached the age of 25.

Since the elimination of slavery by this means was
practicable and would be profitable economically, Campbell asked, *"Is it* [morally] *desirable that it should be
removed?"* He then referred to a passage of Scripture

which he had never used before—at least not in this manner. "Paul once said to a Christian slave,—'If thou
mayest be made free, use it rather.' And to a Christian master the same spirit of wisdom saith,—'If thou,
too, desirest to be made free, use it rather.' "[75]

Describing again some of the burdens which slavery
imposed upon the owners, Campbell declared that "the
emancipation of masters is full as much an object near
to my heart as the emancipation of slaves." "But,
alas!" he said, "masters sometimes, as well as slaves,
hug the chains that enslave them." He was especially
concerned for the welfare of the children of slaveholders.
Their tendency "to take upon them the habits of those
amongst whom they are reared" led him to chide those
parents who recklessly committed their children, "from
the nursery, to the inmates of negro kitchens and negro
cabins . . . [so] degraded in morals and impiety." He
was concerned also about the effect of the master-slave
relationship itself upon growing children.

The intercourse between a master and a slave, however kind
and generous the former, and however pliant and obedient the
latter, is, on the one side, essentially dogmatical, absolute, and
lordly, on the other side, cringing, servile and abject. . . . These
exhibitions are unfavorable to the proper moral education and
development of children.[76]

"Existing laws and institutions in Virginia and Kentucky are greatly adverse to the rights of man and the
rights of Christians," he declared. "The genius of the
age is against Slavery." He hoped that the Christian
people of Kentucky would "speak and vote like Christians at the polls" and bring an end to this evil.[77]

This tract created quite a stir in the South. Once
again Campbell was charged with being an abolitionist.
The July number of the *Millennial Harbinger* carried a
letter from an Abraham Smith canceling his subscrip-
tion and regretting that Campbell had not followed the
advice he gave the New England abolitionists. "I be-

lieve you told them to go home and let the Virginians manage their own business. . . So say we Kentuckians." Campbell replied that he had written to his friends in Kentucky "not as a citizen of Virginia nor as a citizen of Kentucky, but as a citizen of the world and a member of Christ's church." As for slavery itself, he said with spirit:

Men must see (I mean *men*, not boys, nor scraps of men, but *full grown men* must see) that slavery in Kentucky or America is, to say the least of it, contrary to the general moral sense, the moral taste, and the spirit of the present civilized world.

All the orators in the United States could never convince him "that *slavery, as established by our laws,* is either in harmony with the Bible, or the spirit of this age, or the progress of society."[78]

As to the Bible authority for the simple relation of master and slave he had "fully and at all hazards" expressed his views. On that point he felt able to meet any man—not because of his own strength, but because he had "the truth, the Bible, and common sense" with him.

And just as strong feel I . . . in the positions submitted in the aforesaid Tract, that slavery, as now legalized and generally carried out, is not in harmony with what the Lawgiver, and Judge, and Rewarder of all men, has expressed by his Apostles and Prophets to the church and to the world.[79]

Campbell had come a long way from his stand in 1845, when he was quoting from the Apostles to prove the slave relationship "moral." Never before or after did he deal so vigorously with the moral aspects of slavery, although even here he was concerned only with its effects upon the families of slaveholders and not upon the slaves. Here also he made his most explicit statement that American slavery in the concrete was contrary to the will of God.

One of the most violent attacks upon his position was published in Hamburg, South Carolina, in 1851, in the form of a forty-eight page tract, *A Defence of Southern*

Slavery against the attacks of Henry Clay and Alexander Campbell. This pamphlet, "By a Southern Clergyman," contained "a review of Mr. Clay's 'Letter on Emancipation,' and strictures on Mr. Campbell's 'Tract for the People of Kentucky.' " It is noteworthy not for its logic but for its bitterness and for the manner in which it associated together publicly the antislavery pronouncements of Campbell and Clay. The tone of the pamphlet may be seen from its assertion that Clay's object in issuing his letter was "to reach the Presidency by making the degradation of the whole South, the stepping stone to his elevation," and in its insinuation that Campbell was attempting to rally "the tens of thousands of his disciples in Kentucky" on the side of "abolition fanaticism" out of "sycophantic adulation" for Mr. Clay and in anticipation of some office under Clay's administration.[80]

Campbell's "Tract for the People of Kentucky" represents a return to a position similar to that of his writings in 1830 and 1832. With the unity of the churches assured as a result of his defense of Bible slavery in 1845, he seems to have felt free in 1849 to deal once more with the issue of American slavery. There is no basis, however, for the conclusion of some historians that this represents an about-face from his stand in 1845.

THE CHRISTIAN'S DUTY UNDER THE FUGITIVE SLAVE LAW

The passage of the Fugitive Slave Law in 1850 brought the slavery issue before the country once more in a very controversial manner and precipitated a discussion in the *Millennial Harbinger* second only in extent and intensity to that of 1845. Campbell's primary concern in 1851 was not with slavery itself but with order and obedience to law, just as in 1845 it had been with the unity of the church. But again, as an important part of his argument, he turned to the Scriptures to prove that the relationship of master and slave has divine approval. Once more he "leaned the other way" and defended slavery. This time he made more use of the Old Testament—because he had to in order to meet his opponents' arguments and because he had receded farther from his sharp New Testament primitivism. He brought together biblical and natural law arguments for obedience to law—entirely apart from the merits of the particular law in question.

In the opening article of the *Millennial Harbinger* for 1846, Campbell had said that "a question of much importance, and bearing on some minds with great weight," would demand a portion of his attention that year. Related to the slavery issue, the question was this: "How far ought we to obey and submit to our political institutions and rulers—or what is the extent of our allegiance to civil government?"[81] For some unexplained reason he did not take up this matter until 1851 after the Fugitive Slave Law had stirred many individuals and churches in the North to active resistance.

"No law passed by Congress for many years . . . has caused so much excitement as the Fugitive Slave Law," he said.

Large and respectable meetings, ecclesiastic and political, have denounced it as unconstitutional and immoral, and have been advising, or at least countenancing, resistance and insubordination to its requirements. This, indeed, might have been, more or less, expected from those who are not well informed, either on the Constitution of the United States or on that of Christ's Kingdom. But that any one well-instructed in the christian religion could recommend violence, or insubordination to a law, passed by a Congress that merely represents and reflects the will of the sovereign people, is, to me, rather an unexpected development.[82]

This paragraph affords a good introduction to Campbell's discussion of the Fugitive Slave Law, and suggests a convenient outline under which to arrange his somewhat disordered and repetitious remarks. He countered the opposition's arguments that the law was unconstitutional and immoral, and then insisted that resistance was anti-American and unchristian. If the law was constitutional, then resistance was politically indefensible. If it was not immoral, resistance was unchristian.

That the act was constitutional Campbell demonstrated by quoting the second section of the fourth article of the federal Constitution:

No person held to service or labor in one State, under the laws thereof, escaping into another, shall, in consequence of any law or regulation therein, be discharged from such service or labor, but shall be delivered up on claim of the party to whom such service or labor may be due.

This, he declared, "is a precise, definite, and perspicuous article of our constitutional law." The law in question, therefore, must be "to any ordinary mind, most obviously and perfectly constitutional."[83] If not, "have we not a Supreme Court . . . before which its constitutionality can be at once decided?"[84] To enhance the prestige of the Fugitive Slave Law, Campbell appealed to "the immortal Washington" who had subscribed to the law of 1793, and showed that the law of 1851 agreed in principle with that of 1793, differing only in the penalties attached.[85]

Renewing his earlier insistence that the slave relationship was not immoral, Campbell went further and denied "that there is a Jewish law that justifies resistance to the law now before us." The passage of which he had to dispose was Deuteronomy 23:15f—"Thou shalt not deliver to his master the servant which has escaped from his master to thee, etc." "This is one of the special laws of the Jewish nation," he asserted, "and for a special object"—defining who may and who may not enter into

the "congregation of the Lord." The meaning of the
passage is simply that "a servant escaped from his
master was not debarred from the congregation. He was
not, therefore, to be returned." After quoting two biblical scholars in confirmation of his view, Campbell concluded: "This case, then, has no bearing whatever upon
the subject before us . . . [and] can . . . afford no salvo
to the conscience of any intelligent man who will entice,
aid, or allure a servant to run away from his master."[86]

As he continued his scriptural defense of the Fugitive
Slave Law, Campbell seemingly violated his own scheme
of dispensational ethics by use of the Ten Command-
ments and the Mosaic code. The tenth statue—"Thou
shalt not covet thy neighbor's . . . *man servant, nor his
maid servant* . . . nor any thing that is thy neighbors'
property"—proves "the divine recognition and acknowl-
edgment of the relation of master and servant, or of one
man having a rightful property in another."[87]

On the basis of Exodus 21:2-6 he discussed the dilemma of a slave who has been given a wife by his
master, had children by her, and then comes to the end
of his period of servitude. "The day of his freedom ar-
rives! What a dilemma! He has a wife and children;
his by *nature,* and his master's by *right*—by a *jure
divino.* Which shall he choose—freedom or slavery?"
"A modern Abolitionist would say, 'Runaway, my good
sir, and take your dear wife and children with you.'"
Campbell would abide by the clear word of Scripture
and tell the slave he must choose between going forth
alone or remaining in slavery with his wife and children.[88] Here his apologetic for the Fugitive Slave Law
and his scriptural verbalism seem to have led him to for-
get his 1823 opposition to the practice of separating husband and wife and to laws permitting the same.

This second law, from Exodus 21, Campbell recognized
was "not of the same compass nor perpetuity" as the

tenth commandment. It was "a local and temporary arrangement." Yet it shows

what may, in the judgment of God, be consistent with moral rectitude and the purity of the divine law. The God of the New Testament is the God of the Old. . . . That which may be done rightfully for a day, a month, or a year, may be done for a longer period. . . . Christianity is not more just than Judaism.[89]

As he put it later, in discussing the immutability of the moral law: "What a Patriarch, a Jew, or a Christian, may *morally* do, they all may do."[90] This principle, if followed through, would seem to wipe out his whole scheme of dispensational ethics.

Having concluded that the Fugitive Slave Law was neither unconstitutional nor immoral, Campbell logically insisted that resistance was both "anti-American" and "unchristian." He denounced those who advised or countenanced resistance to a law which "merely represents and reflects the will of the sovereign people." Later he took up the argument "that we the sovereign people . . . have all power in our hands" and therefore may refuse to obey a law which we feel to be morally wrong. On the contrary, he argued: "We cannot retain and delegate the same power. . . . When, therefore, our representatives have made laws, we cannot ourselves, individually, annul them." Resistance to the law in question was therefore contrary to the principles of the social compact and the American system of government.[91]

For the benefit of those *Christians* who urged resistance to the Fugitive Slave Law, Campbell quoted Romans 13:1-7 and 1 Peter 2:13-18 on the duty of the Christian to "be subject to the higher powers" and submit himself "to every ordinance of man, for the Lord's sake." He appealed also to the example of Paul in sending Onesimus back to his master, and of the angel of God

who commanded the runaway slave Hagar to "go home
to her mistress."

With these premises before the mind of any christian man,
whatever may be his private opinions on the subject of servitude
or American slavery, I ask how can he, in allegiance to the Lord
Jesus Christ, throw any obstructions in the way of the execution of this law for reclaiming runaway servants? His conscience must, indeed, be very weak and imperfectly enlightened,
if he [thinks he] is, in such acts, pleasing the Lord or promoting the welfare of man.

It was thus a "moral, and even religious" duty for
Christians to obey this law, "because political government is an ordinance of God . . . to be obeyed, for conscience sake." There was no "higher law" involved.
"In the affairs of this life—in all temporal and earthly
matters—the civil law, the social compact, is our rule of
action."[92]

The Christian who was instrumental in putting a slave
back into the hands even of a cruel master was "not
responsible to heaven or earth for the after treatment of
such runaway." He simply had done his duty. It would
then be up to the owner of the returned slave to do his
duty.[93] In defense of this position Campbell later admitted that the law might result in some slaves being
returned to cruel masters. But he asked: "Who has
constituted every citizen a judge of each and every case?
Have the laws of God or of the State, constituted each
and every citizen such judge!"[94] It has already been observed that with the years Campbell came to rank order
above liberty among the ends of government. It might
also be said that in passages like this he ranked it above
justice. He was obviously more concerned about order
and obedience to law in general than he was for the in-
justices that might be involved in particular cases.

The attack upon the Fugitive Slave Law, Campbell
concluded, was "unchristian, impolitic, and anti-Ameri-

can," and he was horrified at the thought that preachers,
of all people, should be preaching resistance. The argument for preserving the union he skillfully turned *against*
the abolitionists, by exclaiming:

That the christian pulpit, *so called,* should preach up rebellion
and violence, and seek to generate or increase a spirit of resistance to the powers that be—to the *ordinance of God*—is what
I never expected to hear from men at the north, so long declaim-
ing against the south for its doctrines of nullification and secession.[95]

Campbell's position on the Christian's duty in relation
to the Fugitive Slave Law was developed in the article
in January, 1851, and then reiterated, amplified, and
defended in a series of articles which ran through the
spring and summer. In March he announced that his
mail from the North was about 50-50 in support of his
stand.

The same issue reported the action of the congregation
at Berrien, Michigan, which had unanimously resolved:
"That Christians are required by their Lord and Master
to yield a cheerful obedience to the 'powers that be,'
provided their laws do not contravene the 'higher
law.'" The congregation was convinced, however,
"that the Fugitive Slave Law . . . *does* obviously conflict
with the Divine Law in several particulars," and, therefore, "that it is not only *not* the duty of Christians to
obey the said law, but a positive dereliction of duty to
their Divine Master, to regard it as of any authority
over them." "Choosing to 'obey God rather than
man,'" the congregation declared: "We will not assist
the master in recapturing 'the servant that has escaped
from his master,' but will feed the poor panting fugitive,
and point him to the North Star, abiding the penalty of
the law." Campbell commented: "We all respect a
conscientious man, even when his conscience is weak and
unenlightened." Once more he rejected the "higher

law'' doctrine, and went on to say that ''a Christian, with a sword in hand, resisting the 'Powers that be,' might have been endured in the light of Cromwell's day, but not in the light of the 19th century.''[96]

In May he took up the question raised by some of his critics whether the Golden Rule, which requires a Christian ''to succor and relieve a brother man, when in distress,'' did not make it impossible to ''sustain or comply with the requisitions of the Fugitive Slave Law.'' He admitted that the whole moral law ''is summed up . . . in doing to another, what, in similar circumstances, we would desire him to do to us.'' But he circumvented the *spirit* of the Golden Rule by reverting to his customary biblicism. The Bible, he said, ''is the only infallible standard by which all the relations of human life, and all the duties and obligations growing out of them, are to be adjudicated.'' To those who appealed to ''the higher law,'' he declared that the Bible itself is *''the highest law.''* ''To it, therefore . . . all questions of moral right and wrong are to be brought for final adjudication.''[97]

Some of the most telling criticisms of Campbell's argument in support of the Fugitive Slave Law came from Isaac Errett, minister in Warren, Ohio, who later became one of the co-editors of the *Millennial Harbinger*. His criticisms and Campbell's feeble answers reveal some of the weaknesses of his position.

Errett's basic question was how Campbell could reconcile his view that God alone is the supreme legislator in matters moral and religious with his doctrine of ''the *absolute* supremacy of the law'' in regard to slavery. Errett introduced Old Testament examples of the violation of orders of ''the powers that be''—the midwives who ''did not as the King of Egypt commanded'' but preserved the male Hebrew children alive, and Obadiah who hid a hundred of the Lord's prophets in a cave to save them from the decree of Ahab and Jezebel. He also questioned Campbell's use of the cases of Hagar and Paul, asking, in regard to the latter, "If Paul were now living in any of the States of the Union, and were to 'harbor' Onesimus, and treat him kindly, and feed him with the bread of life, would he not . . . be liable to a fine of $1,000, and six months' imprisonment?" As to the "immortal Washington," he asked, did he not "lead armies to the fight? Is that any argument for *war*?" Then, too,

> if the heritage of freedom we enjoy was . . . "purchased with the life-blood of the good and the brave," what kind of argument does that furnish for the "absolute supremacy of the law?" And how can we, *in turn*, bequeath inviolate to our descendants, that heritage, by tamely . . . submitting to, unrighteous and oppressive laws?[98]

Campbell's reply evaded all the more crucial issues and contented itself largely with an effort to show the irrelevance of Errett's analogies.

Errett later raised another penetrating question concerning Campbell's use of Scripture. By what right, he asked, did Campbell dispose of Deuteronomy 23:15f as one of the "special laws of the Jewish nation" and yet build his own defense of the Fugitive Slave Law so largely upon the cases of Hagar and Onesimus? "Is there nothing 'special' in these cases . . . ? Is it logical to argue from these peculiar cases to a general conclusion?"[99] Campbell had no convincing answer. An impartial observer must admit that Errett here put his finger upon one of Campbell's weakest points—the rather high-handed manner in which he now disposed of passages that were embarrassing to him and sought scriptural support for his views from whatever source or dispensation he could find it.

Before the end of 1851 the debates on the Fugitive Slave Law had subsided in the pages of the *Millennial*

Harbinger. In his discussion of this issue Campbell had made his most extravagant statements in defense of slavery as a scriptural institution, and his most extreme declarations on the Christian's duty to obey the law of the land without regard to his own judgments and without feeling any personal responsibility for the injustice that might be involved in particular cases.

LATER SECTIONAL TENSIONS

In spite of everything that Campbell and others like him could do, the work of the abolitionists and extreme proslavery advocates bore bitter fruit in the gradual intensification of hatred between South and North. This was reflected in several controversies in which he became embroiled in the middle of the 1850's. He was driven by the exigencies of the situation to stand with the South against the North—even though he opposed the drawing of sectional lines, especially within the church.

Early in 1854 the question of free soil versus slave soil came up in connection with rivalry between Bethany College and Northwestern Christian (now Butler) University, at Indianapolis, Indiana. In a journey through Illinois in the interest of Bethany late in 1853 Campbell discovered that an agent for the rival school, Elder John O'Kane, had apparently appealed to sectional pride and interest in his campaign for funds. As Campbell reported O'Kane's argument it was that "Christians living on *free* soil, should not co-operate with Christians living on *slave* soil, in any seminary of learning."[100] Although the Board of Directors of Northwestern denied espousing the view ascribed to them, Campbell continued to agitate the issue. A correspondent later chastised him for his attitude toward Northwestern and the free-soil issue, charging that "like the politicians from the South, you manifest too much sensitiveness about these matters."[101]

Early in 1856 the *Millennial Harbinger* carried several articles about a disturbance over a slavery discussion at Bethany College. According to Campbell's report of the incident, the policy of the college was "to maintain a strictly literary, scientific and religious character." In keeping with this purpose, "the discussion, by the Students, of difficult and exciting questions of social and public policy, especially those of a sectional peculiarity, has been uniformly discouraged by the Faculty."[102] A small group of ardent abolitionists flaunted this policy, and one of them spoke one Sunday evening "on the true principles of Liberty." His strong antislavery statement led to some disorder. The majority of the students apparently supported the policies of the college, but some from the North issued an ultimatum to the faculty, setting forth the terms on which they would remain as students. Instead of meeting these terms the college dismissed their leaders.

The incident got wide and unfavorable publicity throughout the North and in Scotland. Campbell declared that the stories, which appeared under such titles as "Campbellite Proslaveryism" and "Slavery Intolerance," did not present the situation in its true light. A development which gave him particular pain was the fact that the students who had been dismissed at Bethany were subsequently "received into all the rights, titles, and honors of students in the North-Western Christian University." He rebuked Northwestern for thus "receiving into her bosom, and cherishing in her affection, those dismissed for *immoral* and *unchristian* conduct here."[103]

With the repercussions over this incident the slavery question largely receded from the pages of the *Millennial Harbinger* until the time of the Civil War, with only occasional reiterations of Campbell's seemingly proslavery point of view. His weariness with the whole subject was revealed in an article in 1854 in which he excused himself for not paying any attention to the issues posed by the Nebraska Bill. It did not come within the province of his thought or studies, he said. Admitting that there were strong arguments on both sides, he concluded that

time, that great revolutionist; and worldly interest, that special pleader; and philanthropy, that eloquent orator; and Divine Providence, that Sovereign Arbiter, will one day decide this question and disperse this dark cloud, whether by its own lightenings and thunders, or by the bright shining of the Sun of Righteousness and Mercy on our fallen and bewildered world."[104]

As the curtain fell upon his discussions of slavery, Campbell was leaning rather far in support of that institution—not for its own sake, but as a means of insuring obedience to law. He still looked upon slavery as an evil and longed for its elimination. But in 1851, as in his earlier years, he was "fully satisfied that the only rational—that is, practicable—way of abolishing slavery in America, if it ever can be done, is that proposed by the American Colonization Society."[105]

In his later years he said little about the evils of slavery. There was doubtless an element of "expediency" in this silence, for with the North turning against him, he was increasingly dependent upon the good will of the South for support of the college. It is worthy of note that after the buildings burned near the end of 1857, and he set out to raise funds to rebuild them, Campbell's itinerary was exclusively in the South.

The most striking fact about his treatment of the slavery issue is that he almost never dealt with the subject from the point of view of its effects upon the slaves. Rather he was always concerned primarily with the effects of the system upon the slaveholder and his family, or upon the well-being of society in general, the unity of the church, or order in the state.

This preoccupation with the welfare of social institutions rather than of the slaves may help account for the fact that this is one of the very few issues on which Campbell departed significantly from his early mentors, John Locke and James Hay Beattie. Locke opposed slavery as a violation of the rights of man. Beattie felt very strongly that slavery was "utterly repugnant to every principle of reason, religion, humanity and conscience," and admitted that "in protesting against such a practice it is not easy to preserve that leniency of language and coolness of argument which philosophy recommends."[106] Campbell, for the most part, had no such difficulty—because he almost never looked at the institution from the point of view of the slave.

CHAPTER XIV

CAPITAL PUNISHMENT

IN 1846, during a lull in his slavery discussions, Alexander Campbell directed his attention briefly to the subject of capital punishment. Considerable agitation had arisen against the death penalty during the 1840's as part of the general humanitarian impulse of the period. The number of crimes punishable by death was greatly reduced, being limited generally to murder, treason, arson, and rape. Several states went so far as to abolish capital punishment entirely.

The first notice in the *Millennial Harbinger* of reform movements in this field occurred in a brief item in September, 1845, reporting that "imprisonment for life, in place of hanging or capital punishment, seems to be getting popular at the North."

The question is a troublesome one. It is a little more merciful to take away life than to put a man in solitary confinement for life; and when we read of such a murder as that of Frank Combs by O'Blennis, we think there is especial force in the scriptural denunciation, "Whoso sheddeth man's blood, by man shall his blood be shed."[1]

A few months later Campbell took up the subject in a carefully wrought essay prepared for the Washington Literary Institute, of Washington, Pennsylvania, and published in the *Millennial Harbinger* for March, 1846, because of the "immediate claims" of the question "upon the attention of the whole community."[2]

Among the issues then before the American public, he declared, none was more important than the question "IS CAPITAL PUNISHMENT SANCTIONED BY DIVINE AUTHORITY? or, in other words, *Has man a right to take away the life of man on any account whatever?''* This was a question involving the very "foundation of civil government.''[3]

PRAGMATIC CONSIDERATIONS

Though "we are not, in the first instance, to take into account the consequences of any decision, as having any direct authority to influence our reasonings upon the question," Campbell started out with a pragmatic examination of the issue. If capital punishment is not permissible, then three things follow. For one thing, an officer of justice

has no right to punish at all in any way, if he may not, in that punishment, lawfully take away the life of him that is subjected to it. He has not even the right to imprison . . . a person. . . . [For] How many die in jails, workhouses, and penitentiaries, from causes to which they would not have been exposed but in those places of punishment![4]

In the second place, if it should be proved that capital punishment is not sanctioned by divine authority, then "nations . . . have no right to go to war in any case, or for any purpose whatever." Wars are

originated and conducted on the assumption that man has a right, for just cause, to take away the life of man. For . . . man cannot rightfully kill by the thousand, or by the million, if he cannot lawfully kill one individual.

Campbell did not want to be misunderstood; he was not arguing the legitimacy of war. "Wars might cease and universal peace spread its halcyon wings all over the earth, and still the murderer be rightfully, and, by the supreme authority, put to death." One might be a pacifist, as he was, and "still argue against the abolition of capital punishment." His point was simply that "an end of all wars, offensive and defensive, follows instantly upon the national conviction that men have no right to kill those who have killed their neighbors.''[5]

His third consideration was based upon the second.
For

if nations may not rightfully go to war . . . in what dishonor-
able attitude stands the sainted patriots of all Christian lands—
their Hampdens, their La Fayettes, their Washingtons? And
where stand the men of faith . . . the Joshuas, the Sampsons,
the Baraks, the Gideons, the Davids?

Even those who do honor to the memory of such military
leaders, and eulogize "our own revolutionary heroes"
are guilty if it is contrary to God's law to take the life
of a murderer.[6] Here the equivocal nature of his argument is apparent. While he did not approve of war, he
used these points as arguments that would carry weight
with those who did.

THEORIES OF OPPONENTS EXAMINED

The arguments and speculations of the "theorists"
who opposed capital punishment were then considered.
Campbell rejected the view that "the sole end of punishment is the reformation of the offender." "Punishments
ought, in all cases, to be enacted and enforced with a
very special regard to the reformation of transgressors"
but not with an "*exclusive* regard. . . There must also
be a very special and a supreme regard to the safety of
the state, the protection of the innocent and unoffend-
ing." How these two objectives might best be secured
was a matter "not yet agreed," but Campbell was convinced that "a sentence of perpetual imprisonment is
no guarantee of protection or safety to the state." Life
imprisonment gives society no guarantee "that the monster who has been guilty of one murder may not murder
some of his attendants or fellow-prisoners in hope of
escape." Then, too, "the professedly reformed and
pardoned criminal" has sometimes been guilty of a
second or even a third murder. In view of these con-

siderations, Campbell maintained that society "demands a higher pledge of safety . . . the life of the murderer."[7]

He denied the contention of some opponents of capital punishment that life imprisonment is worse than death. If this were true, then life imprisonment would not be lawful, for "neither the *lex talionis,* nor the Bible, nor right reason . . . would authorize any punishment severer than death."[8]

At the same time he agreed with those who opposed capital punishment "for any other crime than murder." "Much of the excitement and indignation against capital punishment," he felt, "arises from two sources:—The many crimes that have been judged worthy of death; and from the fact, that the innocent sometimes suffer while the guilty escape." There ought to be some correspondence between offenses and their punishment. He could not see the

> expediency of a horizontal tariff, awarding one and the same punishment to each and to every one of a hundred crimes. We would not hang one man for stealing a shilling, and only hang another man for treason, sacrilege, rape, or murder.

The scriptural phrases, "worthy of stripes," "worthy of a sorer punishment," and "worthy of death," sustain his position, he declared, and form "a sound and irrefutable argument in support of capital punishment." He advocated "a scale of punishments . . . ascending up to capital punishment, only in the case of wilful and deliberate murder, not to be extenuated in any case by passion, intemperance, or any temptation whatsoever." He further urged a tightening up of legal procedures so that the innocent might not suffer or the guilty escape.[9]

Thus far Campbell reasoned on the basis of "expediency, and rational propriety." But because of the differences in judgment among equally earnest individuals, it was necessary to "appeal to a higher court, and await the decision of the Supreme Lawgiver and Judge of the universe."[10]

What Do the Scriptures Say?

He turned then to the question, *"What punishment does the Supreme Lawgiver and Judge award to the murderer?"* Capital punishment was sanctioned in the patriarchal age by the voices of reason, conscience, and God. Cain recognized that his act of murder had placed him beyond the pale of divine protection. "It shall come to pass that every one that findeth me shall kill me." Whether Cain understood this through "the voice of reason, the voice of conscience, or the voice of God," was immaterial. Campbell believed it was "the voice of them all." The song of Lamech (Genesis 4:23f) gives further evidence that "death for murder was the established justice of the antediluvian world."[11]

After the flood

The first act of legislation in setting up the new world . . . was *an act against murder.* This was an act not for Jew or Gentile— not for Egyptian, Chaldean, Greek, or Roman; but [being enacted] before any of them existed, for the whole human race.

In Genesis 9:5f, "God gave to man, by a positive and express precept, the power, the authority, and the injunction to cut off all murderers." *"At the hand of every man's brother will I require the life of man. Whoso sheddeth man's blood, by man shall his blood be shed: for in the image of God made he man."* Said Campbell: "No statute was ever more free from ambiguity."[12]

How can a command so "express, so authoritative, and peremptory" as this be set aside by those "seized with a morbid philanthropy, or charmed with the fascinations of a new theory"? It was done "by the magic of a single assumption—'Christianity is more mild, and generous, and philanthropic than the law of Moses.'" But this injunction is not Mosaic, he insisted. It is more fundamental still. It is part of the immutable moral law of the universe.

The constitution that guaranties the continuance of day and night and the seasons of the year, also secures and protects the life of man from the violence of man, by a statute simultaneously promulged . . . for the benefit of the whole human race.[13]

"Still more convincing and decisive" was "the *reason* assigned by the Divine Author of the statute commanding capital punishment. . . . 'FOR IN THE IMAGE OF GOD MADE HE MAN.' " This reason is of "perpetual validity." "So long as it stands true that man was created in the image of God, so long it will bind every religious and moral people to take away the life of the murderer."[14]

Turning next to the Jewish dispensation Campbell quoted Numbers 35:9-33 and pointed out that two great objects were contemplated and secured by the institution of cities of refuge—"a refuge for the innocent, and a *caveat* against manslaughter." The cities of refuge afforded no asylum whatever to the murderer. On trial and conviction he was in all cases taken away and put to death. Attention was again called to the reason connected with the ordinance—"*The land cannot be cleansed of the blood that is shed therein* BUT BY THE BLOOD OF HIM THAT SHED IT." This also Campbell said, "has no respect to time, place, or circumstance. It exclusively belongs to no age, to no nation or people. It is a reason, too, why murder shall not be pardoned" in the subsequent centuries.[15]

He turned finally to the Christian dispensation and asked whether, as is sometimes assumed, Jesus abolished capital punishment. This is

an outrage upon the character of the Messiah! True, indeed, he came not to judge the world, to act the civil magistrate, the civil law giver; or to assume regal authority over any nation or people of this world. His kingdom was spiritual and heavenly. In it he would not have an eye for an eye, tooth for tooth, or stripe for stripe.

But one cannot argue from this for the "abolition of civil government—of civil penalties—or for the abrogation of statutes given to mankind by God himself . . . for the safety of society.''[16]

Campbell had little difficulty in finding plenty of passages in Paul to support his thesis. For example, if the "powers that be are ordained of God," and the magistrate "rightfully wears a sword not his own, but God's," why should he wear a sword "if it be unlawful or unchristian to put any one to death on any account whatever! That would, indeed, be to 'bear the sword in vain.' ''[17]

His conclusion from these scriptural studies was that there is not a single word

in Old Testament or New inhibitting capital punishment, nor a single intimation that it should be done away. On the contrary, reasons are given as the basis of the requisition of life for life, which never can be done away—which are as forcible at this hour as they were in the days of Cain, Noah, Moses, and Jesus Christ.[18]

There remained one passage to be considered—a text used by some as an argument against capital punishment: namely, the sixth commandment. On the contrary Moses himself did not so interpret this precept, Campbell insisted. "For on the very day he descended from the Mount with the autograph in his hand, he commanded the sons of Levi to gird on their swords and kill the idolators . . . of whom no less than three thousand fell that day.''[19]

Campbell next examined another argument used against capital punishment—that no Christian, or other man "of delicate moral sensibility, could execute such a sentence—could despatch to the judgment throne a criminal crimsoned with the blood of his fellow-man." To this left-wing scruple he gave a typical right-wing answer:

It is not the Sheriff's hand—it is not the sword of the executioner. It is the hand of God—it is the sword of his justice that takes away that life which he himself gave, because it has murderously taken away a life which it could not give.[20]

Of those who were so fastidious about taking the life of a murderer Campbell asked: "Is the hand of a man purer than the hand of an angel? And who was it, that, in one memorable night, passing through the land of Egypt, by a single stroke smote to death the first born of all the realms of Pharaoh"? Similarly Moses, Joshua, Samuel, David, Joab, and many others of "the purest, the holiest, and the best of men" God used as "executioners of His justice." Even Jesus, "as governor of the world . . . despatched Titus with a Roman army, and laid siege to Jerusalem and other cities in Judea. . . . [and] killed more than one million" of the rebellious Jews.[21]

Capital punishment, Campbell concluded, was "not only countenanced by innumerable [biblical] precedents, but . . . also most positively enjoined upon all persons to whom God has revealed his will, who are entrusted with the government of the world." This makes it "a divine precept and requisition, to which we are bound to yield our cordial assent."[22]

It is as beneficial as it is just. "The first and paramount concern of every intelligent and moral community on earth" is the protection and safety of human life. The death sentence for murder serves a function not unlike efforts to make highways safe. Society, he pointed out, has immense stakes in the lives of

such men as Christopher Columbus, Martin Luther, Sir Francis Bacon, Sir Isaac Newton, Benjamin Franklin, Robert Fulton, George Washington and many others. Suppose that each of these had fallen in with some Aaron Burr, as did Alexander Hamilton . . . what would have been the present condition of the world?[23]

In conclusion, Campbell entreated every

patriot, philanthropist, and Christian in our country, to use his best endeavors to create a sound public opinion on the obligations resting on every State government to exterminate the crime of murder by a firm, persevering, and uniform execution of the murderer, according to the divine precept.

At a time when many were for "taking away the greatest restraint and for substituting a less one, under the most preposterous assumption that man is wiser than God," he called upon "the real friends of man" to speak out.[24]

After publishing this essay in the *Millennial Harbinger* for March, 1846, Campbell paid no further attention to the issue until the early months of 1847 when he attempted to meet some of the objections to his views. In returning to the subject he mentioned that six or seven thousand copies of the essay had been circulated throughout the country, that it had been republished in England, and there as well as here presented to a number of distinguished men in government. In meeting the arguments of his critics, he re-examined the Scripture passages and precedents which he had used in the original essay but added nothing new to his earlier statements.[25] He then allowed the matter to drop out of his area of public concern.[26]

In his attitude toward capital punishment, Campbell took the right-wing natural law line following Calvin, Locke, and Beattie. He showed the same arbitrary use of Scriptures as he did on the subject of slavery, and a tendency to turn more and more to Old Testament texts for support of his views. By the simple device of interpreting an Old Testament command as part of the immutable moral law and "an essential element in a wise, just, and benevolent jurisprudence," he was able to justify the use of Old Testament norms under the Christian dispensation.

Chapter XV

WAR

THE ISSUES of capital punishment and war are closely related in Christian ethics. Both involve the taking of life and thus pose a fundamental moral problem. Both are justified as essential means to the attainment of fundamental ends of the state—the protection of the lives of its citizens. On the basis of the first similarity Alexander Campbell recognized that "peacemen are generally, if not universally, in favor of the total abolition of capital punishment."[1] On the basis of the second those who approve of capital punishment might logically be expected to approve at least of defensive war. Campbell remained an ardent pacifist even though he approved of capital punishment.[2]

The subject of war received much more frequent and extended attention from him than that of capital punishment. In fact he dealt with it from the first issue of the *Christian Baptist* down to his last written comments in the *Millennial Harbinger* in the midst of the Civil War.

EARLY ANTIWAR SENTIMENTS

Among the anomalies of contemporary Christianity of which he wrote in 1823 was the so-called

Christian General, with his ten thousand soldiers, and his Chaplain at his elbow, preaching, as he says, the gospel of good will among men; and . . . praying that the Lord would cause them to fight valiantly and render their efforts successful in making as many widows and orphans, as will afford sufficient opportunity for others, to manifest the purity of their religion by taking care of them!!![3]

242

Earlier in this article he had referred to Jesus as inculcating a morality which "checks every principle that would lead to war, oppression, or cruelty."[4]

The following month he referred to the Crusades as "chimerical and wicked projects."[5]

In 1825 he published with some zest a "Third Epistle of Peter" with its ironical advice to preachers:

If a brother shall [raise] up the banner of war against brother, and Christians against Christians, rebuke them not: but be some of you on the one side and some on the other; and tell the one host that God is on their side, and the other host that he is on their side: so make them bold to kill. And even among swords and lances, let your black robes be seen.

Preach ye not "peace on earth and good will to men," but preach ye glory to the victor, and victory to the brave.[6]

The following year he criticized an orator at the laying of the cornerstone of Western Reserve College for praying that that institution might send out "a proportionate number of 'Calvins and Knoxes' in the theological department, and of 'Washingtons and Bolivars' in the field." "Orthodoxy and war!—holy and happy alliance!" Campbell exclaimed.[7]

Still more significant was his announcement of a new journal of Christian pacifism. In 1829 he advised:

Those who think it is a duty for *christian* nations to kill one another, and to wage war for *miney* and *thiney;* and that they ought, and, from necessity, must, fight and war for goods and chattels—had better treat themselves to a copy of the *Christian Patriot and Advocate of Peace,* published from No. 99, South Second street, Philadephia, by William Stavely.[8]

His pacifist spirit found expression in the Fourth of July oration in 1830. The cardinal principle of the Messiah's kingdom, he said, is love.

Philosophy as well as religion teaches us that to conquer enemies is not the work of swords, nor lances, nor bows of steel. . . . *To conquer an enemy is to convert him into a friend. . . .* To do this all arms and modes of warfare are impotent, save the arms and munitions of everlasting love.

Accordingly Campbell called upon his hearers to imitate him "who did not lift up his voice in the streets—who did not use so much as a broken reed. . . In that spirit of mildness, meekness, and unostentatious heroism, let us fight the good fight of faith."[9]

The chief source of his pacifism in this period, apart from the Bible, seems to have been the writings of Soame Jenyns which he had probably read before coming to America. In the debate with Owen he quoted a long passage from Jenyns on such "pagan" virutes as valor and patriotism with the conclusion that war can have no place "in the catalogue of christian virtues, being irreconcileable with all its precepts."[10] In the midst of his excerpts from Jenyns, he turned aside to speak approvingly of the Sermon on the Mount. To the scoffer who declares, "Pretty thing, indeed . . . to be commanded 'to turn the other cheek . . .' and to go 'two miles . . .'" he replied: "Yes, indeed, a pretty thing for the proud and retaliating! But the question is, Which is the speedier way to end the controversy?" Campbell was convinced that the "controversy will be sooner terminated, and less danger will be incurred by turning the other cheek than by striking back."[11]

The only issue on which Campbell consistently turned to the teachings of Jesus and the Sermon on the Mount for directives for the Christian's duties as a citizen was in the matter of war. Even here he disavowed any obligation to take the precepts literally, and based his acceptance of them upon pragmatic grounds.

REFLECTIONS OF THE AMERICAN PEACE CRUSADE

In 1834 Campbell began to show signs of direct indebtedness to the American peace movement. He quoted and

endorsed articles like one from the *Moral Lyceum* on the
"Duty of Laboring Assiduously and Praying Unceas-
ingly for the Abolition of War."[12] Even more significantly he quoted with approval the views of Thomas
S. Grimke, one of the leading spokesmen for the peace
movement.

The American peace crusade began in 1815 with the
organization of the New York Peace Society and the
Massachusetts Peace Society. In the years that followed such societies were organized in many parts of the
country. By 1818 there were eight of them in the state
of Ohio, and Elisha Bates was publishing his *Moral
Advocate* at Mt. Pleasant not far from Campbell's home
and the scene of his debate with Walker two years later.

The American Peace Society was organized in New
York in 1828 on a broad and inclusive basis which did
not exclude those who were prepared to support a defensive war. This particular issue was placed squarely before the peace movement by the address of Thomas S.
Grimke, of Charleston, South Carolina, at New Haven,
Connecticut, in May, 1832. Grimke took an uncompromis-
ing stand against all war, defensive as well as offensive,
and asserted flatly that the Revolutionary War was both
unnecessary and unchristian.

Campbell's indebtedness to Grimke for the point that
Anglo-Saxon superiority derives from Protestantism
and the emphasis upon the Bible as a textbook in the
schools has already been noticed. In August, 1834, Campbell quoted two of the "Notes" to the published edition
of Grimke's address on the Bible as a textbook. The
first contrasted the war spirit with that of Robert Raikes,
and was reprinted under the title "The Spirit of the
Nations of Antiquity Was the Spirit of Selfishness, of
Rapine, and of War." The second, headed "Christian
Scheme of Education," contrasted the spirit of the
Gospel, which is "essentially the spirit of peace and

humility, of love and forbearance," with "the spirit that lives and moves throughout the classical models . . . the spirit of war, foreign and civil."[13]

Grimke exerted considerable influence upon Campbell's thought in this period. Campbell's copy of the New Haven address is in the portion of his library which has been preserved to this day. Also extant is his copy of Jonathan Dymond's *Inquiry into the Accordancy of War with the Principles of Christianity,* which converted Grimke to the absolutist position and which Grimke edited for its first American edition. There are echoes of Grimke in Campbell's objections to the American Eagle as a national emblem in the debate with Purcell,[14] and in his later suggestion that if Washington and the other Revolutionary heroes had been better "educated" they might have achieved their purposes without the shedding of blood.[15]

Campbell revealed his familiarity with the materials of the peace crusade by many items quoted or reprinted in the *Millennial Harbinger* during the latter part of the 1830's. In this period he also referred to war as "a consecrated evil,"[16] to Alexander as belonging to "that class of licensed murderers, called *heroes,*"[17] and to the power of music to stir up the war spirit.[18] Yet in the discussion of callings uncongenial to the Christian and inimical to the welfare of society, Campbell was willing to admit that there *may* be a difference between the manufacture of the armor of national defense and that of instruments of private murder and vengeance like the stiletto, dirk, and Bowie knife.[19]

In 1839 one of his correspondents asked Campbell's views on the subject of nonresistance. In setting forth the opinions of "some honest-hearted well-meaning men amongst us," M. Winans spoke first of their views as to the impropriety of the Christian's voting or holding public office, and then of their feeling that, when "commanded to muster or march in the army," the Christian should *"suffer the penalty of disobedience."*[20]

After a characteristic study of the Scriptures, Thomas Campbell, who answered these queries for his son, concluded that the radical sect view set forth by Winans is "certainly unscriptural." Nonresistance in personal relationships is taught by both Testaments. But all this is

without any interference with our political duties; as the subjects of civil government. For he that said, "Resist not evil;" also said . . . "Render to Cesar the things that are Cesar's." And by his Apostles, Peter and Paul, he has given us the most solemn charges to honor kings, to obey magistrates, to be ready to every good work.[21]

On this reply by his father Alexander Campbell made no comment, and there is no way of knowing whether this typically Lutheran distinction between public and private duties expressed his viewpoint at the time or not. He did accept this general distinction in the case of capital punishment, but nowhere in his writings is there a suggestion as to its validity in regard to war. He affirmed that when an executioner kills a murderer it is not his hand that does it, but God's; but nowhere did he admit that when a soldier kills another in war his being an agent of the state or of God relieves him of the responsibility or guilt. On the contrary the implication everywhere seems to be that the soldier is personally responsible for any and all murders he commits.

Issue Raised By the Mexican War

Although he had given indications of his views on war from the very beginning of his editorial career Campbell did not face the issue in any systematic or straightforward manner until the time of the Mexican War. War was declared on May 13, 1846, and the August issue of the *Millennial Harbinger* reported: "Queries on the subject of War as a Christian duty, continue to come into our office." He seemed surprised that his readers were left in any doubt as to his stand on the matter. "My views of *war* . . . have long since been suggested, and in some degree exemplified."[22]

In November he made a start at setting forth his views on the subject

of war in general, and of the present American Mexican Republican war in particular; a war kindly undertaken for the benevolent purpose of acquiring more territory for the improvement of the condition of African slaves, and for civilizing and Christainizing the priest ridden Mexicans.[23]

This statement, with its transparent irony, gives a clear indication of Campbell's attitude toward the Mexican War—the attitude of the American Peace Society and a majority at least of northern peace men. Whereas on the subject of slavery Campbell's position tended to be rather typically southern, upon that of war (as of dueling) it was more characteristically northern.

For the present he retreated from the immediate issue to the more abstract and academic issue of war in general —as he had done with the slavery issue in 1845.

While I must, for more reasons than one, decline the task of scrutinizing the *existing war* either in its object, character, or tendency, I feel it due to those claiming my views, to give them freely on *the whole subject of war* as compatible or incompatible with the genius of the Christian religion.

He need scarcely define his position for those who had been reading him for the last quarter century, he said, quoting his statement in the first issue of the *Christian Baptist* on the anomaly of a Christian general. "From this view of the subject my observations and reflections ever since, have subtracted nothing. On the contrary . . . my convictions have rather become stronger than weaker."[24]

As for the arguments of those who justify war from the Bible, "volumes to this effect only convince me of the ignorance of some and the hypocrisy of others." On the basis of his distinction between the two dispensations, he declared that while

we can justify many of the Old Testament wars . . . so long as any man admits the dying testimony of Jesus Christ to be true, he must, I contend, give up his 'Christian wars,' 'Christian armies,' 'Christian navies,' 'Christian victories,' and military glory.

Jesus' statement in John 18:36 "ought to settle the question forever." Jesus prohibited his servants from fighting for him not because he was "born to die a violent death as a sacrifice for sin" but because his kingdom *"is not of this world."* Campbell turned then to the Sermon on the Mount as an "exponent of the Saviour's mind and will on the subject of war. If he would not have any of them to render evil for evil, and if he pronounced the highest honor and blessing on the peacemakers, who can imagine that he would be a patron of war!"[25]

Having said all this, he recognized that he had still not met all of the issues involved.

Although the teaching of the Master addressed to his followers was all in favor of peace and against war . . . still, it is alleged that in the discharge of our duties to the state, we may, BY THE FORCE OF OTHER PRECEPTS, be constrained to bear arms in defence of our country—or in obedience to the *"powers that be."*

Although we cannot as Christians,

become soldiers, and engage in broils and battles for our own sake, or for the sake of religion . . . may we not volunteer to fight and kill our neighbors for the good of the state? Or, at least, when commanded by those in authority, must we not act as soldiers, and endeavor to destroy men's lives for the honor of our country, or for the maintenance of our rights? On this important question we must reflect for another moon.[26]

Campbell did not return to this question after "another moon." In fact he did not resume the inquiry until eighteen months later in the address on "War." When he did, he explained his silence by saying that the issue "so soon became a party question, that, preserving as I do, a strict neutrality between party politics . . . I finally determined not to touch the subject till the war was over."[27] This is a grave weakness in Campbell's policy in regard to controversial political issues. Like the Arkansas traveler, when it was raining, he was unable to patch the roof, and when the storm was over, there was no urgency for him to do so. He deferred discussion of war when the issue was a live one, and returned to it only when the crisis was past. This was merely a variation of the technique of evasion which he used in the case of slavery. Then he retreated from the *concrete* issue of American slavery to the *abstract* and antiquarian issue of Bible slavery. There were suggestions in 1846 that he might follow this same course in relation to the Mexican War, turning from a discussion of the particular war to a discussion of war in general. He finally chose instead the technique of postponement.

That he was not entirely satisfied with his course in the matter is clear from further remarks in his address of 1848. After explaining his reasons for delay, he went on to confess that he was "sorry" and "ashamed" to think that he had not spoken out his views or written an essay on this subject earlier. "Probably even this much published by me some three years, or even two years ago, might have saved some lives that have been thrown away in the desert," he said.[28]

In the meantime he had continued to reprint brief excerpts on war and to make passing allusions to it in addresses and articles. In the peroration of his Baccalaureate Address of 1847 he said to the graduates:

I call not upon you . . . to furnish yourselves with swords and spears, with the weapons of desolation and death for the impending conflict. This is not the work of scholars, or philos-

ophers, or Christians. Your profession is not to kill and to
destroy, but to redeem and to rescue men from evil. . . . The
weapons of this our warfare are not swords and spears, but
reason, truth, persuasion.[29]

In one of his letters from Europe he lamented the fact
that St. Paul's cathedral in London was really sacred to
"Mars the god of War, rather than to the Prince of
Peace, and his humble friend the true and veritable St.
Paul." A walk through this cathedral

is incomparably better adapted to make heroes than saints,
warriors than Christians, sons of thunder rather than sons of
peace. It is, indeed, a grand pageant—a sublime delusion—a
monstrous insult to the person whose fame it falsely celebrates.[30]

THE ADDRESS ON WAR

After allowing the subject of war to rest for many
"moons" after it was first raised in November, 1846,
Campbell set forth his views in a thoroughly pacifist address before the Wheeling Lyceum, May 11, 1848.

"Has one Christian nation a right to wage war against
another Christian nation?" He approached this "momentous question" with some reluctance but admitted
that he had often

and with intense interest, reflected on the desolations and horrors of war, as indicated in the sacrifice of human life, the ago-
nies of surviving relatives, the immense expenditures of a people's wealth, and the inevitable deterioration of public morals,
invariably attendant on its existence and career.[31]

He was not satisfied that the question was properly
stated. Specifically he asked whether there is any such
thing as a *"Christian* nation." There are many nations
that have Christian communities in them, and by a common figure of speech we refer to such nations as Christian. But speaking more accurately, "a proper literal
Christian nation is not found in any country under the
whole heavens." So he rephrased the question—*"Can
Christ's kingdom or church in one nation wage war*

against his own kingdom or church in another nation?"
When it is stated thus, he asked: "Where is the man
so ignorant of the letter and spirit of Christianity as to
answer . . . in the affirmative."[32]
Even this form of the question did not meet

the exact state of the case, as now impinging the conscience of
very many good men. . . . "Suppose," say they, "England pro-
claims war against our nation, or that we proclaim war against
England, have we a *right, as Christian men,* to volunteer, or
enlist, or, if drafted, to fight against England?". . . Or has our
government a *right* to compel us to take up arms?

Refusing to be drawn aside into an abstract definition
of natural right, he insisted upon taking "the surer and
well established ground—of a divine warrant, or a right
founded on a *divine* annunciation." Thus, as one would
expect, he converted the issue into a scriptural one and
turned to the Bible as "that ultimate tribunal to which
we make our appeal."[33] The results of his study of the
Bible's teachings on war he summarized in the conclusion of his address under six heads, to which were added
two points of a more pragmatic character.

In the first place, he argued:

The right to take away the life of the murderer does not of itself warrant war, inasmuch as in that case none but the guilty
suffer; whereas in war the innocent suffer not only with, but
often without the guilty. The guilty generally make war and
the innocent suffer its consequences.[34]

This was Campbell's rational basis of discrimination between war and capital punishment. He approved the
death penalty because it is presumably inflicted only
upon those who have been proved guilty of murder. But
a war is waged against a whole people, and even if the
enemy started it by killing citizens of one's own country,
only those of the enemy nation are guilty and worthy of
death who were *personally* responsible for the killings.
Since war seldom reaches the guilty and always involves

the slaughter of the innocent, Campbell was unable to
approve it on the grounds upon which he justified capital
punishment.

His second point was that

the right given to the Jews to wage war is not vouchsafed to
any other nation; for they were under a theocracy, and were
God's sheriff to punish nations: consequently no Christian can
argue from the wars of the Jews in justification or in extenua-
tion of the wars of Christendom.[35]

While he granted that the wars of the Old Testament
were right because commanded by God, he insisted that
"what the God of Abraham did . . . before he gave up
the sceptre and the crown to his Son Jesus Christ, is of
no binding authority now."[36] The contrast between the
Mosaic and Christian dispensations was of much more
practical importance for Campbell in regard to war than
in relation to slavery, capital punishment, or economic
ethics. In his discussion of these other issues he recognized no significant departure in the New Testament
from the commands and usages of the Old. But in the
case of war he found a complete reversal which laid the
basis for his radical pacifism and set him off from the
traditional natural law acceptance of the just war. An
important consideration is that on this issue he turned
within the New Testament not to the precepts and precedents of the Apostles but to those of Jesus himself.

After having insisted that the Old Testament commands do not justify Christian participation in war,
Campbell rephrased his question, in its third form, as
follows:

Has the Author and Founder of the Christian religion enacted
war, or has he made it lawful and right for the subjects of his
government to go to war . . . for any national object, at the
bidding of the present existent political authorities of any nation in Christendom?

As he had done earlier, he again refused to admit any
distinction between aggressive and defensive war—"for

a mere grammatical, logical, or legal quibble, will make any war either aggressive or defensive, just as the whim, caprice, or interest of an individual pleases."[37]

In the third through the sixth points of his summary he quickly called attention to the inconsistencies between war and the regulations of the "present Monarch of the Universe."

The prophecies clearly indicate that the Messiah himself would be "THE PRINCE OF PEACE," and that under his reign "wars should cease," and "nations study it no more."

The gospel, as first announced by the angels, is a message which results in producing "peace on earth and good will among men."

The precepts of Christianity positively inhibit war—by showing that "wars and fightings come from men's lusts" and evil passions, and by commanding Christians to "follow peace with all men."

The beatitudes of Christ are not pronounced on patriots, heroes, and conquerors; but on "peace-makers", on whom is conferred the highest rank and title in the universe—"Blessed are the PEACE-MAKERS, for they shall be called THE SONS OF GOD."[38]

His seventh point dealt with the question from a pragmatic, rather than scriptural, point of view. War is *folly*, because "it can never be the criterion of justice or a proof of right,"[39] "it can never be a satisfactory end of the controversy," and "peace is always the result of negociation."[40]

Under the eighth head he argued the *wickedness* of war on the rational and pragmatic grounds that "those who are engaged in killing their brethren, for the most part, have no personal cause of provocation whatever"; "they seldom . . . comprehend the right or the wrong of the war" and act therefore "without the approbation of conscience"; "the innocent are punished with the guilty"; the soldier is constrained "to do for the state that, which, were he to do in his own case, the state would condemn him to death"; and wars "are the pioneers of all other evils to society, both moral and physical."[41]

After setting forth these eight summary statements, Campbell exclaimed: "No wonder, then, that for two or three centuries after Christ all Christians refused to bear arms." Justin Martyr, Tatian, Clement of Alexandria, Tertullian, Origin, and others, were called as witnesses to this fact of history.[42]

In the course of his address Campbell had discussed in a moving passage the horrors of war—

the battle field itself, covered with the gore and scattered limbs of butchered myriads . . . the wounded lying upon one another, weltering in their blood . . . invoking death as the only respite from excruciating torments . . . the enduring wail of widows and orphans.

All these, he declared, "say to the Christian, How can you become a soldier? How countenance and aid this horrible work of death?"[43]

He brought together in his indictment both the professional soldier and the volunteer—"the professional and licensed butcher of mankind, who, for his eight dollars a month, or his ten sous per day, hires himself to lay waste a country, to pillage, burn, and destroy," and "the vain and pompous volunteer, who for his country, 'right or wrong,' hastens to the theatre of war for the mere plaudits of admiring multitudes."[44]

The role of propaganda—"the infatuation of public opinion and popular applause"—was recognized in the case of the latter. But even after making due "allowance for false education, for bad taste, for the contagion of vicious example," Campbell concluded that those who were "deluded by such sophistry, however good their motives," deserve only "compassion and forgiveness." He referred critically to "the softer sex allured, fascinated by the halo of false glory thrown around these worshipped heroes!" He spoke with pity of "the young mother arraying her proud boy 'with cap and feather, toyed with a drum and sword, training him for the ad-

mired profession of a man-killer!' '' But it was not only
in the home that this "false spirit" was inspired. "Our
schools, our academies, our colleges" play their part.
The church also lends its aid in cherishing the delusion
by its eulogies on fallen heroes and its services for "the
mighty dead.''

Not only [are] prayers . . . offered up by pensioned chaplains on
both sides of the field, even amid the din of arms; but, Sabbath
after Sabbath, for years and years, have the pulpits on one side
of a sea or river, and those on the other side, resounded with
prayers for the success of rival armies, as if God could hear them
both, and make each triumphant over the other, guiding and
commissioning swords and bullets to the heads and hearts of their
respective enemies!

All this he viewed as a desecration of "the religion of
the Prince of Peace, by causing it to minister as the
handmaid of war.''[45]

Even if he were not a Christian Campbell would still
plead the cause of peace "on the ground of political economy.'' He was impressed by the good that could be
accomplished if money spent on wars were to be used in
clearing and restoring waste lands, rebuilding cities, en-
dowing schools and colleges, and building meetinghouses,
public halls, lyceums, and libraries.

Beat your swords into ploughshares, your spears into pruning-
hooks; convert your warships into missionary packets; your ar-
senals and munitions of war into Bibles, school-books, teachers,
and professors of literature, science, and art; and then ask,
What would be wanting on the part of man to "make the wilderness and solitary place glad;'' to cause the "desert to rejoice
and blossom as the rose.''[46]

But how are national disputes to be settled? Campbell had his answer—an answer furnished him by the
peace crusade literature with which he was familiar.
"Why not have a *by-law-established Umpire?*'' he asked
—"a Congress of Nations and a High Court of Nations
for adjudicating and terminating all international mis-

understandings and complaints, redressing and remedy-
ing all wrongs and grievances?'' There seemed to him
not a ''physical or a rational difficulty in the way.''
These proposals have a modern ring. There was also a
hint of the philosophy of the twentieth-century War
Resister's League in his quotation from Shakespeare,

> War is a game that, were their subjects wise,
> Kings would not play at.[47]

''We have all much interest in the question,'' he continued. ''We can all do something in it, and it is every
one's duty to do all the good he can.'' He called upon
his hearers to ''inspire a pacific spirit, and show off on
all proper occasions the chief objections to war.''[48]
Again he stressed the importance of public opinion, as
he had done in his discussions of the public school issue,
capital punishment, and, on occasion, slavery.

He concluded with a quotation from ''the eloquent
Grimke'' and the plea,

Let every one, then, who fears God and loves man, put his hand
to the work; and the time will not be far distant, when—

> ''No longer hosts encount'ring hosts
> Shall crowds of slain deplore;
> They'll hang the trumpet in the hall,
> And study war no more!''[49]

It is obvious that Campbell had much more of a crusading spirit on the subject of peace than he had on any
other public issue with which he dealt, with the possible
exception of public education. He used the arguments
and literature of the peace crusade freely and without
the reservations and critical spirit which he showed toward the arguments and literature of the anti-Catholic
crusade.

T<small>HE</small> I<small>NTERVAL OF</small> C<small>OMPARATIVE</small> S<small>ILENCE</small>

Unlike most of his other statements on controversial
issues, publication of the address on ''War'' was not

followed by any protracted discussion in the pages of the *Millennial Harbinger*. This may indicate either that it met with general approval, or that Campbell decided it would be wise not to prolong the discussion by answering his critics—probably the former. Not only did he fail to defend his position on war, but he made almost no references to the subject and reprinted only a few items dealing with it during the next dozen years. This reflects the curve of declining interest in the peace movement throughout the nation.

In December, 1849, he published excerpts from the address by Victor Hugo at the opening session of the Paris International Peace Congress that fall. In introducing this material he reiterated the fact that he was "morally and religiously a Peace Man—against savage and civil war" and commended the portions of this address to the "perusal and grave consideration" of all his readers.[50]

The following September he attempted to assess the costs of the Mexican War in terms of the earning power of those who were killed. Admitting that it was impossible to measure the sorrows and the demoralization it caused, he concluded that "our very victories are, not unfrequently, misfortunes. . . . It is not all gold that glitters, nor every triumph that is either an honor or an advantage."[51]

Nine years later, he reprinted reports of a battle between Francis Joseph of Austria and Emperor Napoleon exclaiming, "These belligerents are commonly called Christian nations! What a satire on Christianity!!" In impassioned language he went on to picture the anomaly of supposedly

Christian nations . . . settling their disputes and contentions at the cannon's mouth, with myriads of swords and bayonets, covered with the blood of slaughtered legions, whose bereaved widows and fatherless sons and daughters doomed to penury and wretchedness, must, in most cases, drag out a lingering life of unmitigated misery and wretchedness![52]

REACTIONS TO THE CIVIL WAR

Campbell was holding a meeting at Charlottesville, Virginia, when he learned of the attack on Fort Sumter on April 12, 1861. He at once abandoned his tour and returned to Bethany, observing signs of preparation for war on the way. Weakened by age, he was stunned by the course of events that followed.

By this time more youthful and vigorous spirits had taken over major responsibility for the *Millennial Harbinger*. In November, 1860, Isaac Errett had become one of the coeditors and he along with W. K. Pendleton and A. W. Campbell (Alexander's brother) were the ones who dealt most realistically and forcefully with the new situation. The June, 1861, issue contained the text of an address from the Peace Society of London to the people of the United States published under the title "A Cry from London."[53] The same month A. W. Campbell recognized the duty of the Christian citizen to be obedient to the "powers that be" in all things, *provided* the obedience required does not contravene the laws of the Prince of Peace. In the case of war there is such a contravention, and the editor appealed to Christians not to fight "in the ranks of so unholy a warfare."[54] In July Isaac Errett reviewed and criticized a war sermon, and W. K. Pendleton issued an impassioned "Plea for Peace."[55]

The editorial policy of the *Millennial Harbinger* throughout the Civil War was thoroughly pacifist, and from letters, circulars, and addresses published in its pages it is evident that there was rather general support for this position—at least upon the part of most of the journal's correspondents. Early in the war fourteen leaders from Missouri issued a ringing pacifist manifesto in the form of a circular letter.[56]

This pacifist spirit among Disciples of Christ was due in large part to their New Testament orientation and to the lead given them by Alexander Campbell. Geographical factors probably entered in, too, for they were strongest in the border states where enthusiasm for war was at a lower pitch among people in general, due to milder and mixed counsels on the issues involved and the ties of friendship which linked individuals and communities across the lines. Among Disciples of Christ there had been an extensive interchange of leaders and much traveling back and forth across the Mason-Dixon line by ministers and laymen alike, so that the war actually presented itself as a conflict between Christian brothers.

Campbell's own remarks in relation to the Civil War were quite pathetic. As early as 1856 some of his northern critics on the slavery issue had characterized him as the victim of "imbecile old age."[57] In a memorial address delivered after his death in 1866, D. S. Burnet spoke of the "almost imperceptible decay" of Campbell's intellectual powers and admitted that "the Campbell of the last fifteen years never compared with the Campbell of the preceding thirty-five."[58]

By the year 1860 his writings showed unmistakable signs of age and the weakening of his intellectual penetration. His statement "To our Readers and Patrons" in December of that year was pitifully diffuse. This became increasingly characteristic of his writing after the outbreak of the Civil War. He tended more and more to elaborate etymological studies, long quotations from Scripture, and straying from the subject. These qualities are evident in his reply to a letter from Australia in January, 1862, where, in the midst of a discussion of the gospel definition of Christianity, the contrast between preaching and teaching, the quotation of the whole of the fifty-third and fifty-fourth chapters of Isaiah, and sundry other matters, Campbell brought himself up sharp with the remark, "But, my dear brother, in this excursive style I seem to have forgotten myself."[59] The

following year, in a discussion of the "Apostolic Definition of Faith," after two pages of wandering, he asked,
"But whither have we strayed."[60]

In these disconnected and rambling discussions Campbell frequently reverted to the subject of war and lamented its horror and evil. His first notice of the Civil
War occurred in an article, relatively long as his writings at this period went, in the issue for June, 1861, on
"Wars and Rumors of Wars." There seemed to be "a
necessity, an insuperable necessity," laid upon him "to
attempt to analyze the whole rationale of war," he said.
After ranging briefly over the subjects of creation and
the rebellion and ruin of Adam and Eve, he spoke of
civil war as the greatest atrocity. In his characteristic
etymological manner he asked, "And pray what is *civil
war!*" Webster "places it in the category of *civilities!*"
Yet it is a very "incivil" thing!

It is said by the great dramatist that a rose by any other name
would smell as sweet. And in the present case we presume
that a stroke from a *civil* bullet, from a civil musket, would
wound or kill a person well aimed at, and duly striken, as
though it had been discharged by a savage rifle.

He went on to discuss the source whence wars and fighting come (on the basis of James 4:1), the fact that the
first war in the universe began in heaven, the various
names by which the rebel spirit is characterized in Scripture, and the subject of foreknowledge versus foreor-
dination. Finally he affirmed that wars "are now, and
very generally have been, unprofitable and non-paying
concerns" and declared that he had been "at least for
fifty years . . . an advocate of arbitration by elected
parties" and therefore a believer that "those called
Christian nations, or Christian states," should adopt
"pacific means and measures" for settling their disputes. With feeling he continued:

Of all the monstrosities on which our sun has ever shown, that
of professedly *Christian* nations, glutting their wrath and ven-

geance on one another, with all the instruments of murder and slaughter, caps the climax of human folly and gratuitous wickedness. Alas! Alas! man's inhumanity to man has made, and is still intent on making, countless millions mourn!![61]

Except for the fact that he had not quoted from "the distinguished Soame Jenyns," this passage is quite typical of the eight or ten references which Campbell made to war during the closing months before he was compelled to give over the editorship to W. K. Pendleton in January, 1864.[62] He died March 4, 1866.

His views on war represent the most consistent and pronounced left-wing strand in all of Campbell's practical political ethics. Although he showed marked right-wing tendencies in regard to economic ethics, slavery, and capital punishment, in the matter of war he adhered to the characteristic radical sect position even to the end. This was due largely to the seeds planted in his mind by his reading of Soame Jenyns and perhaps William Godwin, to his own pacifist temperament,[63] and to the influence of the literature of the peace crusade. Another important subconscious influence was the fact that throughout his lifetime the United States was never in serious danger of attack from without.

He had no room for the natural law concept of a "just war." Even in his day he saw that no war can meet the requirement of being waged only against those who are guilty and actually worthy of death. This was also the basis for his discrimination between capital punishment as approved, and war as disallowed, by the patriarchal provision calling for the death of the murderer.

In the case of war Campbell's position was that of most New Testament primitivists. Neither his usual preference for Acts and the Epistles, nor his more mature tendency to revert to Old Testament precepts and precedents, diverted him from an acceptance of the radical pacifism of the Sermon on the Mount. The result is that on this subject he stood farthest removed from the position of Calvin with whom, on other subjects, he tended toward a rapprochement.

On the surface Campbell's pacifism appears to have been purely of the legalist-absolutist type, based upon a strict adherence to the letter of Scripture. But supporting this biblicism were rational and pragmatic factors that cannot be minimized—his Enlightenment faith in the inherent rationality of man, his view of war as supremely foolish and irrational, his belief in the obvious superiority and practicability of the way of reason and arbitration, and his faith that wars would cease if men refused to fight. There were also suggestions of a holiness note and a revulsion against the contamination of blood in his frequent, vivid pictures of the gore of the battlefield.

His pacifism qualified at one important point Campbell's more mature insistence upon the Christian's duty of unquestioning obedience to the constituted authorities. But this had little practical significance under the circumstances of his generation. It is interesting to speculate what his position would have been on the whole subject of war if he had lived in the middle of the twentieth century.

CONCLUSION

ALTHOUGH his basic concepts in both religion and politics were largely derived from his reading and experience in the British Isles, Alexander Campbell's more mature thought was hammered out on the anvil of his experience as a churchman and a citizen in this new country. Constant interaction went on between his views of religion and his concerns as a churchman and his political theories and environment.

Historically considered his attitudes on political matters and public issues were representative of a large body of opinion at the time—outside as well as within his own particular religious movement. He was sensitive to prevailing currents of thought and had a gift for giving vivid expression to ideas that had wide acceptance among those of his own geographical and social position. This was true not only of his views as expressed at the Virginia Constitutional Convention, but also of his party alignments and his attitudes on most of the special topics dealt with in Part Three of this volume.

From the point of view of the sociology of religion, Campbell's political ethics represent the emergence of a type of Christianity which conforms to neither of the basic categories of Ernst Troeltsch, but exemplifies rather clearly the "denominational" type set forth by Joachim Wach. While some American religious leaders and groups came to this *via media* from an ecclesiastical-body position, Campbell moved to it from a thorough-going sect position. This sect element remained prominent to the end—especially in his preference for biblical norms and in his advocacy of withdrawal from political life. In practice his biblicism was modified by his concessions to natural law. As a Christian citizen, he showed a lively interest in the problems of society and accepted a considerable measure of responsibility for political decisions. That is to say, his practice was essentially denominational, even at points where his theory remained rather strongly of the sect type.

Although Campbell never abandoned the characteristic left-wing insistence upon separation of church and state, he put great value upon the indirect contributions which the church and religion make to the community and state, and in his later years he stressed very strongly the Christian's responsibility to be in subjection to the powers that be.

The transition from a sect to a denominational position in his political ethics was facilitated by the peculiar turn taken by his New Testament primitivism—his preference for Acts and the Epistles as over against the Gospels and the Sermon on the Mount, and also by the ecclesiastical activism supported by his eschatology. As he became more and more concerned with the building of a college, a missionary society, and the other institutions of a millennial church, and as he gave more and more hostages personally to the *status quo,* in the form of his increasing wealth and social prestige, he came inevitably to take a more positive—i.e., conservative—attitude toward society and the state.

His change from a sect to a denominational view of the church preceded and prepared the way for his transition from a sect to a denominational view of the Christian's relation to government. His shift of emphasis from the rights of the individual to order and obedience, in both church and state, paralleled the general cultural movement of the West as the frontier psychology, with its ultra-individualism and emphasis upon freedom, gave way to that of a more settled region, concerned with the building of stable community life. Campbell's practical political ethics, then, cannot be understood in terms

purely of religious causation, but represent the result of
the interaction between his theories of religion and his
theories of the state, *and of both* with the dynamics of
an evolving churchmanship and of a maturing cultural
and political environment.

THE NORMS OF CHRISTIAN POLITICAL ACTION

One of the perennial problems for Christianity has
been the relevance of the Bible to life. This is especially
true for the denominational-type Christian who does not
feel obliged to follow the Bible too literally or rigorously,
but who believes that Christianity involves more than
mere common-sense, natural law ethics.

Campbell made a promising start in meeting this problem by his use of what today would be called "lower
criticism." This led to his recognition of development
in biblical ethics, his distinction between the three dispensations, and his insistence that the New Testament,
rather than the Old, is the rule for Christians.

Yet his very biblicism had the effect of making ethics
static. There was no room for further revelation of
God's will once the New Testament canon was closed.
Campbell spoke of religion and morality as "sciences . . .
wholly unsusceptible of improvement"[1] and everywhere
assumed that the New Testament contains the last word
on Christian ethics.

His verbalism made him a slave to the *letter* of Scripture. He seldom made use of the *spirit* of the Gospel,
or the "tendency of Christianity," in seeking to discover the Christian's duty. It was invariably some *ipse
dixit* or some form of words setting forth a scriptural
precedent, which finally settled the issue for him.
Tangled up with precepts and precedents, he seldom
took note of the great underlying ethical *principles* of
Scripture.

The radical distinction between the Old and New
Testaments was largely blurred over—for social and po-

litical ethics, at least—by his view that the moral law, in contrast to the positive or ritual law, is, for the most part, immutable. This led him back in the direction of a rather generous use of Old Testament norms—in some instances to an almost Calvinist equation of the Decalogue with the moral law.

He concentrated upon the socially conservative portions of both Testaments—the Epistles in the New, and the books of Genesis and Exodus in the Old. Almost never did he turn to the teachings of Jesus or the Sermon on the Mount, and his only use of the Old Testament prophets was to prove that Jesus appeared in fulfillment of prophecy. Thus the radical prophetic note in biblical ethics, Old Testament and New, was largely lost.

For his political theory as such, Campbell turned to the natural rights philosophy of Locke, Beattie, Montesquieu, and the Virginia Bill of Rights. The latter he accepted almost as a divine revelation, and applied to it the same methods of exegesis and interpretation that he applied to Scripture. As the Bible sets forth the will of God for the conduct of the individual Christian and the church, so the Bill of Rights was assumed to set forth eternally valid principles for the organization and conduct of the state.

Only at the Virginia Convention did Campbell speak or write "as a politician," or from the point of view of political theory. Elsewhere he generally dealt with public issues from the point of view either of the individual Christian citizen or of the church. In these cases he almost always based his discussion upon the Bible rather than the Bill of Rights.

While he customarily justified his views of Christian duty—even on social and political matters—upon the basis of the Bible, and claimed to have derived his views from that source, there are indications that he was sometimes influenced by what seemed "right" to him on the basis of reason or natural law. The theoretical basis for this practice was his view that the moral law is more or less discernible by the use of reason—a part of his inheritance from Locke and from the "common sense" philosophy of Reid and Beattie.

For the most part Campbell felt that biblical ethics and those of natural law or common sense run along parallel lines, although there were times when he recognized a conflict between them and admitted that the dictates of good Christianity were opposed to those of good politics. This was especially true in his earlier years before he reached a synthesis based upon a more conservative social philosophy.

The result of this conflict, where it existed, was an internal bifurcation of life. The individual Christian was left torn between his duty as a Christian and his duty as a citizen. Campbell offered little guidance or help in this situation. He never developed, or attempted to develop, a truly Christian political ethic—that is, an ethic for Christians in political life that would be both good Christianity and good politics, or that would represent the best possible adjustment between the two. Except in the case of education and capital punishment, he was generally more concerned to safeguard the scriptural integrity of the individual Christian or the scriptural unity of the church than to point the way toward what might be a more statesmanlike or a more Christian policy for the state.

A fundamental weakness of his method of deriving norms for Christian action in political matters is that it left him with relatively little tension between what *is* and what *ought to be*. As has been observed he made use of the socially most conservative portions of the Bible. "Natural law" thinking also often tends in the direction of social conservatism, as it did in his case— at least in his later years. As a result he had no objective, radically Christian principle and no creative secular principle by which to measure and criticize existing social practices and institutions. His views thus tended to be quite conservative. Even his radical views on war were sufficiently "safe" under the circumstances of the time.

The Christian today can well begin where Campbell began, but ought not to stop where he stopped. The contemporary Christian will do well to follow Campbell in a reverent yet critical approach to the Bible, a recognition of development in the divine revelation, and a sincere and earnest loyalty to the will of Christ. But then he will go on and, making use of the best critical and historical studies of the Bible, pay more attention than Campbell did to the radical, prophetic element in biblical ethics. He will also seek to get behind the particular precepts and precedents of Scripture to the enduring ethical principles to be found there. He will make an earnest effort to understand the facts and forces, the principles and potentialities in contemporary social and political life, making use of the best studies and insights of the social and political sciences. Then, upon the basis of his understanding of Christian ethical principles on the one hand, and of social facts and forces on the other, he will seek to develop a creatively Christian ethic for social and political life that will be concerned not primarily with the personal holiness of the individual or the scriptural purity and unity of the church, but rather with building a more Christian community and way of life for all—or at least a community which will be conducive to the maximum achievement of Christian values, social and personal.

If this is a rather large task for the individual Christian working alone, it merely points to a second question.

The Role of the Church

How adequate for present-day Christians is Campbell's view of the role of the church in relation to social and political issues? Once again, it must be said that he made a promising start. While the church, as a church, was to take no part in politics, the individual Christian, in his capacity as a citizen, was to act according to the law of Christ. Here the distinction between faith and opinion served a useful purpose. As long as members of a church agreed upon fundamental matters of faith, they were free to disagree upon matters of opinion; i.e., those about which the Scriptures are not explicit. Since Christianity does not prescribe the political duties of Christians, and since nothing can be made a matter of faith that is not based upon a clear and unmistakable command of Scripture, political decisions were left almost entirely in the realm of opinion and individual judgment. This is the position held by most denominational-type Christians and groups.

Building upon this foundation Campbell might have gone on to urge Christians to study together the issues involved in vital public questions upon the basis of their common faith and commitment to Christ and of their differing social perspectives, areas of experience, and competence. Frankly facing their differences, they might have sought together for the most Christian course of action under existing circumstances. This would have been a thoroughly democratic procedure and, without dictating to the individual, would have helped him reach a more intelligent understanding of both his duties and opportunities as a Christian citizen. It would also have been quite in line with Campbell's fundamental principles and his Enlightenment faith in reason.

But other factors entered into the picture to block this development. In the early years the most important was his extreme left-wing fear of the amalgamation of church and state. Later it was a denominational concern for the unity of the church, coupled with an increasingly "aristocratic," socially conservative fear of anything that might lead to change. The result was that Campbell actually *discouraged* Christians from discussing social and political questions *as Christians,* and opposed their joining with others outside the church for any form of Christian political action.

From the perspective of contemporary Christianity, this is probably one of the gravest weaknesses of his position. The result of this policy was to leave it to the individual Christian to resolve the conflict between his duty as a Christian and his duty as a citizen as best he could, with almost no guidance from his church, and to leave the public issues themselves to be settled largely on the basis of economic, social, and political interests, with no effective means of bringing religious and moral influences to bear upon them.

The wisdom of attempting to stifle the discussion of vital moral issues within the church is open to serious question. Church historians point out that most religious bodies entered upon a period of revitalization and advance after their debates and divisions over slavery. Disciples of Christ, on the contrary, went into a period of stagnation and controversy and finally divided over such relatively insignificant questions as open or closed communion, the title of "Reverend," the use of the organ, and the legitimacy of missionary societies. This division might have taken place anyway, but it is a question whether frankly facing a live social issue— even a controversial and divisive one—may not be more wholesome for the life of the church than seeking to maintain unity at the cost of moral evasion. If Christians do not get excited over the "weightier matters of the law," they may expend their energies instead in Pharisaic concern for the tithing of "mint and dill and cummin."

With the safeguard of Campbell's distinctions between the areas of individual and church action, and between matters of faith and opinion, there is no reason why the church need choose between evasion and division. With creative leadership, the church should be able to play a much more positive role in political and moral issues than Campbell advocated. Its primary function in this field will remain that of developing educational procedures better to equip the individual members of the church for their role as Christian citizens. But it has the additional task of helping mould public opinion outside the church upon issues where Christian moral principles are at stake—a field in which Campbell himself, as an individual, was often very active—and in general of bringing its collective influence to bear upon the side of social righteousness and welfare. Many churches in the religious body of which Campbell was the outstanding early leader are doing this today, and getting valuable assistance and leadership from the agencies of their brotherhood itself.

THEORY OF GOVERNMENT

There is little point in attempting a critical evaluation of the present-day validity of Campbell's theories of government and of the state as such. He made no original contributions in this field, and to evaluate his views on this subject would be to evaluate those which were rather generally held in America at the time. In any event, no one today is likely to look to him as a fountain of inspiration in this matter.

It is clear that Campbell accepted rather uncritically the prevailing atomistic, utilitarian view of the state as based upon a rational compact. There was little appreciation of the state as an historically given reality, rooted in the instinctual life of man and society, with an existence and inner dynamic of its own. Like others of his time he tended to look upon government more as an infringement upon the natural rights and liberties of man than as a source of human freedom.

For all of his recognition of the dangers of power and the need for checks and balances within government, he had no profound recognition of the role of power in political life. Government was thought of rather largely as required for the restraint of evil men, and there was little sense of the need for restraint upon the impulses and conduct of good men. His emphasis upon welfare represents something of an advance over the then-prevailing view of government as existing almost solely for the protection of life and property.

Some elements in Campbell's political theory are certainly worthy of being preserved: his constitutionalism, with its emphasis upon government by laws rather than by men; his belief in the inherent dignity and rights of the individual; his concern for education and freedom of speech, press, and conscience; his insistence upon the separation of church and state; and his passion for peace and the development of agencies of world organization. Many of these furnish wholesome correctives to contrary tendencies in the world today and even in the United States of America.

At the same time his rather "aristocratic" distrust of the common man and his later tendency to place order above freedom, and even above justice, are dubious guides for the present. As for the Christian citizen's relation to government, Campbell's *theory* in his early and middle years called, if anything, for too much reserve, while in his later years it called for too uncritical an obedience to the powers that be.

But when all has been said Campbell must not be judged from the point of view of our own time, or of any one author's theories of Christian political action. While his conclusions were certainly not final, he did grapple earnestly and honestly with some of the basic and perennial problems of the denominational-type Christian who is content neither to withdraw and establish a little colony of heaven encapsulated from the world, nor to accept uncritically and sanctify in the name of the Lord most of the institutions and ways of the world. The present-day Christian can learn much from Campbell—both by way of guidance and of warning.

Seen in the perspective of his own time—and in the light of history—Campbell stands forth as a fine example of American religious leadership. His primary loyalty was to Jesus Christ and his chief concern was always for the building up of his church in preparation for the dawn of the Christian millennium. At the same time he was wholly committed to the fundamental principles of American democracy, had a real sense of the mission of America in the world, and did all that he could to insure that his adopted land would measure up to its high dreams and destiny. He was convinced that there were not only historical but also inescapable contemporary interrelationships between Protestant Christianity and democracy, and that a vital Christianity is essential to the health and perpetuity of democratic institutions.

NOTES

INTRODUCTION

1. Robert Richardson, *Memoirs of Alexander Campbell, Embracing a View of the Origin, Progress and Principles of the Religious Reformation Which He Advocated* (2 vols.; Philadelphia: J. B. Lippincott & Co., 1868-70), II, 548.
2. *Millennial Harbinger*, 1866, p. 131.
3. *Ibid.*, 1832, p. 87.
4. *Ibid.*
5. Joachim Wach, *Church, Denomination and Sect: The Inaugural Lecture: M. Dwight Johnson Memorial Lectureship in Church History* (Evanston, Ill.: Seabury-W e s t e r n Theological Seminary, 1946), pp. 8-19.
6. *Ibid.*, p. 16.
7. *Ibid.*, pp. 22f.
8. Throughout this study the terms ''denomination'' and ''sect'' will be used in their technical sociological s e n s e. Since it would not be practical to write on a subject like this without using the term ''church'' in its more general sense (e.g., ''church and state''), the term ''ecclesiastical body'' will be used to indicate the ''church type'' of Christian fellowship, along with the terms ''church-type'' and ''right wing.'' In the same way the terms ''sect'' and ''left wing'' will be used interchangeably.
9. Wach, *op. cit.*, p. 19.
10. The method followed in this study was the inductive one to which Campbell was devoted.

All of the extant materials from his lips and pen were combed and those that have to do directly or indirectly with his political thought were read with care. The attempt was then made to discover the patterns that emerge from this material, both chronologically and topically, and to interpret Campbell accordingly.

At the same time an effort was made to identify and examine some of the more important sources for his political views, and histories of the various subjects with which he dealt were consulted in an attempt to understand him in relation to contemporary movements of thought.

Campbell was a voluminous writer. He edited a monthly magazine called the *Christian Baptist* from 1823 to 1830, and followed that with a more ambitious journal, the *Millennial Harbinger*, from 1830 to 1863. He was an eager debater, and his public debates with John Walker (1820), W. L. Maccalla (1823), Robert Owen (1829), John B. Purcell (1837), and N. L. Rice (1843) were all published. Other volumes of special significance for this study include his *Christianity Restored* (1835), *C h r i s t i a n System* (3rd. ed., 1840), *Christian Baptism* (1852), *Popular Lectures and Addresses* (1863), and *Familiar Lectures on the Penta-*

teuch (1867). Another significant primary source is the *Proceeding and Debates of the Virginia State Convention of 1829-30,* which includes three major addresses by Campbell, besides numerous briefer statements, motions, and resolutions, and his votes on all the issues before that constitution-making body. One secondary source, especially valuable for the period before 1823, is Robert Richardson's *Memoirs of Alexander Campbell,* which preserves much information and many quotations that would otherwise have been lost.

Except in his addresses at the Virginia Convention, most of Campbell's political theory as such was expressed only incidentally as he used political analogies to illuminate his discussions of church polity, or in the casual observations in the "Notes" on his frequent speaking tours. Nowhere did he attempt to set forth a systematic political theory. He did deal directly, and in some cases rather systematically, with many of the great moral issues of his time.

Campbell was quite inconsistent in his spelling and capitalization. He seldom read the proofs of his articles before they were published. The result is that his periodical articles especially are filled with typographical errors. These are reproduced in passages quoted in this volume but are not commented upon unless they render the meaning unclear.

Students who may wish further documentation or detail may consult the author's dissertation, copies of which are deposited in the library of Yale University, New Haven, Connecticut, and in the archives of the Disciples of Christ Historical Society, Nashville, Tennessee.

CHAPTER I

1. Roland H. Bainton, "The Left Wing of the Reformation," *Journal of Religion,* XXI (April, 1941), 124-134.

2. *A Debate on the Roman Catholic Religion: Held in the Sycamore-Street Meeting House, Cincinnati, From the 13th to the 21st of January, 1837, Between Alexander Campbell of Bethany, Virginia, and the Rt. Rev. John B. Purcell, Bishop of Cincinnati* (Cincinnati: J. A. James & Co., 1837), p. 68. See also pp. 66-69. This debate will hereafter be referred to as the *Campbell-Purcell Debate.*

3. *A Debate Between Rev. A. Campbell and Rev. N. L. Rice, On the Action, Subject, Design and Administrator of Christian Baptism; Also, on the Character of Spiritual Influence in Conversion and Sanctification, and on the Expediency and Tendency of Ecclesiastical Creeds, as Terms of Union and Communion Held in Lexington, Ky., from the Fifteenth of November to the Second of December, 1843* . . . (Lexington, Ky.: A. T. Skillman & Son, 1844), p. 873. This will hereafter be referred to as the *Campbell-Rice Debate.*

4. *A Debate on the Evidences of Christianity; Containing an Examination of the "Social System," and of All the Systems of Scepticism of Ancient and Modern Times. Held in the city of Cincinnati, Ohio, from the 13th to the 21st of April, 1829: Between Robert Owen, of New Lanark, Scotland, and Alexander Campbell, of Bethany, Virginia, with an Appendix, Written by the Parties* (2 vols.; Bethany, Va.: Alexander Campbell, 1829), II, 5. This will hereafter be referred to as the *Campbell-Owen Debate*. See also *Campbell-Rice Debate*, p. 795.
5. *Millennial Harbinger*, 1844, pp. 11f.
6. *Campbell-Owen Debate*, II, 5.
7. *Christian Baptist*, II, 40.
8. *Ibid.*, p. 41.
9. Richardson, *op. cit.*, I, 466.
10. *Christian Baptist*, II, 41.

15. *A Debate on Christian Baptism, Between the Rev. W. L. Maccalla, a Presbyterian Teacher, and Alexander Campbell, Held at Washington, Ky., Commencing on the 15th and Terminating on the 21st Oct. 1823, in the Presence of a Very Numerous and Respectable Congregation. In Which Are Interspersed and to Which Are Added Animadversions on Different Treatises on the Same Subject, Written by Dr. J. Mason, Dr. S. Ralston, Rev. E. Pond, Rev. J. P. Campbell, Rector Armstrong, and the Rev. J. Walker* (Buffaloe, [Va.]: Campbell & Sala, 1824), p. 381. Hereafter this will be referred to as the *Campbell-Maccalla Debate*.
16. *Campbell-Rice Debate*, p. 795; see also p. 873.
17. *Millennial Harbinger*, 1833, p. 469.

CHAPTER II

1. *Christian Baptist*, II, 40.
2. Richardson, *op. cit.*, I, 143, 340; see also pp. 374ff.
3. *Christian Baptist*, I, 184, 188.
4. Alexander Campbell, *A Connected View of the Principles and Rules by which the Living Oracles May Be Intelligibly and Certainly Interpreted: of the Foundation on which all Christians May Form One Communion: and of the Capital Positions Sustained in the Attempt to Restore the Original Gospel and Order of Things; Containing the Principal Extras of the Millennial Harbinger, Revised and corrected* (Bethany, Va.: M'Vay and Ewing, 1835), p. 97. This will hereafter be referred to as *Christianity Re-*

stored, under which title it is usually bound.
5. Richardson, *op. cit.*, I, 448.
6. *Millennial Harbinger*, 1846, pp. 495-521.
7. *Campbell-Owen Debate*, II, 97-124. Campbell covered some of the points more adequately in a series of "Essays on Man in His Primitive State," which ran intermittently in the *Christian Baptist* from August, 1828, to the final issue in June, 1830, and also in the *Millennial Harbinger*, 1834, pp. 387-427.
8. *Christian Baptist*, VI, 90.
9. *Campbell-Owen Debate*, I, 105.
10. *Millennial Harbinger*, 1846, p. 500.
11. Alexander Campbell, *The Christian System, in Reference to the*

Union of Christians, and a Restoration of Primitive Christianity, As Plead in the Current Reformation (3d. ed.; Pittsburgh: Forrester & Campbell, 1840), p. 90.

12. *Millennial Harbinger*, 1848, pp. 368, 383.
13. *Campbell-Owen Debate*, II, 107.
14. *Millennial Harbinger*, 1846, pp. 133-138.
15. *Campbell-Owen Debate*, II, 98.
16. *Ibid.*, p. 101.
17. *Christian Baptist*, VII, 16.
18. *Campbell-Owen Debate*, II, 101f.
19. *Millennial Harbinger*, 1848, p. 373.
20. *Christian Baptist*, VII, 265.
21. *Infant Sprinkling Proved to Be a Human Tradition; Being the Substance of a Debate on Christian Baptism, between Mr. John Walker, a Minister of the Secession, and Alexander Campbell, V. D. M., a Regular Baptist Minister, Held at Mount Pleasant, Jefferson County, Ohio, on the 19th and 20th June, 1820, in the Presence of a Very Numerous and Respectable Congregation. To Which is Added, a Large Appendix* (Steubenville, Ohio: James Wilson, 1820), p. 47. Hereafter this will be referred to as the *Campbell-Walker Debate.*

22. *Millennial Harbinger*, 1834, p. 410.
23. *Ibid.*, pp. 417f.
24. *Christian Baptist*, VII, 16, capitals mine.
25. *Ibid.*, I, 148.
26. *Millennial Harbinger*, 1830, p. 83.
27. Campbell, *Christian System*, p. 92.
28. *Millennial Harbinger*, 1831, p. 207.
29. *Ibid.*, 1834, p. 410.
30. *Ibid.*, 1845, pp. 108, 193, 237, *passim.*
31. *Christian Baptist*, III, 194-197.
32. *Millennial Harbinger*, 1832, pp. 114-116; see also *Campbell-Owen Debate*, II, 116f, and *Millennial Harbinger*, 1848, pp. 422f.
33. *Millennial Harbinger*, 1832, p. 15.
34. Campbell, *Christian System*, p. 94.
35. *Millennial Harbinger*, 1845, p. 108.
36. Alexander Campbell, *Popular Lectures and Addresses* (Philadelphia: James Challen & Son, 1863), p. 361.
37. *Millennial Harbinger*, 1833, p. 120.

Chapter III

1. *Christian Baptist*, I, 270; see also pp. 91-96, 109-112, *passim.*
2. *Campbell-Walker Debate*, p. 185.
3. *Ibid.*, p. 186.
4. *Ibid.*, p. 194; see also *Millennial Harbinger*, 1833, pp. 319, 467; 1837, pp. 17-19; *Campbell-Purcell Debate*, pp. 113-275; *Campbell-Rice Debate*, pp. 305-355; Alexander Campbell, *Christian Baptism, With Its Antecedents and Consequents* (Bethany, Va.: Alexander Campbell, 1852), pp. 170f, 113, 239ff, *passim.*
5. *Christian Baptist*, VI, 65; *Millennial Harbinger*, 1839, p. 431; 1842, p. 94; 1845, p. 234.
6. *Millennial Harbinger*, 1831, p. 207.
7. *Campbell-Walker Debate*, p. 187.

8. *Millennial Harbinger*, 1843, pp. 98ff.
9. *Ibid.*, pp. 109, 105.
10. *Ibid.*, 1844, p. 238.
11. *Campbell-Walker Debate*, p. 189.
12. *Ibid.*, p. 195.
13. *Ibid.*, p. 188.
14. Richardson, *op. cit.*, II, 29.
18. *Ibid.*, p. 470.
19. William Warren Sweet, *Religion in Colonial America* (New York: Charles Scribner's Sons, 1942), pp. 322f.
20. Richardson, *op. cit.*, I, 517.
21. *Ibid.*, p. 523.
22. *Ibid.*, pp. 523f, 528.
23. *Ibid.*, p. 526.
24. *Christian Baptist*, VI, p. 203.
25. *Ibid.*, p. 201.
26. *Millennial Harbinger*, 1832, pp. 614f.
27. *Ibid.*, 1837, p. 271.
28. *Christian Baptist*, III, 59f, 64.
29. *Campbell-Maccalla Debate*, p. 216.
30. *Christian Baptist*, III, 204f.
31. *Ibid.*, II, 143, 264.
32. *Ibid.*, p. 143.
33. *Ibid.*, p. 262; III, 17.
34. *Ibid.*, II, 156f.

35. *Ibid.*, IV, 12.
36. *Ibid.*, pp. 15f; see also *Ibid.*, II, 215.
37. *Ibid.*, IV, 265; *Millennial Harbinger*, 1851, p. 473.
38. John Locke, *Four Letters on Toleration* (7th ed.; London: Alexander Murray, 1870), p. 5.
39. *Millennial Harbinger*, 1830, pp. 305f.
40. Locke, *op. cit.*, pp. 7, 10.
41. Marriage, being both a civil and a religious institution, presented certain problems. Campbell believed that it is the duty of the state to make laws regulating marriage. If the laws of the state permit a minister to celebrate the rites of matrimony, then "it is every way consistent and expedient that such persons attend upon this service as *ministers of the body politic.*" *Millennial Harbinger*, 1834, p. 141.
42. Ernst Troeltsch, *The Social Teachings of the C h r i s t i a n Churches*, trans., Olive Wyon (2 vols.; New York: The Macmillan Co., 1931), II, 638.

CHAPTER IV

1. Robert Frederick West, in his *Alexander Campbell and Natural Religion* (New Haven: Yale University Press, 1948), is the first student of Campbell to deal at all adequately with this phase of his thought. West devotes the third part of his study to Campbell's "Philosophy of History," pp. 163-217.
2. *Millennial Harbinger*, 1830, pp. 1f.
3. *Ibid.*, 1843, pp. 73f.
4. *Ibid.*, 1841, p. 9.
5. *Ibid.*, 1842, pp. 44f.
6. *Ibid.*, 1841, p. 9.

7. *Ibid.*, 1842, p. 59.
8. *Ibid.*, 1843, p. 74.
9. *Christian Baptist*, II, 156.
10. *Campbell-Owen Debate*, II, 123.
11. *Millennial Harbinger*, 1831, p. 211.
12. *Ibid.*, 1833, p. 12.
13. *Ibid.*, pp. 121, 521.
14. *Ibid.*, 1839, pp. 575f.
15. *Ibid.*, 1838, p. 474.
16. *Ibid.*, 1839, p. 8.
17. *Ibid.*, 1831, p. 179.
18. *Ibid.*, 1850, p. 219; see also *Ibid.*, 1859, p. 432.
19. *Ibid.*, 1856, p. 670.
20. *Ibid.*, 1848, p. 668.

21. *Ibid.*, 1853, p. 606.
22. *Ibid.*, 1845, p. 316.
23. *Ibid.*, 1846, p. 4.
24. *Ibid.*, 1840, p. 413.
25. *Ibid.*, pp. 414f.
26. *Ibid.*, pp. 102f.
27. *Ibid.*, 1857, p. 174.
28. *Ibid.*, 1845, p. 108.
29. *Ibid.*, 1848, p. 352.
30. *Ibid.*, 1836, p. 282.
31. *Ibid.*, 1845, p. 505.
32. *Campbell-Owen Debate*, II, 167.
33. If his preoccupation with the responsibilities of constructive churchmanship led him to minimize the place of politics in the life of the Christian, it also led him to stress patient and passive obedience to *the powers that be* in the interim before the millennium. Since both church-type and denominational factors contributed to this emphasis, its discussion will be deferred until the denominational elements in his thought are considered in Part Three.

CHAPTER V

1. John Locke, *Of Civil Government; Two Treatises*, ed. William S. Carpenter (Everyman ed.; London: J. M. Dent & Sons, 1924), pp. 119, 159, 164.
2. *Ibid.*, pp. 120, 179f.
3. *Ibid.*, pp. 123, 127, 180.
4. *Ibid.*, p. 118.
5. James Hay Beattie, *Elements of Moral Science* (2 vols.; Philadelphia: Mathew Carey, 1792-1794), II, 112, 115f.
6. *Ibid.*, p. 119.
7. *Ibid.*, pp. 161f.
8. *Ibid.*, p. 163.
9. *Ibid.*, pp. 164f. This is almost a perfect summary of Campbell's views on the whole subject.
10. *Ibid.*, p. 182.
11. *Ibid.*, p. 183.
12. *Ibid.*, pp. 190f.
13. *Ibid.*, pp. 195f.
14. *Campbell-Owen Debate*, II, 132.
15. See p. 140.

CHAPTER VI

1. Hugh B. Grigsby, a fellow delegate, in speaking later about the personalities of the convention, devoted nearly half of the time given to Campbell in discussing the traditional "prejudice" in the public mind in Virginia "on the subject of an union of religious and political functions in the same person," and of the stir caused by Campbell's election. "It was feared that by the presence of a popular divine in the Convention the element of religion might be mixed up with topics sufficiently exciting in themselves. But the course of A L E X A N D E R CAMPBELL s o o n dispelled such fears." Pointing out that Campbell, though belonging to "a sect the most numerous in the Union," was a "schismatic," he concluded: "There was no danger to religious freedom from him. He needed it more than any body else." "The Virginia Convention of 1829-30, A Discourse Delivered before the Virginia Historical Society at Their Annual Meeting, Held in the Anthenaeum

in the City of Richmond, December 15th, 1873," *Virginia Historical Reporter*, I, 79-91.

2. Charles Henry Ambler, *Sectionalism in Virginia from 1776 to 1861* (Chicago: University of Chicago Press, 1910), pp. 5f.

3. *Ibid.*, p. 137.

4. Richardson, *op. cit.*, II, 319f.

5. Charles Edward Merriam, *A History of American Political Theories* (New York: The Macmillan Co., 1903), p. 190.

6. *Proceedings and Debates of the Virginia State Convention, of 1829-30, to Which Are Subjoined the New Constitution of Virginia, and the Votes of the People* (Richmond: Ritchie & Cook, 1830), p. 53. This volume will henceforth be referred to as the *Virginia Convention Debates*.

7. *Ibid.*, p. 64.

8. "He had a great fund of humor. . . . He was a fine scholar, and, with the younger members of the body who relished his amusing thrusts, his pleasant address and social feelings rendered him very acceptable. As a controversialist he had some great qualities; he was bold, subtle, indefatigable, and as insensible to attack as if he were sheathed in the hide of a rhinoceros." Grigsby, *op. cit.*, pp. 79-81.

9. *Virginia Convention Debates*, p. 117.

10. *Ibid.*, p. 118.

11. *Ibid.*, pp. 119f.

12. *Ibid.*, pp. 120f.

13. *Ibid.*, pp. 121f.

14. *Ibid.*, p. 122.

15. *Ibid.*

16. *Ibid.*, pp. 122f.

17. *Ibid.*, pp. 123f.

18. *Ibid.*, p. 124.

19. *Ibid.*, pp. 496f.

20. *Ibid.*, p. 831.

21. *Ibid.*, p. 850.

22. As a compromise he did support the Doddridge motion which would have put representation on a white basis in the House and on the basis of the "federal number" in the Senate.

23. *Virginia Convention Debates*, p. 350.

24. *Ibid.*, p. 383.

25. *Ibid.*, p. 385.

26. *Ibid.*

27. *Ibid.*, pp. 385f.

28. *Ibid.*, p. 386.

29. *Ibid.*

30. *Ibid.*, p. 387.

31. *Ibid.*, pp. 387f.

32. *Ibid.*, p. 389.

33. *Ibid.*, p. 390.

34. *Ibid.*

35. *Ibid.*, p. 440.

36. *Ibid.*, p. 441.

37. *Ibid.*, p. 651.

38. Campbell opposed setting any minimum tax or any minimum valuation upon the freehold estate necessary to qualify one to vote. On three different motions he voted against "capitation taxes" against which he had inveighed in his own address on suffrage when he suggested that the tax levied by the Turks upon the pilgrims to the Holy Sepulchre furnished the first model "and is the true origin of the Virginia 'poll-tax.'" *Ibid.*, p. 387.

39. *Virginia Convention Debates*, p. 526.

40. *Ibid.*

41. *Ibid.*, pp. 526f.

42. *Ibid.*, p. 527.

43. *Ibid.*

44. *Ibid.*, p. 528.

45. *Ibid.*, pp. 527f.

46. *Ibid.*, p. 528.

47. *Ibid.*, pp. 528f.

48. *Ibid.*, pp. 529f.

49. *Ibid.*, p. 530.
50. *Ibid.*, pp. 604f. The following day when Littleton W. Tazewell moved an amendment to leave one supreme court a constitutional court, and all the inferior courts legislative ones, Campbell spoke in behalf of the amendment, which was defeated 56 to 29.
51. Campbell seems to have been less concerned for the job security of judges than many of his colleagues. He favored setting a maximum age for judges to serve and opposed paying salaries to those whose courts had been abolished or whose judicial duties had been terminated.
52. *Virginia Convention Debates*, p. 34.
53. He also voted for the popular election of sheriffs, for a one-year term for the governor, for the selection of the secretary of state by joint vote of both houses, and for leaving the matter of succession in the hands of the General Assembly.
54. *Virginia Convention Debates*, p. 40.

55. *Ibid.*, p. 707.
56. But see his discussion of the "incongruity" of "Lords spiritual" sitting in the British House of Lords. *Millennial Harbinger*, 1847, pp. 579f.
57. *Virginia Convention Debates*, p. 460.
58. *Ibid.*, pp. 708f.
59. In the final stage of the debates before the house, William F. Gordon moved to amend the legislative proposal by lowering the minimum age for senators from thirty to twenty-five. This was defeated 45 to 51, with Campbell, Doddridge, and Wilson voting for the age thirty and Morgan for twenty-five.
60. *Virginia Convention Debates*, p. 750.
61. *Ibid.*, p. 787.
62. *Ibid.*, p. 777.
63. *Ibid.*, p. 784.
64. Richardson, *op. cit.*, II, 320.
65. His nephew, Archibald W. Campbell, a graduate of Bethany College and an abolitionist, was one of the leaders in the West Virginia statehood movement.

CHAPTER VII

1. *Campbell-Rice Debate*, pp. 579f.
2. *Christian Baptist*, III, 14.
3. Campbell, *Popular Lectures and Addresses*, p. 80.
4. *Christian Baptist*, VII, 4; *Millennial Harbinger*, 1830, p. 302.
5. *Campbell-Owen Debate*, II, 130.
6. *Millennial Harbinger*, 1830, p. 304.
7. *Campbell-Rice Debate*, p. 580.
8. *Millennial Harbinger*, 1841, p. 440.
9. *Ibid.*, 1833, p. 224; see also *Ibid.*, 1834, p. 402.
10. *Ibid.*, 1841, p. 440.
11. See p. 189.
12. *Millennial Harbinger*, 1851, p. 15.
13. *Ibid.*, 1834, p. 403.
14. *Ibid.*
15. *Ibid.*, 1843, p. 258; 1848, p. 213.
16. *Christian Baptist*, VII, 15.
17. *Campbell-Owen Debate*, II, 130.
18. Campbell, *Christian Baptism*, p. 92.
19. *Campbell-Owen Debate*, II, 131; see also *Millennial Harbinger*, 1835, pp. 472f.

20. *Campbell-Rice Debate*, p. 580.
21. *Christian Baptist*, VII, 4.
22. *Campbell-Rice Debate*, p. 580.
23. *Christian Baptist*, I, 284.
24. *Millennial Harbinger*, 1851, pp. 27, 29.
25. *Ibid.*, p. 28.

26. *Ibid.*, 1834, pp. 401f.
27. *Ibid.*, p. 401.
28. *Ibid.*, 1857, p. 587.
29. *Ibid.*, 1851, p. 29.
30. *Ibid.*, 1846, p. 124.
31. *Virginia Convention Debates*, p. 385.

CHAPTER VIII

1. *Millennial Harbinger*, 1831, pp. 237f.
2. *Ibid.*, pp. 436-438.
3. *Ibid.*, 1835, pp. 164-171.
4. *Ibid.*, 1840, pp. 502-504; 1841, pp. 45-47, 532-537.
5. *Ibid.*, 1838, pp. 126-128.
6. *Ibid.*, 1839, p. 325.
7. *Ibid.*, 1840, p. 335.
8. *Ibid.*, 1844, p. 226.
9. *Ibid.*, 1843, pp. 216f.
10. *Ibid.*, 1837, pp. 411-414, *passim*.
11. *Ibid.*, 1839, pp. 211f.
12. *Ibid.*, 1847, p. 31.
13. *Ibid.*, 1852, p. 211.
14. *Campbell-Walker Debate*, p. 46.
15. *Millennial Harbinger*, 1841, pp. 340-342.
16. *Ibid.*, pp. 346f.
17. *Christian Baptist*, II, 75.
18. *Campbell-Owen Debate*, II, 131.
19. *Ibid.*, p. 135, italics mine.
20. Thomas Reid, *The Works of Thomas Reid, D.D. Now Fully Collected, With Selections From His Unpublished Letters; Prefixed by Stewart's Account of the Life and Writings of Reid.* Edited with Preface, Notes and Supplementary Dissertations by Sir William Hamilton (6th ed.; 2 vols.; Edinburgh: MacLachlan and Stewart, 1863), I, 638.
21. *Millennial Harbinger*, 1838, p. 70.
22. See pp. 143-145.
23. *Millennial Harbinger*, 1840, p. 35.
24. *Christian Baptist*, I, 284.
25. *Millennial Harbinger*, 1845, p. 240.
26. *Ibid.*, p. 272. Wrongly numbered 260, since the paging is off from pages 252 to 300 in this volume.
27. *Ibid.*, p. 315.
28. *Ibid.*, 1851, p. 29.
29. *Ibid.*, 1846, pp. 123f.
30. *Ibid.*, p. 124.

CHAPTER IX

1. Richardson, *op. cit.*, I, 207.
2. *Ibid.*, pp. 465f. In 1811, as soon as he took up residence in the state of Virginia, he took out his first papers for naturalization, and became a citizen two years later. *Ibid.*, p. 465. As he put it: "I became a citizen of Virginia as soon as the laws of the state permitted, and have continued such until this day." *Christian Baptist*, II, 40f.
3. *Christian Baptist*, VII, 3f.
4. *Millennial Harbinger*, 1830, pp. 305, 307.
5. Campbell, *Christianity Restored*, pp. 208ff.
6. *Millennial Harbinger*, 1830, p. 43.
7. *Ibid.*, p. 554.
8. *Ibid.*, pp. 45f.; see also p. 257.

9. *Ibid.*, 1832, p. 240.
10. *Christian Baptist*, VI, 29f.
11. *Millennial Harbinger*, 1831, p. 39.
12. *Ibid.*, 1833, pp. 520f.
13. *Ibid.*, 1835, p. 66.
14. *Ibid.*, 1830, p. 427.
15. *Ibid.*, 1837, pp. 447f.
16. *Ibid.*, 1844, p. 410.
17. *Ibid.*, 1847, pp. 421, 431f.
18. *Ibid.*, p. 526.
19. *Ibid.*, p. 574.
20. *Ibid.*, p. 552.
21. *Ibid.*, p. 578.
22. *Ibid.*, p. 611.
23. *Ibid.*, 1850, p. 407.
24. *Ibid.*, pp. 267f.
25. *Ibid.*, 1852, pp. 449, 458f.
26. *Ibid.*, p. 486.
27. *Ibid.*, 1845, p. 195.
28. *Ibid.*, 1851, p. 225.
29. *Ibid.*, 1846, p. 4.
30. *Virginia Convention Debates*, p. 119.
31. *Millennial Harbinger*, 1845, p. 351.
32. *Ibid.*, 1848, p. 650, wrongly numbered 550. The immediate occasion of Campbell's remarks was probably Tyler's vetoes, which, according to Ambler (*op. cit.*, p. 232), exasperated the nationalists of western Virginia.
33. *Millennial Harbinger*, 1835, pp. 594f.
34. *Ibid.*, 1836, p. 331.
35. *Ibid.*, p. 506.
36. *Ibid.*, 1839, p. 7.
37. Richardson, *op. cit.*, II, 642f.
38. *Millennial Harbinger*, 1855, p. 221.

39. *Ibid.*, 1839, p. 60.
40. *Ibid.*, 1856, p. 88.
41. *Ibid.*, 1860, p. 98.
42. *Ibid.*, p. 427.
43. *Opinions of Lord Brougham, on Politics, Theology, Law, Science, Education, Literature, etc., etc. As Exhibited in His Parliamentary and Legal Speeches, and Miscellaneous Writings* (London: Henry Colburn, 1837), pp. 45f.
44. *Millennial Harbinger*, 1843, p. 64.
45. *Ibid.*, 1844, pp. 359f.
46. Quoted by Merriam, *op. cit.*, p. 156.
47. *Millennial Harbinger*, 1844, p. 584.
48. *Christian Baptist*, IV, 10. This seems in strange contrast to his faith in the ability of the common man in matters of religion during the same period.
49. *Millennial Harbinger*, 1850, p. 232.
50. *Ibid.*, 1846, p. 406.
51. *Ibid.*, 1844, p. 45.
52. *Ibid.*, 1850, p. 6.
53. *Ibid.*, 1854, pp. 203-206; 1856, pp. 311, 314.
54. *Ibid.*, 1845, pp. 49f.
55. *Christian Baptist*, VI, 47.
56. *Ibid.*, VII, 49.
57. *Millennial Harbinger*, 1842, p. 186.
58. *Ibid.*, p. 431.
59. *Ibid.*, 1845, pp. 291f, wrongly numbered 279f.
60. *Ibid.*, 1850, p. 219.
61. *Ibid.*, 1858, p. 71; see also p. 157.

CHAPTER X

1. Ray Allen Billington, *The Protestant Crusade, 1800-1860: A Study of the Origins of American Nativism* (New York: The Macmillan Co., 1938), pp. 1-3.

2. Richardson, *op. cit.*, I, 49f. 102, 209f.
3. *Christian Baptist*, VI, 213.
4. *Millennial Harbinger*, 1832, p. 397.

5. *Ibid.*, 1833, p. 288.
6. *Ibid.*, pp. 538f.
7. *Ibid.*, p. 539.
8. *Ibid.*, 1835, pp. 65f.
9. *Ibid.*, p. 66.
10. *Ibid.*, p. 114.
11. *Ibid.*, pp. 410f.
12. *Ibid.*, 1836, pp. 579f.
13. *Campbell-Purcell Debate*, p. viii.
14. *Ibid.*, pp. 48, 76, *passim.*
15. *Ibid.*, pp. 66-69, 77.
16. *Ibid.*, p. 113.
17. *Ibid.*, pp. 203f, 218.
18. *Ibid.*, pp. 303f.
19. *Ibid.*, pp. 280, 302.
20. *Ibid.*, p. 279.
21. *Ibid.*, p. 294.
22. *Ibid.*, p. 311.

23. *Ibid.*, p. 329.
24. *Ibid.*, p. 312.
25. *Ibid.*, p. 314.
26. *Ibid.*
27. *Ibid.*, p. 315.
28. *Ibid.*, p. 323.
29. *Ibid.*, p. 281.
30. *Ibid.*, p. 324.
31. *Ibid.*, pp. 324, 333.
32. *Ibid.*, p. 331.
33. *Ibid.*, p. 333.
34. *Ibid.*, p. 351.
35. *Millennial Harbinger*, 1837, pp. 185-187, 322-325.
36. *Ibid.*, 1843, pp. 182f.
37. *Ibid.*, 1844, p. 410.
38. *Ibid.*, 1848, pp. 671f.
39. *Ibid.*, 1855, p. 536.
40. *Ibid.*, 1851, pp. 541f.

CHAPTER XI

1. *Millennial Harbinger*, 1853, p. 425.
2. *Ibid.*, pp. 426-428.
3. Elwood P. Cubberley, *Public Education in the United States: A Study and Interpretation of American Educational History; An Introductory Textbook Dealing with the Larger Problems of Present-Day Education in the Light of their Historical Development* (Boston: Houghton-Mifflin Co., 1919), pp. 128f.
4. *Millennial Harbinger*, 1830, p. 555.
5. *Ibid.*, p. 556.
6. *Ibid.*
7. *Ibid.*, 1836, pp. 481f.
8. *Ibid.*, 1837, p. 65.
9. *Ibid.*, 1838, p. 422.
10. Ambler, *op. cit.*, pp. 273f.
11. *Ibid.*, p. 276.
12. *Millennial Harbinger*, 1841, p. 434.
13. *Ibid.*, p. 448.

14. *Ibid.*, p. 449.
15. *Ibid.*, p. 452.
16. *Ibid.*
17. *Ibid.*, p. 453.
18. *Ibid.*, pp. 453f.
19. *Ibid.*, p. 456.
20. *Ibid.*, 1846, p. 407.
21. *Ibid.*, 1853, p. 134.
22. *Ibid.*, 1835, p. 66. Campbell's emphasis upon the Bible as a textbook in the public schools may have been inspired in part by Thomas S. Grimke's address, ''The Expediency and Duty of Adopting the Bible as the Text Book of Duty and Usefulness, in Every Scheme of Education, from the Primary School to the University,'' from the notes to the published edition of which Campbell quoted at some length in the *Millennial Harbinger* for 1834, pp. 342f.
23. *Millennial Harbinger*, 1836, pp. 596f.

24. *Ibid.*, p. 597.
25. *Ibid.*, 1837, p. 258. Cf., William Chillingworth, *The Religion of Protestants, a Safe Way to Salvation, Or An Answer to a Booke Entitled Mercy and Truth, or, Charity Maintain'd by Catholiques, Which Pretends to Prove the Contrary* (Oxford: Leonard Lichfield, 1637), p. 101.
26. *Millennial Harbinger* 1837, p. 568.
27. There were striking similarities between Campbell and Horace Mann not only in their attitudes toward free public schools for all and the use of the Bible in these schools, but in their general economic and social philosophies as well.
28. *Millennial Harbinger*, 1850, p. 168.
29. *Ibid.*, 1854, p. 77.
30. *Ibid.*, 1856, pp. 639f, 642.
31. Merle Eugene Curti, *The Social Ideas of American Educators* ("Report of the Commission on the Social Studies," X; New York: Charles Scribner's Sons, 1935), pp. 64-71.

CHAPTER XII

1. Benjamin Lyon Smith, *Alexander Campbell* (St. Louis: The Bethany Press, 1930), p. 147.
2. Francis Wayland, *The Elements of Political Economy* (4th ed.: Boston; Gould and Lincoln, 1855). Campbell's views generally agreed with those of Wayland except on the propriety of the government's establishing interest rates.
3. *Christian Baptist*, III, 33; see also pp. 136-138.
4. *Millennial Harbinger*, 1831, p. 14.
5. *Campbell-Owen Debate*, II, 136.
6. *Millennial Harbinger*, 1845, p. 136.
7. *Ibid.*, 1837, p. 270.
8. *Ibid.*, 1838, pp. 286f.
9. *Christian Baptist*, V, 126.
10. *Millennial Harbinger*, 1843, p. 215.
11. *Ibid.*, 1838, p. 387.
12. *Ibid.*, 1839, pp. 16f.
13. *Ibid.*, 1835, p. 383.
14. *Ibid.*, 1839, p. 316.
15. *Ibid.*, pp. 316f.
16. *Ibid.*, pp. 317f.
17. *Ibid.*, p. 339.
18. *Ibid.*, pp. 340f.
19. *Ibid.*, pp. 403f.
20. *Ibid.*, 1840, pp. 209-211.
21. *Ibid.*, p. 274.
22. *Ibid.*
23. *Ibid.*, 1842, pp. 295f.
24. *Ibid.*, p. 296; Cf. Beattie, *op. cit.*, II, 147f.
25. *Millennial Harbinger*, 1853, pp. 586f.
26. *Ibid.*, p. 587.
27. *Ibid.*, 1843, pp. 255-258.
28. *Ibid.*, p. 258.
29. *Ibid.*, p. 255.
30. *Ibid.*, p. 258.
31. *Ibid.*, pp. 258f.
32. *Ibid.*, p. 259. Cf., Beattie, *op. cit.*, II, 145.
33. *Millennial Harbinger*, 1848, p. 213.
34. *Ibid.*, 1830, p. 553, italics mine.
35. *Ibid.*, 1856, p. 238.
36. *Ibid.*, 1851, pp. 577f; but see *Ibid.*, 1834, pp. 54-56.

37. *Campbell-Owen Debate*, II, 117; *Millennial Harbinger*, 1848, p. 668.
38. *From Max Weber: Essays in* *Sociology*, trans. and ed. H. H. Gerth and C. Wright Mills (New York: Oxford, 1946), pp. 302-322.

CHAPTER XIII

1. *Christian Baptist*, III, 228.
2. *Millennial Harbinger*, 1840, p. 61.
3. *Christian Baptist*, I, 25.
4. *Millennial Harbinger*, 1832, p. 86.
5. *Ibid.*, 1849, p. 243.
6. *Ibid.*, 1830, pp. 128f.
7. *Ibid.*, pp. 131f; see also p. 47.
8. *Ibid.*, pp. 189-191.
9. Ambler, *op. cit.*, p. 196.
10. *Millennial Harbinger*, 1832, p. 14.
11. *Ibid.*, p. 15.
12. *Ibid.*
13. *Ibid.*, p. 86.
14. *Ibid.*, pp. 87f.
15. *Ibid.*, p. 88.
16. *Ibid.*, 1835, p. 588.
17. *Ibid.*, pp. 588f.
18. *Ibid.*, pp. 589f, italics mine.
19. *Ibid.*, 1849, p. 242.
20. Gilbert Hobbs Barnes, *The Antislavery Impulse, 1830-1844* (New York: D. Appleton-Century Co., 1933), p. 11.
21. *Ibid.*, p. 161.
22. *Millennial Harbinger*, 1835, p. 331.
23. *Ibid.*, 1840, p. 233.
24. *Ibid.*, 1835, p. 587.
25. *Ibid.*, 1840, p. 99.
26. *Ibid.*, pp. 99f.
27. *Ibid.*, pp. 98f.
28. *Ibid.*, pp. 102f.
29. *Ibid.*, p. 235.
30. *Ibid.*
31. *Ibid.*, 1835, p. 17. Later he was to speak of it as "a misfortune entailed upon us, rather than a crime perpetrated by us." *Ibid.*, 1851, p. 429.
32. *Ibid.*, 1839, p. 113.
33. *Ibid.*, 1842, p. 375. A decade earlier, at the time of the Southampton Insurrection, he had devoted many pages to the slavery issue, even though it was not "so directly in the train of our labors." Then he had asked for the "indulgence of our readers out of the precincts of Virginia . . . while we give one push to the car of liberty now in motion." *Ibid.*, 1832, p. 87.
34. *Millennial Harbinger*, 1845, p. 51.
35. *Ibid.*, p. 233.
36. *Ibid.*, p. 195.
37. *Ibid.*, p. 274, wrongly numbered 262.
38. *Ibid.*, p. 51; see also p. 313.
39. *Ibid.*, p. 236.
40. *Ibid.*, p. 275, wrongly numbered 263.
41. *Ibid.*, p. 52.
42. *Ibid.*, pp. 69f.
43. *Ibid.*, p. 145.
44. *Ibid.*, p. 193.
45. *Ibid.*, p. 145.
46. *Ibid.*, pp. 233f.
47. *Ibid.*, p. 235.
48. *Ibid.*, pp. 269-271, wrongly numbered 257-259.
49. *Ibid.*
50. *Ibid.*, p. 271, wrongly numbered 259; see also *Ibid.*, 1831, p. 435.
51. *Ibid.*, 1846, p. 473.
52. *Ibid.*, 1845, p. 284, wrongly numbered 272.
53. *Ibid.*, p. 240.
54. *Ibid.*, pp. 237ff.

55. *Ibid.*, p. 313.
56. *Ibid.*, 1846, p. 593.
57. *Ibid.*, 1848, p. 176.
58. *Ibid.*, 1847, pp. 627-631.
59. *Ibid.*, p. 648. For the full story of this incident see Richardson, *op. cit.*, II, 551-566, and Campbell's own account in his "Letters from Europe" in the *Millennial Harbinger*, 1847, pp. 626-648, 683-685; 1848, pp. 45-53.
60. *Millennial Harbinger*, 1840, p. 234.
61. Merriam, *op. cit.*, pp. 227-248.
62. *Millennial Harbinger*, 1845, p. 145.
63. *Ibid.*, 1848, p. 88.
64. *Ibid.*, 1847, p. 630.
65. *Ibid.*, 1845, p. 274, wrongly numbered 262.
66. *Ibid.*, 1851, p. 627.
67. *Ibid.*, 1845, p. 274, wrongly numbered 262.
68. Campbell's views of the origins of Slavery show the influence of Locke and Beattie. "The first wars of a public character were wars of extermination. . . . In process of time the captives were respited from death, and made to serve; so that slavery was substituted for death. Hence slavery became a matter of commutation, and finally of contract." *Ibid.*, pp. 418f.
69. *Millennial Harbinger*, 1845, p. 49.
70. *Ibid.*, 1830, p. 129.
71. *Ibid.*, 1849, pp. 242, 252.
72. *Ibid.*, pp. 241f.
73. *Ibid.*, pp. 246f.
74. *Ibid.*, p. 247.
75. *Ibid.*, p. 248.
76. *Ibid.*, pp. 249-251.
77. *Ibid.*, p. 252.
78. *Ibid.*, pp. 413f.
79. *Ibid.*, p. 414.
80. [Iveson L. Brooks], *A Defence of Southern Slavery, Against the Attacks of Henry Clay and Alex'r. Campbell, in Which Much of the False Philanthropy and Mawkish Sentimentalism of the Abolitionists Is Met and Refuted, In Which It Is Moreover Shown That the Association of the White and Black Races in the Relation of Master and Slave Is the Appointed Order of God, as Set Forth in the Bible, and Constitutes the Best Social Condition of Both Races, and the Only True Principle of Republicanism*, by a Southern Clergyman (Hamburg, S. C.: Robinson and Carlisle, 1851), pp. i, 28, 37.
81. *Millennial Harbinger*, 1846, p. 6.
82. *Ibid.*, 1851, p. 27.
83. *Ibid.*, p. 30.
84. *Ibid.*, p. 28.
85. *Ibid.*, pp. 53, 389.
86. *Ibid.*, pp. 31f; see also pp. 429f.
87. *Ibid.*, p. 202.
88. *Ibid.*, pp. 204-206.
89. *Ibid.*, p. 206.
90. *Ibid.*, p. 249.
91. *Ibid.*, pp. 27, 29.
92. *Ibid.*, pp. 28-31.
93. *Ibid.*, p. 31.
94. *Ibid.*, p. 624.
95. *Ibid.*, p. 32.
96. *Ibid.*, pp. 171f.
97. *Ibid.*, pp. 247-249.
98. *Ibid.*, pp. 224f.
99. *Ibid.*, p. 630.
100. *Ibid.*, 1854, p. 42.
101. *Ibid.*, p. 587.
102. *Ibid.*, 1856, p. 54.
103. *Ibid.*, pp. 112f.
104. *Ibid.*, 1854, p. 351.
105. *Ibid.*, 1851, pp. 529f.
106. Beattie, *op. cit.*, II, 76.

CHAPTER XIV

1. *Millennial Harbinger*, 1845, p. 424. In a passage in the *Christian Baptist* for December, 1826, he had assumed the justice of capital punishment in the case of a murderer. *Christian Baptist*, IV, 97f.
2. *Millennial Harbinger*, 1846, p. 121.
3. *Ibid.*, pp. 124f.
4. *Ibid.*, p. 125.
5. *Ibid.*, pp. 125f.
6. *Ibid.*, pp. 126f.
7. *Ibid.*, pp. 127f.
8. *Ibid.*, p. 129.
9. *Ibid.*, pp. 130-132.
10. *Ibid.*, p. 132.
11. *Ibid.*, pp. 133-135.
12. *Ibid.*, pp. 135f.
13. *Ibid.*, p. 136.
14. *Ibid.*, pp. 137f, italics mine.
15. *Ibid.*, pp. 140f.
16. *Ibid.*, pp. 142f.
17. *Ibid.*, p. 143.
18. *Ibid.*, pp. 143f.
19. *Ibid.*, p. 144.
20. *Ibid.*, pp. 144f.
21. *Ibid.*, pp. 145-147.
22. *Ibid.*, p. 147.
23. *Ibid.*, pp. 148-151.
24. *Ibid.*, p. 151.
25. *Ibid.*, 1847, pp. 61-70, 158-160.
26. He did occasionally insert a brief note or exchange item which was consistent with his point of view on the matter. *Ibid.*, 1846, p. 705; 1848, p. 575; 1850, p. 594.

CHAPTER XV

1. *Millennial Harbinger*, 1846, p. 126.
2. Francis Wayland, whose texts Campbell used in his teaching at Bethany College, was another pacifist who favored capital punishment. See his *Elements of Moral Science* (2d ed.; New York: Cooke and Co., 1835), pp. 440-444.
3. *Christian Baptist*, I, 24.
4. *Ibid.*, p. 18.
5. *Ibid.*, p. 48.
6. *Ibid.*, II, 283.
7. *Ibid.*, IV, 11.
8. *Ibid.*, VI, 143.
9. *Millennial Harbinger*, 1830, pp. 304, 309.
10. *Campbell-Owen Debate*, II, 116.
11. *Ibid.*, p. 118.
12. *Millennial Harbinger*, 1834, pp. 306-309.
13. *Ibid.*, pp. 341-343.
14. ''Although I prefer the American Eagle to the British Lion, I would rather fight the battles of my king, under the device of a milk white dove, on an azure flag, as more consonant to the genius of the Reign of heaven. War, however, is wholly barbarous. Nations at war, are at best but partly civilized, and, therefore, they generally choose beasts of prey for their insignia.'' *Campbell-Purcell Debate*, p. 256. Cf., Thomas Smith Grimke, *Address on the Truth, Dignity, Power, and Beauty of the Principles of Peace, and on the Unchristian Character and Influence of War and the Warrior; Delivered in the Centre Church at New-Haven, During the Session of the Legislature of Connecticut, at the Request of the Connecticut Peace Society, on Sunday Evening, the 6th of May, 1832* (Hartford: George F. Olmsted, 1832), p. 43.

15. "Yet had that Washington and his illustrous compeers been still better educated than was the age in which they lived, and from which they took their counsels and their examples, who can tell but that without so much blood and so many years of suffering, by other policies and principles all that we enjoy might have been secured to themselves and their posterity for many generations! Another Franklin, of another category, might have arisen, who could have stolen from the breast of kings the electric fluid of a monarch's wrath by a conducting rod that would, without the lurid flash of scathing lightenings and the mighty peals of angry thunders, have sent it secretly and quietly into the bosom of mother earth." *Millennial Harbinger*, 1841, p. 437. Cf., Grimke, *op. cit.*, p. 42.

16. *Millennial Harbinger*, 1836, p. 283.

17. *Ibid.*, 1837, p. 157.

18. *Ibid.*, 1842, p. 229.

19. *Ibid.*, 1839, p. 316.

20. *Ibid.*, p. 575.

21. *Ibid.*, pp. 576f.

22. *Ibid.*, 1846, p. 473.

23. *Ibid.*, p. 638.

24. *Ibid.*, pp. 638f, italics mine.

25. *Ibid.*, pp. 640f.

26. *Ibid.*, pp. 641f, capitals mine.

27. *Ibid.*, 1848, p. 385.

28. *Ibid.*

29. *Ibid.*, 1847, p. 432.

30. *Ibid.*, pp. 619f.

31. *Ibid.*, 1848, pp. 361f.

32. *Ibid.*, pp. 364f.

33. *Ibid.*, pp. 367f.

34. *Ibid.*, p. 383, wrongly numbered 283.

35. *Ibid.*

36. *Ibid.*, p. 370.

37. *Ibid.*, p. 371.

38. *Ibid.*, p. 383.

39. If it could, nations at war would save millions of dollars and thousands of lives if each would select "one of their genuine Simon Pure *patriots* and *heroes*" and let them meet in single combat before a competent number of witnesses to decide which side was right. *Ibid.*, p. 373.

40. *Millennial Harbinger*, 1848, p. 383.

41. *Ibid.*, pp. 383f.

42. *Ibid*, p. 384.

43. *Ibid.*, pp. 378f; cf. William Godwin, *Enquiry Concerning Political Justice, and Its Influence on Morals and Happiness* (2d ed. corrected; 2 vols.; London: O. G. and J. Robinson, 1796), II, 167.

44. *Millennial Harbinger*, 1848, pp. 379f.

45. *Ibid.*, pp. 380f.

46. *Ibid.*, p. 384.

47. *Ibid.*, pp. 382f.

48. *Ibid.*, p. 385.

49. *Ibid.*, p. 386.

50. *Ibid.*, 1849, p. 703.

51. *Ibid.*, 1850, p. 524.

52. *Ibid.*, 1859, p. 519.

53. *Ibid.*, 1861, pp. 334f, wrongly numbered 234ff.

54. *Ibid.*, pp. 338f.

55. *Ibid.*, pp. 380-387, 405-410.

56. *Ibid.*, 477f, 583-590, 593-596, 649-651, 654f, *passim*.

57. *Ibid.*, 1856, pp. 227f.

58. *Ibid.*, 1866, p. 315.

59. *Ibid.*, 1862, p. 24.

60. *Ibid.*, 1863, p. 221.

61. *Ibid.*, 1861, pp. 345-348.

62. *Ibid.*, pp. 412f, 715; 1862, pp. 23f, 49f, 82f, 168f, 196f, 439.

63. Richardson reports that Campbell always went unarmed on his

travels, and recounts an incident on one of his trips on horseback through Ohio when he fell in with a rough-looking traveler. When the other rider made what appeared to be a menacing move, Campbell produced a New Testament from his pocket and engaged him in conversation about the protection which its divine Author promises to those who trust in him. In reporting the incident Campbell declared: ''It is the carrying of arms that creates the idea of the possession of money and invites attack, but the being without arms has the directly contrary effect, and I am persuaded that many persons lose their lives simply from carrying arms.'' Richardson, *op. cit.*, II, 661-663.

CONCLUSION

1. *Millennial Harbinger,* 1846, p. 123.